CONSPIRACY THEORIES

A Primer

JOSEPH E. USCINSKI

University of Miami

ROWMAN & LITTLEFIELD
Lanham • Boulder • New York • London

Executive Editor: Traci Crowell
Assistant Editor: Deni Remsberg
Higher Education Channel Manager: Jonathan Raeder

Credits and acknowledgments for material borrowed from other sources, and reproduced with permission, appear on the appropriate page within the text.

Published by Rowman & Littlefield
An imprint of The Rowman & Littlefield Publishing Group, Inc.
4501 Forbes Boulevard, Suite 200, Lanham, Maryland 20706
www.rowman.com

6 Tinworth Street, London SE11 5AL, United Kingdom

British Library Cataloguing in Publication Information Available

Library of Congress Cataloging-in-Publication Data

Names: Uscinski, Joseph E., author.
Title: Conspiracy theories : a primer / Joseph E. Uscinski.
Description: Lanham : Rowman & Littlefield, 2020. | Includes bibliographical references and index. | Summary: "Analyzes current arguments and evidence while providing real-world examples so students can contextualize and visualize the debates. Each chapter addresses important current questions, provides conceptual tools, defines important terms, and introduces the appropriate methods of analysis"— Provided by publisher.
Identifiers: LCCN 2019041421 (print) | LCCN 2019041422 (ebook) | ISBN 9781538121191 (cloth) | ISBN 9781538121207 (paperback) | ISBN 9781538121214 (epub)
Subjects: LCSH: Conspiracy theories.
Classification: LCC HV6275 .U73 2020 (print) | LCC HV6275 (ebook) | DDC 001.9—dc23
LC record available at https://lccn.loc.gov/2019041421
LC ebook record available at https://lccn.loc.gov/2019041422

∞™ The paper used in this publication meets the minimum requirements of American National Standard for Information Sciences—Permanence of Paper for Printed Library Materials, ANSI/NISO Z39.48-1992.

Contents

Preface

Conspiracy theories currently present two problems. The first is that the believers can act on their beliefs, sometimes with deadly intent. The second is that the aversion to conspiracy theories—particularly by those in power—endangers freedom of speech and press, as well as the free exchange of ideas on the internet.

Recently, an FBI report about conspiracy theorists was leaked. The report showed that the FBI was beginning to see conspiracy theorists as a potential terror and security threat. Shortly following the release of the report, a deranged man killed twenty-two people and injured twenty-four others; the shooter was acting on a form of the "white genocide theory," a conspiracy theory that claims that whites are being replaced by cheaper minority workers. Following the shooting, there have been numerous calls to purge conspiracy theories from the internet and from public discussion forums. Should those who want to ban conspiracy theories get their way, a large swath of ideas that meet the definition of *conspiracy theory* will be banned. This concerns me because while most conspiracy theories are false, and some even dangerous, most are benign, and some are even helpful or true.

This short book is a primer—it cannot cover every conspiracy theory (there are an infinite number) or every circumstance brought on by conspiracy theories (these are also too numerous). While a book of this length cannot provide a complete picture, it does provide, I believe, a *complete-enough* picture. I cover the major terms and concepts, and attempt to dispel some of the myths that have developed around conspiracy theories. I note also that this book is a polemic, and not by intention. It addresses truth and power, two topics that frequently spark disagreement. I expect the book to upset not only believers of specific conspiracy theories but also partisans. I will likely be accused of excusing the conspiracy theorizing of one group or another; referring to real conspiracies as conspiracy theories; denigrating conspiracy theorists; and shilling for the establishment. None of these are my intention, but such accusations are all par for the course. For not agreeing with others' conspiracy theories, my inbox is filled with: "I'm not saying you are in on it, I'm saying you seem like a very, very lazy researcher and should not be teaching anyone anything"; "You are the enemy of the people"; "You've decided to join the losing team right before they're led to the gallows"; and "Utterly stupid or actively participating in a conspiracy of silence?" This is how the study of conspiracy theories goes and is exactly why it needs to be done even-handedly, with both compassion and understanding.

It is likely that everyone reading this book has a relative, friend, or acquaintance who has strong conspiracy beliefs. Many people contact me about how conspiracy theories are destroying a relationship. I have heard from parents and wives whose sons and husbands have become consumed by conspiracy theories to the point where they can no longer hold jobs, have civil conversations, or maintain familiar relationships. I wish, of course, that I had an answer for these people, a magic bullet or antidote. But I don't. Maybe sometime in the future, such a corrective will avail itself, but for now, we are left with nothing more than the ability to empathize with others. Social scientists have made many discoveries about conspiracy theories in the last decade; I have catalogued those here. I hope that by doing so, I will spark the next generation of scholars to seek out newer and better answers.

Acknowledgments

I would like to thank those who reviewed the book proposal: Lee Basham (South Texas College/University of Texas, Rio Grande Valley), M. R. X. Dentith (New Europe College), Marius Raab (University of Bamberg), Alfred Moore (University of York), Joanne Miller (University of Delaware), Kathryn Olmsted (University of California, Davis), and Hugo Drochon (University of Cambridge).

About the Author

Joseph E. Uscinski is associate professor of political science at the University of Miami's College of Arts and Sciences in Coral Gables, Florida. He studies American politics, mainly conspiracy theories, fake news, and misinformation. He is the author of two books, *American Conspiracy Theories* (2014) and *The People's News: Media, Politics, and the Demands of Capitalism* (2014), as well as editor of *Conspiracy Theories and the People Who Believe Them* (2018).

Professor Uscinski studies one question: Why do people believe conspiracy theories? He uses national surveys and experiments to understand the factors that drive people to either adopt conspiracy beliefs or not.

Professor Uscinski teaches undergraduate courses on conspiracy theories, mass media, public opinion, and elections. Each election year in the fall, he team-teaches a large course focusing on the political campaigns. He also takes UM students to London every summer for a study-abroad course.

Professor Uscinski's essays have appeared in the *Washington Post, Politico,* the *Los Angeles Times, Newsweek,* and the *Miami Herald* and on *NBC News Online* and *CNN Online.* He has been interviewed more than five hundred times by major local, national, and international news outlets. The *Miami New Times* recently wrote an article on Professor Uscinski: "America's Conspiracy Theory Expert Is a UM Professor, and His Phone Is Ringing Off the Hook."

Professor Uscinski has published more than twenty peer-reviewed articles. He created and oversees the Truth in Politics initiative at the University of Miami; in doing so, he brings high-profile politicians to campus to meet with students and alumni.

Professor Uscinski received his PhD from the University of Arizona in 2007, his MA from the University of New Hampshire in 2003, and his BA from Plymouth State College in 2000. He lives in beautiful downtown Miami with his wife and two dogs.

1

Why Study Conspiracy Theories?

I n what is commonly considered one of the greatest achievements of humankind, Neil Armstrong and Buzz Aldrin broke out of Earth's atmosphere, traveled more than 237,000 miles through space, and then walked on the moon. Perhaps even more astonishing, their achievement was watched by an estimated 530 million people on live television.[1] Upon returning to Earth, the astronauts received a hero's welcome for their bravery, and the success of the Apollo 11 moon landing led to five more missions to the moon.

But did this actually happen? Did American astronauts *really* leave the atmosphere, travel to the moon, walk on it, and return safely home? Is traveling to the moon even possible? Or was this all just an elaborate hoax?

For most Americans, the moon landings are a point of pride: a sign of American ingenuity and a testament to their resolve during the Cold War. But for others, the moon landing is not what it seems. Some argue that the United States, intending to defeat the Soviet Union, devised a plan to trick their rivals into believing that US technological capacity had actually surpassed the Soviets'.[2] Others, reaching for a supernatural explanation, contend that demonic forces are faking moon missions to trick the world into doubting the cosmological pronouncements in the Bible.[3] Still others think that the moon can't be landed on because it is actually a base occupied by malevolent alien overlords who watch over us from afar.[4]

Other observers contend that the moon landings did happen, but just not in the way authorities would have us believe. Some claim that the astronauts found alien bases but that this amazing discovery is being kept from the public.[5] Others contend that the camera footage of the moon landing was faked to guarantee a more positive image of the event. To wit, the acclaimed director Stanley Kubrick is often accused of creating footage for

1

the government and then admitting (in secret code) to his involvement in the iconic film *The Shining*.[6]

The moon landing is not the only major historical event to be questioned. Elections, wars, natural disasters, terrorist attacks, and mass shootings, for example, attract denials and alternative accounts. The assassination of President John F. Kennedy on November 22, 1963, is a perfect example: even though the Warren Commission ruled that the shooting was carried out by one man, Lee Harvey Oswald, many have postulated opposing narratives not only about the assassination, but also about those who investigated it. A long list of characters have been accused of being coconspirators: then–Vice President Lyndon Johnson, the military, defense contractors, Fidel Castro, the Soviet Union, the FBI, the CIA, the Secret Service, the Dallas Police, the Mafia, Richard Nixon, the New Orleans gay community, and a defrocked pedophile priest.[7] An even greater number of actors have been accused of taking part in a decades-long cover-up.[8]

Such alterative accounts—which in this book we will call "conspiracy theories"—suggest either that (1) powerful actors are seeking money or power at the expense of the unsuspecting public or that (2) epistemological authorities such as government bodies, the media, scientists, and academia—those responsible for discovering and disseminating truth—are corrupt, untrustworthy, and engaged in active deception. In the first case, the accusations scapegoat and demonize a group of people based upon dubious evidence. In the second case, the accusations discredit expertise, facts, and the methods we use to generate reliable knowledge.

Conspiracy theories surround most events that receive prominent news coverage. The assassinations of President John F. Kennedy and his brother Robert Kennedy have since the 1960s been lightning rods for conspiracy theories. The high-profile shootings in Orlando and Parkland, Florida, Las Vegas, and Sandy Hook, Connecticut, are often referred to as "false flag" attacks.[9] Such theories allege that these shootings did not take place as reported, did not take place at all, or were carried out by the government with a political agenda in mind. Election outcomes, in the United States and abroad, are often called into question by conspiracy theories claiming that the contest was rigged in favor of the winner.[10] Downed airplanes typically attract conspiracy theories (e.g., TWA Flight 800, United Airlines Flight 93, Amelia Earhart's final voyage). For example, the disappearance of Malaysia Airlines Flight 370 quickly became fodder for conspiracy theorists after it vanished from radar, and crews failed to locate wreckage.[11] Terror attacks such as those of September 11, 2001, in New York and Washington, DC; July 7, 2005, in London's Underground; or December 12, 2015, in Paris have all attracted conspiracy theories from those who think that the attacks were coordinated by governments to justify the sapping of personal liberties.[12]

Conspiracy theories also surround smaller, lesser-known events that don't leave as big a mark on history. Less newsworthy events such as minor crimes and local deaths spark conspiracy theories, too, but such theories tend to have less traction than theories attached to more widely known events.[13]

Conspiracy theories frequently drive policy discussions, and there are few policy areas that do not have at least a few conspiracy theories attached to them. Some people believe that bicycle-sharing programs and land-use policies are designed to wrestle local control from residents and hand power to corrupt international organizations intent on instituting tyranny.[14] Debates have raged for more than fifty years about the regulation of fluoride in local drinking water: many on the political right feared that communists were using fluoride to "dumb down" the population; more recent left-wing activists believe big corporations are behind a plot to poison people.[15] Immigration policy is often intertwined with conspiracy theories: many Europeans believe the "white replacement theory" that says that governments and corporations are replacing whites with cheap foreign labor.[16] Some individuals have acted on these conspiracy theories by committing violent atrocities, such as the mass shooting in Christchurch, New Zealand. In the United States, a caravan of immigrants seeking asylum at the southern border attracted conspiracy theories involving billionaire philanthropist George Soros; these ideas led Robert Gregory Bowers to murder eleven innocents at the Tree of Life Synagogue in Pittsburgh.[17]

Government agencies, particularly powerful ones, attract the ire of conspiracy theorists. The US Federal Reserve, the CIA, and the military have long been targeted by conspiracy theories; across the pond, the European Union is frequently accused of hiding secret plans of further integration and of building a clandestine army.[18] Wars are often questioned with conspiracy theories. Some people believe that President Franklin Roosevelt allowed the attack on Pearl Harbor so he could justify entering World War II; many opposed the 2003 US invasion of Iraq because they believed it was secretly a war for oil.[19]

Besides specific events, circumstances such as wealth inequality, racial and gender disparities, and other social conditions can spark accusations of coordinated manipulation. US senator and presidential candidate Bernie Sanders emphatically claims that the "one percent" have rigged the entire American economic and political systems and in doing so have made it hard for regular Americans to "survive."[20] Sanders's liberal counterpart in the United Kingdom, Labour Party leader Jeremy Corbyn, has claimed much of the same.[21] Some feminist activists claim that a secret group of power-wielding males, "the patriarchy," subverts the interests of women.[22] To explain their political and economic disenfranchisement, some African Americans have at various times turned to conspiracy theories involving, among other things, the government and Jews.[23]

Photo 1.1   Some people believe that the Earth is a disc rather than a globe.
© iStock / Getty Images Plus / kevron2001

Even scientific findings backed by the majority consensuses of scientists are called into question by conspiracy theories. A small number of people believe that the Earth is flat, not spherical. The "flat earthers" contend that the flat Earth "disc" is surrounded by an ice barrier (which keeps the oceans from pouring over the edge).[24] Flat Earth conspiracy theories ignore the findings of every government agency and airplane pilot on the planet, along with consensuses of geographers, physicists, and astronauts.

A much larger percentage of Americans believe that the Earth is not warming due to manmade carbon emissions, but is either not warming, or is warming due to some factor unrelated to human activity. To make their case, climate deniers usually accuse the scientific authorities either of faking findings to get grant money, or of being pawns in a plan to enslave the planet under communist rule.[25]

Similar accusations have been made of scientists who study the safety of genetically modified organisms (GMOs): despite extensive studies attesting to their safety and usefulness, scientists are said to fake their research for powerful interests.[26] Some people argue that biotech companies are profiting from selling unhealthy GM vegetables; others contend that biotech interests want to take over the world by depopulating the planet.[27] Vaccines, once held in high regard because they save millions of lives, are now vilified by conspiracy theories. Anti-vaxx conspiracy theories, as they are known, are partially responsible for recent outbreaks of diseases once thought cured.[28] Celebrities such as Robert De Niro, Jenny McCarthy, and Jim Carrey have brought much attention to these conspiracy theories.[29] More generally, conspiracy theories also attack the effectiveness of modern medicine, suggesting that the medical establishment is hiding alternative natural treatments to either get rich or kill people.[30]

There is an infinite number of conspiracy theories out there. They run the gamut in terms of what they attempt to explain, and in doing so, collectively accuse nearly everyone of taking part in one conspiracy or another. In the United States, frequent targets of prominent conspiracy theories have included Jews, Catholics, Muslims, Mormons, Christians, Atheists, women's groups, Republicans, Democrats, conservatives, liberals, extremists, the rich, the poor, government agencies, foreign governments, foreigners, and the media. I could continue, but you get the point: conspiracy theories accuse many people of many things.

Why Are Conspiracy Theories Important?

Conspiracy theories can be entertaining or even funny. They are tales of schemes and skullduggery, of foul villains and sympathetic victims. By offering a glimpse into a world of intrigue, they dazzle our imaginations. Many popular movies and television series have been based on conspiracy theories; *The X-Files, Lost, Fringe, In Search Of, Ancient Aliens*, and Oliver Stone's *JFK* come to mind. One can even book a cabin on the annual Conspira-Sea Cruise, which allows passengers to not only heal from all of the conspiracies that have been perpetuated upon them but also watch for alien visitors in the night sky.[31] This being said, conspiracy theories are more than just "parlor games about who shot John Kennedy or who probed whom at Roswell, New Mexico."[32]

Conspiracy theories posit a powerful enemy whose goals may pose an existential threat to humanity. It is therefore reasonable to expect that such theories would motivate believers to take action. Thus, there are many reasons we should be interested in, if not outright concerned with, conspiracy theories.

The first reason for concern is that foiling, exposing, and preventing real conspiracies are of the upmost importance. If a conspiracy theory is true, and widespread fraud or serious attacks upon our basic ground rules are indeed taking place, then the public should be made aware so that such mischief is less likely to occur in the future. It is imperative that the conspirators be stopped, held accountable for their misdeeds, and, if possible, made to make amends.

But what if a conspiracy theory is not true? Does it still have truth value? The answer is yes. Our epistemic authorities are not right all the time. Sometimes they are unintentionally wrong, but other times, they are wrong on purpose. In either case, the only way of ferreting out mistakes is through advocacy. Even if a specific conspiracy theory is wrong, it can form the basis of a successful appeal and overturn an incorrect verdict. Conspiracy theories, even when they miss the mark, can make the case for increased transparency. For example, we know far more about the Kennedy assassination and 9/11 terror attacks because conspiracy theorists questioned the official narratives and demanded further details.[33] Over the long term, conspiracy theories could potentially incentivize good behavior: if the powerful intend to conspire, conspiracy theorists will be watching, investigating, and publicizing. This is a job that the press should be doing, but journalists have their own blind spots. Conspiracy theorists can bring to the fore problems that journalists miss.

The second reason we should be concerned with conspiracy theories is that beliefs inform actions, at both the individual and collective levels. If actions are driven by views disconnected from our shared reality, then those actions will not only be unwise and unnecessary but also potentially dangerous.

At the collective level, democracy requires that people make informed choices. If beliefs about voter fraud lead people to abstain from voting, then democracy will function poorly because large portions of the electorate will not take part. This is currently the case in the United States, where conspiracy-minded citizens are less likely than other citizens to register, vote, volunteer, or donate to campaigns, or even put up yard signs.[34] Their willful absence from the system likely alienates them further, thereby increasing their willingness to engage in conspiracy theorizing to explain their isolation. The simplest solution to this problem might be to encourage conspiracy theorists to participate, but this could have terrible consequences as well. If majorities make decisions based on dubious conspiracy theories, those decisions become binding on everyone.

Consider the United Kingdom's European Union membership referendum in 2016, also known as the "Brexit" vote. Many Brits who voted to leave the EU did so under false pretenses; for example, they believed that the true levels and costs of immigration into the UK were being hidden.[35] Forty-six percent of the people who supported the "Leave" position believed that they should mark their ballot in ink because if they were to vote in pencil, their ballot would be altered.[36] The consequences of this vote—52 percent in favor of leaving the EU—will have far-reaching consequences for Britain, Europe, and the world.

Voters in Turkey, responding to conspiracy theories about a "deep state," an "interest rate lobby," and Western agitators not only elected Recep Erdoğan president, but also voted him more powers so he could dismantle the supposed conspiracies. The conspiracy theories were made real by an actual conspiracy to remove Erdoğan from the presidency. The resultant policies led to the violation of rights on a mass scale, including the jailing of college professors thought to be part of the plot, and the overturning of valid election results.[37]

The leaders elected by conspiracy-minded voters may feel compelled to address their supporters' theories. Consider Texas governor Greg Abbott, who gave in to conspiracy theories about a federal government takeover. Many local residents believed that the military, under the direction of Barack Obama, was on the verge of invading Texas. Abbott, by directing the Texas State Guard to monitor US military exercises in the Jade Helm region of Texas, responded in a way that gave credence to the conspiracy theories. Ironically, many of those theories were sparked by a Russian conspiracy to agitate Texans with fake news.[38]

Elected officials in other instances act more aggressively on citizens' conspiracy beliefs. And sometimes officials concoct and push conspiracy narratives themselves to justify actions they would have taken regardless. Conspiracy theories involving GMOs have driven state and local governments in the United States to adopt strict labeling and other restrictions on foods that have been repeatedly proven safe, efficient, and better for the environment. These policies—without any real benefit—have led to higher food costs and less choice for consumers.[39] Europe has banned the importation of genetically modified foods, and this has severely injured Africa, which cannot use GM seeds to farm more efficiently because it cannot sell such products abroad. Economists estimate this has led to the deaths of hundreds of Africans.[40] Local officials, buckling under the pressure placed on them by conspiracy theorists, have removed or refused to add fluoride to their water supplies. Teeth have paid a price for these policies: cities that cease fluoridation experience an increase of tooth decay.[41]

Climate change is perhaps the biggest collective danger faced by the planet, yet as many as 40 percent of Americans reject anthropogenic climate change, believing instead that all this talk of climate change is a carefully orchestrated hoax perpetrated by communists, globalists, and unscrupulous government officials to sap our money, freedom, and standard of living.[42] Because much of the American public rejects the idea of climate change, Congress is unable to pass meaningful legislation to address it.

Since 2016, the United States has instituted severe restrictions on the internet, supposedly to combat immense (but largely fictitious) sex-trafficking rings.[43] The FBI recently seized control of Backpage.com, a site often used by sex workers to connect with clients safely. The government charged that Backpage facilitated child sex trafficking, despite (1) there being little evidence of such and (2) the fact that Backpage was actively cooperating with the FBI to detect sex trafficking.[44] Some of these beliefs about child trafficking are tied to more extreme conspiracy theories such as the Pizzagate and QAnon theories, which allege that massive child-sex-trafficking rings are run by high-ranking government officials.[45] Such conspiracy theories about sex-trafficking gangs have (1) made conditions worse for sex workers who are already vulnerable, (2) created an incorrect public perception that traffickers are actively running vast sex slave operations and kidnapping children, (3) led authorities to violate rights on a massive scale, and (4) motivated gangs of individuals to harass and threaten violence against supposed (and sometimes fictitious) sex traffickers.[46] No doubt there is some sex trafficking in the United States (which should be stopped), but the government's pronouncements about it go beyond the available evidence and have created a panic.[47] Now, rights are being violated.

Going back in history, American colonists, importing the practice from Europe, hanged and crushed "witches" for supposedly conspiring with Satan.[48]

Photo 1.2 The QAnon movement has become a cult that analyzes the clues provided by an anonymous poster.
© iStock / Getty Images Plus / BackyardProduction

As the trials dragged on, governments raised the evidentiary standards at trials, thereby excluding the use of spectral evidence (visions, revelation, and demonic voices). In much the same way, overblown fears of communist influence led the US government to engage in unconstitutional practices during the 1950s.[49] Anxieties eventually subsided when it became clear that the threat was not as menacing as previously thought. As for outside the United States, consider the conspiracy-theory-drenched propaganda Adolf Hitler used to justify his genocidal actions against the Jews, or the conspiracy theories used by Stalin to justify killing, starving, and imprisoning his detractors. I could unfortunately provide multiple examples, but the point is that conspiracy theories can be most harmful when adopted by government officials, because a government is able to act on those conspiracy theories as a monopoly of authoritative force.

Conspiracy theories can also be thorny when individuals or small groups act upon them. For example, conspiracy theories have been shown to lessen people's willingness to reduce their carbon footprint or to engage in pro-social behaviors.[50] Conspiracy theories can aggravate people and make them want to quit their jobs.[51] Worse, conspiracy theories can convince people to put themselves at risk by forgoing modern medical treatments such as vaccines and cancer treatments.[52]

On the extreme end, individuals strongly influenced by conspiracy theories have been shown more likely to (1) possess a toxic mix of psychological characteristics, (2) possess a willingness to conspire to achieve goals, and (3) accept violence against the government.[53] Further, anger can be a motivating factor for those engaging with conspiracy theories.[54]

Take, for example, Timothy McVeigh: he was angry with the government's actions at Ruby Ridge and Waco, Texas; he believed the government was conspiring to take away gun rights to control people and thought that the army had implanted a monitoring chip in his body to spy on him.[55] In response to what McVeigh saw as a government conspiracy against himself and all Americans, he conspired against the government by killing 168 people and injuring 700 others by bombing the federal building in Oklahoma City.

In 2016, Edgar Maddison Welch traveled from his home in North Carolina to a Washington, DC, restaurant to foil a supposed conspiracy he had learned of on Reddit. He had read that Democrats, including Hillary Clinton, were running a satanic child-sex-trafficking ring beneath the Comet Ping Pong Pizza shop. When Welch entered, he fired a round and opened a door expecting to find the entrance to a sex dungeon. He found a broom closet instead. After his arrest, Welch was sentenced to four years in prison.[56]

In 2017, James Hodgkinson attacked a congressional baseball-team practice, shooting several people, including Republican representative Steve Scalise. Hodgkinson was apparently motivated by anti-Trump conspiracy theories.[57] In 2018, having been motivated by conspiracy theories about satanic sex-trafficking rings (the same ones Welch was concerned with), a group of armed men began patrolling the Arizona desert looking for the child sex slaves and their traffickers. These satanic sex traffickers have yet to be captured, but the group insists they have found conclusive evidence (authorities disagree, however).[58]

When told that powerful shadowy forces are operating against the innocent, some people are going to fight fire with fire. Lucky for us, conspiracy beliefs don't always, or even often, lead to violence. Political violence is thankfully rare (in most Western nations), and conspiracy-driven violence seems to be even more so. But conspiracy theories do occasionally lead some people to act. Conspiracy theories can also drive otherwise rational individuals to take part in mass panics, witch hunts, and mob violence.[59]

A Misunderstood Topic

Despite their historical and contemporaneous significance, social scientists are only beginning to understand conspiracy theories.[60] They did not become an object of study until historian Richard Hofstadter examined extremist groups in the late 1950s and 1960s; he concluded that a "paranoid style" was characteristic of American political thought.[61] A few historians dabbled in the topic during the decades that followed, but a concerted research agenda did not develop until the 1990s when cultural scholars showed an interest.[62] Philosophers followed, around the turn of the century, mostly examining the criteria for judging the veracity of conspiracy theories.[63] It was not until 2007 that psychologists began to study the topic in earnest, with political scientists and sociologists later trailing along. As of 2019, new academic studies on the topic are being published every week.

Scholars have shed much light on conspiracy theories, and this book will detail the breadth of our current knowledge. With that said, scholars have much to discover. There are many unanswered questions, and the answers researchers provide today may be supplanted by better answers as new evidence is discovered. Nonetheless, the available body of evidence, despite its weaknesses, shows that many of the oft-repeated claims about conspiracy theories are either untrue or unsupported. Let's take a look at some of these.

Conspiracy Theories Are More Popular Now/There Are More Conspiracy Theories Now

Journalists often claim that "now" is the time of conspiracy theory. Al Jazeera claimed in 2018 that "today conspiracy theories have become the true 'opium of the masses.'"[64] In 2013, *New York Times* editor Andrew Rosenthal summed up US conspiracy beliefs in five words: "No Comment Necessary: Conspiracy Nation."[65] In 2011, the *New York Daily News* declared the United States a "conspiratocracy. . . . [Conspiracy theories] have never spread this swiftly across the country. They have never lodged this deeply in the American psyche. And they have never found as receptive an audience."[66]

A year prior, columnist David Aaronovitch argued that the West was "going through a period of fashionable conspiracism."[67] Six years before that, the *Boston Globe* claimed we were then in the "golden age of conspiracy theory."[68] A decade before that, in 1994, the *Washington Post* claimed that Bill Clinton's first term "marked the dawn of a new age of conspiracy theory," when only two years earlier the *Post* had said that we were then living "in an age of conspiracy theories."[69] In 1977, the *Los Angeles Times* believed that the United States had "become as conspiracy prone . . . as the Pan-Slav nationalists in the 1880s Balkans," and in 1964 the *New York Times* was sure that that was the year of conspiracy theories because they had "grown weed-like."[70] For journalists, it's always fashionable to report a conspiracy panic, but the reports above are based on little more than feelings. There is no systematic evidence supporting any of them. How can anyone know that the United States has become as conspiracy minded as the "Pan-Slav nationalists in the 1880s"? What existing data could possibly support such a claim?

Further, claims that "now" is the apex of conspiracy theorizing are made without any precision; they seem to confuse the number of conspiracy theories, the number of people who believe those theories, and the salience of those beliefs. An increase in any one of these would indicate something different and would be measured differently. To wit, few measurements have been made of any of these concepts, yet journalists have been quick to authoritatively declare that they are all rising.

Conspiracy Theories Are Extreme

Journalists often characterize conspiracy theories as extreme views, or as stemming from believers' extreme political ideologies. For example, commentators often refer to the QAnon conspiracy theory—alleging that a pedophilic deep state is working against President Trump—in this way.[71] But such claims depend first on how we define "extreme" and if we apply that definition consistently. For example, Oliver Stone's mainstream movie *JFK* is based on a conspiracy theory asserting that a pedophilic deep state conspired against President Kennedy.

It is true that people on the political extremes believe conspiracy theories, but some conspiracy theories attract moderates. JFK assassination theories consistently garner majorities in US polls; the "white replacement" theory polls close to 50 percent in France; and a majority of Brits believed that the EU was hiding secret plans of further integration.[72] People who have middle-of-the-road political views believe such conspiracy theories; the theories are therefore not strictly the province of society's political extremists.

We could define the *content* of conspiracy theories as extreme, but in order to do so, we would need an objective way to categorize some content as extreme and other content as not. However, such categorizations are often applied subjectively, if at all. For example, many people who believe that George W. Bush was behind the destruction of the Twin Towers on 9/11 also argue that the Birther theory—that Barack Obama faked his birth certificate—is too extreme to be believed.[73] But I am not sure on what evenly applied metric such a claim could be made. Is accusing one president of killing three thousand of his own people less extreme than accusing another of usurping the presidency? Is accusing one president of setting explosives in one of the world's busiest cities, undetected, less extreme than accusing another of forging documents and hiding his true birthplace? I don't want to suggest that either of these two conspiracy theories is likely, but I do want to suggest that making clear distinctions between the two is a more difficult task than it first appears.

Conspiracy Theories Are for the Mentally Ill

Many journalists dismiss conspiracy theories as a form of mental illness.[74] Pejoratives like *paranoid*, *crazy*, and *delusional* are occasionally used. But there is little evidence to link conspiracy theories to any psychopathology (i.e., a mental or behavioral disorder). First, polls suggest that everyone believes in at least one or a few conspiracy theories. Unless we want to label everyone as mentally ill, then we should not suggest that conspiracy theories indicate a psychopathology.

Second, people who are truly ill tend not to be driven by conspiracy theories per se. According to Dr. Ken Duckworth, medical director of the National Alliance of Mental Illness, "most people with major mental illness don't believe in conspiracy theories."[75] The mentally ill tend to engage in delusions that are self-centric, such as "the mailman is after me," rather than group-centric conspiracy theories: "the postal workers are all out to get us."[76] Also, according to Duckworth, many of the theories that conspiracy theorists believe would be laughed at by people suffering from mental illness.[77]

Conspiracy Theories Are Believed by Conservatives More Than Liberals

This claim has been made widely since Hofstadter's famous essays looked at the paranoid style of right-wing groups in the 1950s.[78] However, there has been little systematic evidence showing that the right is more prone to conspiracy theorizing than the left in the United States. We will spend more time discussing this in chapter 5, but for now, polls show that people on the political left (in the United States) are just as prone to conspiracy theories as people on the right.[79] When we do find differences, those differences tend to be small and can be attributed to the way the beliefs were measured. For example, if we only look at beliefs in conspiracy theories that accuse communists, then our data-collection efforts will yield mostly believers on the right, leaving folks on the left looking quite reasonable. However, if we looked at conspiracy theories that impugned corporations or Republicans, then we would find the opposite.[80]

Each side believes in conspiracy theories more or less equally, but they tend to believe in different ones that accuse the opposing side.[81] An important point is that there is nothing inherent in Republicanism, conservatism, or right-wing politics that makes people more conspiratorial in their outlook, so there is no reason is expect that people on the right would partake in conspiracy theories more than anyone else. That said, this is an empirical finding and may change over time and/or vary across geographic context.

Conspiracy Theories Are More Popular in the United States (or in Some Other Place)

Americans like to think of ourselves as being exceptional in many ways, but one way we are not exceptional is in our conspiracy theorizing. While more polling across contexts is needed, the available evidence suggests that conspiracy theories are popular everywhere polling has been done, though not necessarily equally popular.

It can be tempting to label particular nationalities as especially prone to conspiracy theorizing. The *New York Times*, in addition to suggesting that Americans are particularly taken with conspiracy theories, has tarred Mexicans, Arabs, Afghanis, Pakistanis, Bangladeshis, Iraqis, Africans, Egyptians, Russians, Bulgarians, Italians, Yemenis, and the gay community as being particularly prone to conspiracy theorizing.[82] The best the literature can tell us, however, is that no one country or region has a monopoly on the practice. We should avoid casting such aspersions until more data is in.

What This Book Will Do

Thus far, I have attempted to make the case that it is important to study conspiracy theories. In the next chapter, I will provide working definitions for the most frequent terms used to discuss conspiracy theories, starting with, of course, *conspiracy theory*. The remainder of this primer will introduce students to the latest research on conspiracy theories. In chapters 3 and 4, I will discuss the latest polling numbers and research by psychologists and sociologists. Chapter 5 addresses the political causes of conspiracy theorizing and the conspiracy theories endorsed by President Donald

Trump and those surrounding his presidency. In the final chapter, I will discuss the effect of society's information-sources and address ways for mitigating the negative effects of conspiracy theories.

I want to make clear that this short book is a primer—it cannot cover every conspiracy theory or every reason for believing them. A book of this length cannot provide a complete picture, but it does provide a complete-enough picture. Many will consider this book a polemic, but that is not my intention. The following chapters will upset not only believers of specific conspiracy theories, but also partisans. I may have upset *you* already.

I will likely be charged with excusing the conspiracy theories of one group or another, of referring to real conspiracies as conspiracy theories, of denigrating conspiracy theorists, and of shilling for powerful interests. Such accusations are commonplace in the study of conspiracy theories. My punishment for researching this topic is an inbox filled with insults and allegations, perverse offers to spy on family members for my research, pleas for help in deprogramming conspiracy-obsessed family members, and the occasional threat. This is how the study of conspiracy theories goes, and exactly why it needs to be studied with compassion and understanding.

Bibliography

Aaronovitch, David. *Voodoo Histories: The Role of Conspiracy Theory in Shaping Modern History*. New York: Riverhead Books, 2010.

Bailey, Ronald. "Vermont GMO Labeling Hits Kosher Foods." *Reason* (2016). Published electronically July 11, 2016.

BBC Trending. "EU Referendum: 'Use Pens' Plea of Voting Fraud 'Conspiracy Theorists.'" *BBC Trending* (2016). Published electronically June 22, 2016.

Berman, Ari. "The Democratic Primary Wasn't Rigged." *The Nation* (2016). Published electronically June 16, 2016.

Broniatowski, David A., Karen M. Hilyard, and Mark Dredze. "Effective Vaccine Communication during the Disneyland Measles Outbreak." *Vaccine* 34, no. 28 (2016): 3225–28.

Brown, Elizabeth Nolan. "Nabbing Robert Kraft Helped Florida Prosecutors Get Headlines. Now Kraft and Other Orchids of Asia Customers Are Fighting Back." *Reason* (2019). Published electronically April 23, 2019.

———. "Patriots Owner Robert Kraft's Bust Is Being Billed as a Human Trafficking Bust, but It Looks More Like Ordinary Prostitution." *Reason.com* (2019). Published electronically February 22, 2019.

———. "This Is How Sex-Trafficking Panic Gets Made: Reason Roundup." *Reason* (2018). Published electronically October 10, 2018.

Burdick, Alan. "Looking for Life on a Flat Earth." *New Yorker* (2018). Published electronically May 30, 2018.

Butler, Lisa D., Cheryl Koopman, and Philip G. Zimbardo. "The Psychological Impact of Viewing the Film *JFK*: Emotions, Beliefs, and Political Behavioral Intentions." *Political Psychology* 16, no. 2 (1995): 237–57.

Butter, Michael, and Peter Knight. "The History of Conspiracy Theory Research: A Review and Commentary." In *Conspiracy Theories and the People Who Believe Them*, edited by Joseph E. Uscinski, 33–46. New York: Oxford University Press, 2018.

Carstairs, Catherine, and Rachel Elder. "Expertise, Health, and Popular Opinion: Debating Water Fluoridation, 1945–80." *Canadian Historical Review* 89, no. 3 (2008): 345–71.

Chokshi, Niraj. "False Flags, True Believers and Trolls: Understanding Conspiracy Theories after Tragedies." *Washington Post*, December 4, 2015.

Chuck, Elizabeth. "Science Says Fluoride in Water Is Good for Kids. So Why Are These Towns Banning It?" NBC News (2018). Published electronically October 17, 2018.

"Conspira-Sea Cruise." Legendary World Travel, http://www.divinetravels.com /ConspiraSeaCruise.html.

Cox, Lauren, and ABC News Medical Unit. "What's behind Internet Conspiracy Empires?" ABC News (2008). Published electronically December 12, 2008.

Crocker, Jennifer, Riia Luhtanen, Stephanie Broadnax, and Bruce Evan Blaine. "Belief in U.S. Government Conspiracies against Blacks among Black and White College Students: Powerlessness or System Blame?" *Personality and Social Psychology Bulletin* 25, no. 8 (August 1, 1999): 941–53.

Dabashi, Hamid. "Living in a Conspiracy Theory in Trump's America." *Aljazeera .com* (2018). Published electronically November 1, 2018.

Douglas, Karen M., and Ana C. Leite. "Suspicion in the Workplace: Organizational Conspiracy Theories and Work-Related Outcomes." *British Journal of Psychology* 108, no. 3 (2017): 486–506.

Douglas, Karen, and Robbie Sutton. "Does It Take One to Know One? Endorsement of Conspiracy Theories Is Influenced by Personal Willingness to Conspire." *British Journal of Social Psychology* 50, no. 3 (2011): 544–52.

Drochon, Hugo. "Who Believes in Conspiracy Theories in Great Britain and Europe?" In *Conspiracy Theories and the People Who Believe Them*, edited by Joseph E. Uscinski, 337–46. New York: Oxford University Press, 2018.

Dunning, Brian. *Conspiracies Declassified: The Skeptoid Guide to the Truth behind the Theories*. Avon, MA: Adams Media, 2018.

Ebbert, Stephanie. "In Wayland, Suburban Dog-Walking Moms Target Sex Trafficking." *Boston Globe* (2019). Published electronically April 27, 2019.

Edelson, Jack, Alexander Alduncin, Christopher Krewson, James A. Sieja, and Joseph E. Uscinski. "The Effect of Conspiratorial Thinking and Motivated Reasoning on Belief in Election Fraud." *Political Research Quarterly* 70, no. 4 (2017): 933–46.

"8 in 10 French People Believe a Conspiracy Theory: Survey." *France24* (2018). Published electronically January 8, 2018.

Enders, Adam M., and Steven M. Smallpage. "Polls, Plots, and Party Politics: Conspiracy Theories in Contemporary America." In *Conspiracy Theories and the People Who Believe Them*, edited by Joseph E. Uscinski, 298–318. New York: Oxford University Press, 2018.

Ernst, Edzard, and Angelo Fasce. "Dismantling the Rhetoric of Alternative Medicine: Smokescreens, Errors, Conspiracies, and Follies." *Mètode Science Studies Journal-Annual Review*, no. 8 (2017).

Farrakhan, Louis, and Henry Louis Gates Jr. "Farrakhan Speaks." *Transition*, no. 70 (1996): 140–67.

Furnham, Adrian. "Commercial Conspiracy Theories: A Pilot Study." *Frontiers in Psychology* 4 (2013).

Gall, Carlotta. "Turkey Orders New Election for Istanbul Mayor, in Setback for Opposition." *New York Times* (2019). Published electronically May 6, 2019.

Geyer, Georgie Anne. "The Rewriting of History to Fit Our Age of Conspiracy." *Los Angeles Times*, 1977, 1.

Gibson, James L. "Political Intolerance and Political Repression during the McCarthy Red Scare." *American Political Science Review* 82, no. 2 (1988): 511–29.

Goertzel, Ted. "The Conspiracy Theory Pyramid Scheme." In *Conspiracy Theories and the People Who Believe Them*, edited by Joseph E. Uscinski, 226–42. New York: Oxford University Press, 2018.

Gray, Kathleen. "Bernie Sanders: Election Is about Survival of Middle Class." *Detroit Free Press* (2016). Published electronically October 7, 2016.

Haag, Matthew, and Maya Salam. "Gunman in 'Pizzagate' Shooting Is Sentenced to 4 Years in Prison." *New York Times* (2017). Published electronically June 22, 2017.

Hargrove, Thomas. "Third of Americans Suspect 9/11 Government Conspiracy." *Scripps News*, August 1, 2006.

Harmon, Amy. "A Lonely Quest for Facts on Genetically Modified Crops." *New York Times*, January 4, 2014.

Hill, Frances. *A Delusion of Satan: The Full Story of the Salem Witch Trials*. Tantor eBooks, 2014.

Hofstadter, Richard. *The Paranoid Style in American Politics, and Other Essays*. Cambridge, MA: Harvard University Press, 1964.

Hollingworth, Robert M., Leonard F. Bjeldanes, Michael Bolger, Ian Kimber, Barbara Jean Meade, Steve L. Taylor, and Kendall B. Wallace. "The Safety of Genetically Modified Foods Produced through Biotechnology." *Toxological Sciences* 71 (2003): 2–8.

Hurley, Patrick T., and Peter A. Walker. "Whose Vision? Conspiracy Theory and Land-Use Planning in Nevada County, California." *Environment and Planning* 36 (2004): 1529–47.

Icke, David. *Human Race Get Off Your Knees: The Lion Sleeps No More*. Isle of Wight: David Icke Books, 2010.

Jacobsen, Annie. "The United States of Conspiracy: Why, More and More, Americans Cling to Crazy Theories." *NYDailyNews.com*, August 7, 2011. http://articles.nydailynews.com/2011-08-07/news/29878465_1_conspiracy-theories-bavarian-illuminati-nefarious-business.

Johnson, Kevin, Ray Locker, Brad Heath, and Aamer Madhani. "'It's Time to Destroy Trump & Co.': Scalise Shooter Raged on Facebook." *USA Today* (2017). Published electronically June 14, 2017.

Jolley, Daniel, and Karen Douglas. "The Effects of Anti-Vaccine Conspiracy Theories on Vaccination Intentions." *PLoS ONE* 9, no. 2 (2014): e89177.

Kang, Cecilia. "Fake News Onslaught Targets Pizzeria as Nest of Child-Trafficking." *New York Times*, November 21, 2016.

Keeley, Brian. "Of Conspiracy Theories." In *Conspiracy Theories: The Philosophical Debate*, edited by David Coady, 45–60. Burlington, VT: Ashgate, 2006.

"Kenneka Jenkins' Death Photos 'Raise More Questions,' Lawyer Says as Police Close Case." *Chicago Tribune* (2017). Published electronically October 23, 2017.

Klein, Colin, Peter Clutton, and Adam G. Dunn. "Pathways to Conspiracy: The Social and Linguistic Precursors of Involvement in Reddit's Conspiracy Theory Forum." psyarxiv. com/8vesf (2018).

Kloor, Keith. "GMO Opponents Are the Climate Skeptics of the Left." *Slate.com*, September 26, 2012.

Knight, Peter. *Conspiracy Culture: From the Kennedy Assassination to the* X-Files. London: Routledge, 2000.

——, ed. *Conspiracy Theories in American History*, vol. 1. Santa Barbara, CA: ABC-CLIO, 2003.

Krauss, C. "28 Years after Kennedy's Assassination, Conspiracy Theories Refuse to Die." *New York Times*, January 5, 1992, 12.

Krauthammer, Charles. "A Rash of Conspiracy Theories." *Washington Post*, July 5, 1991.

LaCapria, Kim. "Hickory (NC) Walmart Human Trafficking Warning." Snopes.com (2015). Published electronically 2015.

Latner, Richard. "'Here Are No Newters': Witchcraft and Religious Discord in Salem Village and Andover." *New England Quarterly* 79, no. 1 (2006): 92–122.

Leeson, Peter T., and Jacob W. Russ. "Witch Trials." *Economic Journal* 128, no. 613 (2018): 2066–105.

Lind, Dara. "The Conspiracy Theory That Led to the Pittsburgh Synagogue Shooting, Explained." *Vox.com* (2018). Published electronically October 29, 2018.

Lowry, Rich. "Bernie's Conspiracy Theory." *National Review* (2015). Published electronically October 30, 2015.

Marrs, Jim. *Population Control: How Corporate Owners Are Killing Us*. New York: William Morrow, 2015.

Martin, Sean. "UFO Hunters Discover Alien Base on Google Moon Maps—Bizarre Pyramid Found." *Express* (2018). Published electronically September 30, 2018.

McHoskey, John W. "Case Closed? On the John F. Kennedy Assassination: Biased Assimilation of Evidence and Attitude Polarization." *Basic and Applied Social Psychology* 17, no. 3 (1995): 395.

McLaren, Lindsay, Steven Patterson, Salima Thawer, Peter Faris, Deborah McNeil, Melissa Potestio, and Luke Shwart. "Measuring the Short-Term Impact of Fluoridation Cessation on Dental Caries in Grade 2 Children Using Tooth Surface Indices." *Community Dentistry and Oral Epidemiology* 44, no. 3 (2016): 274–82.

McMahon, Darrin M. "Conspiracies So Vast: Conspiracy Theory Was Born in the Age of Enlightenment and Has Metastasized in the Age of the Internet. Why Won't It Go Away?" *Boston Globe*, February 1, 2004.

"MH370 Conspiracy Theories: What Really Happened to the Missing Malaysia Airlines Flight?" *The Week* (2018). Published electronically August 22, 2018.

Miller, Justin. "How Greg Abbott Got Played by the Russians during His Jade Helm Freakout." *Texas Observer* (2018). Published electronically May 3, 2018.

Morton, Brian. "The Guns of Spring." *City Paper Baltimore* (2009). Published electronically April 15, 2009.

Musgrave, Paul. "Conspiracy Theories Are for Losers. QAnon Is No Exception." *Washington Post* (2018). Published electronically August 2, 2018.

NASA. "Apollo 11 Mission Overview." NASA.gov. May 15, 2019. https://www .nasa.gov/mission_pages/apollo/missions/apollo11.html.

Nyhan, Brendan. "9/11 and Birther Misperceptions Compared." *Brendan-nyhan .com/blog* (2009).

Oliver, Eric, and Thomas Wood. "Medical Conspiracy Theories and Health Behaviors in the United States." *JAMA Internal Medicine* 174, no. 5 (2014): 817–18.

Olmsted, Kathryn S. *Real Enemies: Conspiracy Theories and American Democracy, World War I to 9/11*. New York: Oxford University Press, 2008.

Orr, Martin, and Ginna Husting. "Media Marginalization of Racial Minorities: 'Conspiracy Theorists' in U.S. Ghettos and on the 'Arab Street.'" In *Conspiracy Theories and the People Who Believe Them*, edited by Joseph E. Uscinski, 82–93. New York: Oxford University Press, 2018.

Osher, Christopher N. "Bike Agenda Spins Cities toward U.N. Control, Maes Warns." *Denverpost.com*, August 4, 2010.

Pickard, James. "Corbyn Lashes Out at Financial Sector 'Speculators and Gamblers.'" *Financial Times* (2017). Published electronically November 30, 2017.

Rosenthal, Andrew. "No Comment Necessary: Conspiracy Nation." *New York Times* (2013). Published electronically January 17, 2013.

Russakoff, Dale, and Serge F. Kovaleski. "An Ordinary Boy's Extraordinary Rage." *Washington Post* (1995). Published electronically July 2, 1995.

Sabato, Larry J. *The Kennedy Half-Century: The Presidency, Assassination, and Lasting Legacy of John F. Kennedy*. New York: Bloomsbury USA, 2013.

Selk, Avi. "Falsely Accused of Satanic Horrors, a Couple Spent 21 Years in Prison. Now They're Owed Millions." *Washington Post* (2017). Published electronically August 25, 2017.

Shackford, Scott. "Backpage Founder's 93 Charges Lack Actual Sex-Trafficking Claims." *Reason* (2018). Published electronically April 9, 2018.

Shenon, Philip. "Files Will Shed Light on a JFK Shooting Conspiracy—but Not the One You Think." *The Guardian* (2017). Published electronically October 26, 2017.

Smallpage, Steven M., Adam M. Enders, and Joseph E. Uscinski. "The Partisan Contours of Conspiracy Theory Beliefs." *Research & Politics* 4, no. 4 (2017): 2053168017746554.

Stanley-Becker, Isaac. "'We Are Q': A Deranged Conspiracy Cult Leaps from the Internet to the Crowd at Trump's 'Maga' Tour." *Washington Post* (2018). Published electronically August 1, 2018.

Stolworthy, Jacob. "Stanley Kubrick's Daughter Debunks Moon Landing Conspiracy Theory." *Independent* (2016). Published electronically July 6, 2016.

Thomas, Kenn. "Clinton Era Conspiracies! Was Gennifer Flowers on the Grassy Knoll? Probably Not, but Here Are Some Other Bizarre Theories for a New Political Age." *Washington Post*, January 16, 1994.

Tupy, Marian. "Europe's Anti-GMO Stance Is Killing Africans." *Reason* (2017). Published electronically September 5, 2017.

"Turkey Academic Jailed after Raids on Professors and Activists." *Aljazeera.com* (2018). Published electronically November 19, 2018.

Uscinski, Joseph E., Karen Douglas, and Stephan Lewandowsky. "Climate Change Conspiracy Theories." In *Oxford Research Encyclopedia of Climate Science.* Oxford: Oxford University Press, 2017, 1–43.

Uscinski, Joseph E., and Joseph M. Parent. *American Conspiracy Theories.* New York: Oxford University Press, 2014.

van der Linden, Sander. "The Conspiracy-Effect: Exposure to Conspiracy Theories (about Global Warming) Decreases Pro-Social Behavior and Science Acceptance." *Personality and Individual Differences* 87: 171–73.

Victor, Jeffrey S. "Moral Panics and the Social Construction of Deviant Behavior: A Theory and Application to the Case of Ritual Child Abuse." *Sociological Perspectives* 41, no. 3 (1998): 541–65.

"The Warren Commission Report." *New York Times*, September 28, 1964, 1.

Wiles, Tay. "Conspiracy Theories Inspire Vigilante Justice in Tucson." *High Country News* (2018). Published electronically September 12, 2018.

2

What Is a Conspiracy Theory?

This chapter takes on perhaps the most important task of this book: defining our concepts. Definitions are particularly important because arguments about conspiracy theories often turn on what counts as conspiracy theory and what does not. People who believe in a particular conspiracy theory do so because they believe it is true and well evidenced; therefore, they tend to consider it as not conspiracy *theory* at all but rather as conspiracy *fact*. Herein lies the main problem addressed in this short text: people disagree over what is true and what is not. It is possible that this book has already challenged one of your sacred beliefs by referring to it as a conspiracy theory. As I provide a definition for the term *conspiracy theory* in this chapter, I hope you will consider why you categorize and believe the conspiracy theories that you do.

Arguments often hinge on definitions, but they shouldn't. Definitions are not fixed, and words have usages rather than intrinsic meanings. As long as we agree on what the words we use mean, we can communicate effectively. Take a ubiquitous term like *middle class*; it might mean one thing to one person but something entirely different to another. There are few speeches made by politicians in the United States that do not discuss the plight of the middle class. One problem is that most people—rich and poor—consider themselves to be middle class, rendering the term meaningless. Worse is that when asked what they mean by this term (which they use over and over), politicians often can't say.[1] If politicians say they want to give a benefit to, or place a tax on, the middle class, who exactly are they talking about?

Using terms without clear meanings attached to them is a serious problem because the language becomes empty. To avoid this, *conspiracy theory*, its variants, and other related terms are defined below as they will be used in this book, but keep in mind that other people may use these terms slightly differently. It is important when we communicate that we agree on how we are using our key terms, or else we may just talk past each other.

Clarity is made all the more important because the term *conspiracy theory* and its derivatives can be weaponized.[2] Few people want their ideas to be labeled "conspiracy theories" and fewer want to be called "conspiracy theorists." Such labels do little for one's standing.[3] *Conspiracy theory* and *conspiracy theorist* are frequently used to deride ideas and people, and become dangerous when employed by the powerful to deflect (sometimes legitimate) accusations of wrongdoing.

I use *conspiracy theory* and its derivatives because they are common; I intend them neutrally. Some scholars use alternative terms, but they are clunky and confusing (for example, the term *state crimes against democracy* [SCADs] is sometimes used in place of *conspiracy theory*).[4] In using *conspiracy theory*, it is not my intention to adjudicate the truthfulness of any idea, to shield wrongdoers from justice, or to deride conspiracy theorists.

Conspiracy

A conspiracy involves a small group of powerful individuals acting in secret for their own benefit and against the common good. Use of the term both in common parlance and in this text (rather than in legal terminology) suggests a large-scale attempt to inhibit rights, alter bedrock institutions, and commit large-scale fraud, most of which goes beyond traditional legal definitions of conspiracy. Therefore, this definition excludes planning to commit common illegal acts such as robbing a convenience store, killing a family member for the insurance money, or illicitly dealing narcotics. The conspiracies we discuss here can of course violate numerous laws, but that is not a necessary condition: for example, "backward masking" rock 'n' roll albums to create an army of teenage communists does not violate any specific law, but it would count as a conspiracy for our purposes.

Street-gang and Mafia activities are generally excluded from this definition of conspiracy because these groups do not intend to alter bedrock ground rules, but rather operate underneath them; terrorist activities are also usually excluded because terrorists' intentions are typically well known even if their tactics are not.[5] This definition also excludes government lobbying and legislative logrolling because these are normal democratic processes, even if they are an unsavory part of our politics.

Examples that fit our definition of conspiracy include the events commonly referred to as Watergate, Iran-Contra, and the Tuskegee experiments. *Watergate* is a blanket term encompassing a number of activities undertaken by President Richard Nixon and his administration that undermined the rule of law, sought to punish or disadvantage Nixon's opponents for political gain, and then tried to cover up those activities.[6] Iran-Contra was a scheme carried out by the Reagan administration, which sought to—against the wishes of Congress—trade arms to hostile nations in exchange for hostages. The Tuskegee experiments, carried out by the US government, injected syphilis into unsuspecting African Americans.[7] These are three obvious examples, and I unfortunately could go on with many, many more.

I consider the accusatory perception that a conspiracy has occurred to be justified when the appropriate epistemological authority has judged it as having actually occurred. *Epistemology* is the scientific study of how humans gather and build knowledge; it focuses on the difference between justified and unjustified beliefs. An *epistemological authority* generates knowledge claims and consists of a "distributed network of agents, trained in assessing knowledge claims, who make their evidence and processes available to scrutiny, within and beyond the network."[8] An appropriate epistemological authority, therefore, is one that is trained to assess knowledge claims in a relevant area and draw conclusions from valid data using recognized methods in an unbiased way. Physicists, for example, are the appropriate authority for making and evaluating claims pertaining to physics, whereas historians are more appropriate for making claims about history. Having expertise relevant to the subject area is key. Watergate, for example, is referred to as a *conspiracy* because it was deemed as such by Congress, courts, and many other investigative bodies whose hearings and evidence are open to inspection.[9] Many of the conspirators—including Nixon—admitted to their crimes in open forums.

Conspiracies happen frequently and should never be overlooked as an important, though unfortunate, part of our politics.[10] Powerful people occasionally abuse their power, and secret plots are concocted far too often. As concerned citizens, we should always be on the lookout for abuse. This does not mean, however, that all conspiracy *theories* are true.

Conspiracy Theory

Conspiracy theory is an explanation of past, present, or future events or circumstances that cites, as the primary cause, a conspiracy. Like conspiracies, conspiracy theories involve the intentions and actions of powerful people; for this reason, conspiracy theories are inherently political. Conspiracy theories are accusatory ideas that could be either true or false, and they contradict the proclamations of epistemological authorities, assuming such proclamations exist. For example, theories asserting that the George W. Bush administration orchestrated the terror attacks of 9/11/2001 run counter to the proclamations of the FBI, CIA, 9/11 Commission, and *Popular Mechanics* magazine.[11] Therefore, "9/11 Truth theories," as they are often called, are appropriately called "conspiracy theories" rather than "conspiracies."[12]

In cases where the appropriate epistemological authority has yet to investigate or reach conclusions, conspiracy theories assert a conspiracy despite a lack of affirmation. For example, even though the agencies tasked with investigating the disappearance of Malaysian Airlines Flight 370 have yet to determine the causes of the plane's disappearance, the countless theories that assert that the CIA, Vladimir Putin, or North Korea, for example, shot down or hijacked the plane are nonetheless conspiracy theories.[13] Sparked by the break-ins at the Watergate Hotel, journalists Bob Woodward and Carl Bernstein were chasing down a conspiracy theory involving Richard Nixon and his associates until the appropriate agencies determined that there was indeed a conspiracy committed by Nixon and his cronies. Labeling accusations of conspiracy as "conspiracy theories" and withholding belief in those theories are both warranted until the appropriate epistemic authorities deem them true. When that happens, we should refer to them as "conspiracies."

In this same vein, theories asserting that Donald Trump conspired with Russia to rig the 2016 presidential election were conspiracy theories prior to the release of the Mueller Report, and given Mueller's findings, will remain conspiracy theories until the appropriate epistemic authorities over-

Photo 2.1 Richard Nixon directed his underlings to engage in crimes and then to cover up those crimes.
Photofest © Photofest

turn Mueller's findings. If, at some point, the appropriate epistemic authorities find one of the many accusations of conspiracy against Trump to be true, then that one theory will then be deemed a conspiracy and every other Trump/Russia conspiracy theory (of which there are many) will remain appropriately referred to as "conspiracy theories."

The bottom line is that citizens should believe accounts from properly constituted epistemic authorities rather than theories that either (1) directly conflict with the epistemic authorities or (2) assert knowledge that has yet to be deemed authoritative by the epistemic authorities. A conspiracy theory may be true, but people are not justified in believing it until the appropriate epistemological authorities deem it true. Therefore, well-evidenced conspiracy theories may—should they reach a certain evidentiary bar—provide the grounds for investigation, appeal, and reassessment, but they should not be believed outright.

When people believe a conspiracy theory, they tend not to consider it theory at all, but rather fact. (Again, people disagree on what is true and what is not.) Conspiracy theorists often claim that their beliefs are justified because they have evidence. But that evidence may not be convincing to anyone other than true believers, and it may do nothing to convince experts in the relevant fields. David Icke has spent decades researching a conspiracy theory claiming that an ancient bloodline of human-reptilian hybrids rules the planet. Icke has published many long books on the subject, each claiming to provide concrete evidence.[14] While Icke's followers seem convinced, the vast majority of people are underwhelmed by his evidence. The explanation is that each person sets for themselves the standards by which they judge evidence; those standards are quite elastic across different conspiracy theories.

People tend to require more evidence to believe that someone from their own group did something wrong than they do to believe that someone from an opposing group did something wrong. People are also more inclined to believe that they were cheated by someone else, rather than that they cheated someone else. When a nationally representative sample of Americans was asked which presidential campaign engaged in "dirty tricks" during the 2012 campaign, partisans tended to accuse the opposing party rather than their own.[15] A study of attitudes toward the act of stealing campaign yard signs showed that people were more concerned when the other side stole yard signs than when their own side did.[16] A study of attitudes toward a recent football scandal signals the same: New England Patriots quarterback Tom Brady was accused of deflating footballs so they would be easier for his receivers to catch. However, it remains unclear if Brady had engaged in this form of cheating, as the evidence was highly contested. A study of opinions on the matter showed that people from New England (those most likely to be Patriots fans) did not believe Brady did cheat, but people living outside of New England (those most likely to be fans of opposing teams, and therefore jealous of New England's championships) believed that Brady had cheated.[17] The same evidence was out in the media for all to see, but what mattered was how people's loyalties led them to interpret that evidence. In general, people find it easier to agree with arguments that coincide with how they already view the world. When arguments challenge their worldviews, people find ways to wriggle around the contradictory evidence.[18] Truth is not subjective, but people interpret it using their own subjective worldviews and therefore come to very different conclusions about it.

By directly challenging or going beyond authoritative knowledge, conspiracy theories often call into question the very authorities charged with establishing that authoritative knowledge. For example, conspiracy theories that posit a broad conspiracy to assassinate President Kennedy assert, at least by default, that the body tasked with investigating the assassination, the Warren Commission, was duped, deficient, or dishonest. Those who argue in favor of "flat-Earth" theories accuse nearly every knowledge-generating body in the world of being in on a massive scam to trick the entire human population. Epistemic authorities can of course make mistakes. In those instances, conspiracy theories can form the basis of successful appeals. But the best way to remedy incorrect verdicts is with more epistemic authorities, rather than abandoning epistemic authority and adopting conspiracy theory.

The difference between conspiracy and conspiracy theory is sometimes blurry because many people prefer to adopt their own views rather than defer to experts, who could, in their minds, be part of the conspiracy as well. It may seem tautological, but people believe ideas because they think those ideas are probably true. People occasionally misrepresent their beliefs,[19] but it's impossible for people to believe ideas they deem false. It is easy to approach others' conspiracy theories by asking why they believe obvious falsehoods; but to the believers, the ideas are not false at all—their conspiracy theories are true. Put another way, people do not seek out ideas they believe are wrong and then adopt them anyway just so they can offend other people. The believers are not purposely attempting to thwart reality; they are merely intending to find truth, just like everyone else.

The term *conspiracy theory* and its variants carry with them much baggage, and conspiracy theorists are well aware of this. Few people want to be called "conspiracy theorists" even when their ideas clearly count. Thus, it is no wonder that conspiracy theorists have argued that the term *conspiracy theory* was created as part of a CIA conspiracy to discredit JFK assassination conspiracy theories.[20] However, there is little evidence to suggest that the CIA engaged in such a scheme, and the term *conspiracy theory* was used long before the Kennedy assassination.[21] Further, Kennedy assassination theories are among the most popular in the United States; if the CIA was plotting to tamp down on such beliefs with etymology, they did a terrible, terrible job.

Falsifiability

For the same reason that it is difficult to prove a negative, it is difficult to refute a conspiracy theory and show that there is *not* a shadowy conspiracy avoiding detection. For the conspiracy theorist, the fact that we don't have good evidence of a conspiracy only shows that the conspirators are good at covering their tracks. The wealth of evidence showing that the conspiracy doesn't exist only shows that the conspirators are good at misleading the investigators.

Thus, conspiracy theories are *non-falsifiable*. Falsifiability is a hallmark of scientific thinking: if there is no evidence that could disprove a claim, then the claim—according to some philosophers—should be ignored.[22] This might seem counterintuitive at first: Why would not being able to prove a claim wrong make belief in it irrational? The reason—in the simplest terms— is that when evidence cannot prove a claim wrong, evidence can't prove the claim right, either. At that point, the claim enters the realm of theology.

But while the absence of falsifiability does not work in favor of conspiracy theories, it should not be thought of as a death knell, either. We should expect conspirators to confuse investigators with red herrings, to conceal positive proof of their activities, and to compartmentalize their operations to stop leaks. But because of their non-falsifiability, conspiracy theories should not be thought of as true or false, but rather as more or less likely to be true. The evidentiary facts presented to support a conspiracy theory should be deemed true or false. Consider, for example, the work that the staff of *Popular Mechanics* did to address the evidence put forward by 9/11 conspiracy theorists: while they could not disprove a shadowy conspiracy, they could disprove the evidentiary claims (e.g., the angle at which the towers fell) that were used to support the various conspiracy theories.[23]

When you discuss with conspiracy theorists the veracity of their pet theories, an immediate question regarding falsifiability is: What evidence can I show you that would convince you that you are wrong? If their answer is "Nothing," then I advise you to exit the conversation. Consider the resiliency of Birther beliefs. The evidence brought to bear on these claims should have ended Birtherism. But the evidence has not stopped committed conspiracy theorists from moving the goal posts.[24] When Obama came to office, conspiracy theorists alleged he had no birth certificate. When Obama produced his short-form birth certificate, the Birthers claimed that only the long-form version would do.[25] When the long-form birth certificate was produced, conspiracy theorists claimed that he forged it. No evidence could change the mind of a committed Birther because disconfirming evidence could be reasoned away, rendering their beliefs immune to refutation.

Standards for Evaluating Conspiracy Theories

It would be useful to have a uniform standard for separating the zany conspiracy theories from those more likely to be true. Unfortunately, there is no accepted method for doing so. How would one distinguish among unfalsifiable, unauthoritative ideas? Withholding belief from conspiracy theories is therefore the most consistent strategy, because believing some conspiracy theories but rejecting others would almost certainly rely on inconsistent evidentiary standards. On the other hand, to believe in all conspiracy theories would lead one to believe in numerous contradictory and incompatible accounts. This is not to suggest that we should ignore conspiracy theories; some conspiracy theories warrant investigation. When appropriate evidence is gathered and analyzed by the epistemological authorities, then we will have reason to update our beliefs.

With this said, epistemologists have offered a variety of standards for judging conspiracy theories. Some, like Sir Karl Popper, suggest that conspiracy theories should be abandoned because they posit impossible or unfalsifiable claims, contradict epistemic authority, and are usually not the best or most likely explanation for events or circumstances.[26] Other scholars, like philosopher Brian Keeley, don't believe that conspiracy theories should be dismissed outright, but rather should be dismissed when the number of conspirators involved in the theory increases beyond the point that secrecy could be maintained.[27] Keeley notes that many conspiracy theories must be expanded in scope in order to explain why they have avoided exposure (i.e., the entire national media is also in on the conspiracy because they are not allowing the public to see the evidence!). The problem, Keeley notes, is that the more actors involved in any conspiracy, the more likely the scheme is to fail because secrecy cannot be maintained among large groups.[28] Other philosophers suggest that conspiracy theories should be rejected when other explanations seem more likely.[29] For example, philosopher Pete Mandik sums up his argument in two words, "Shit Happens!" and asserts that just because something strange or unusual occurred, it does not mean there was a shadowy conspiracy directing it. Sometimes called "cock-ups," explanations of events and circumstances that put the causal locus on coincidence, chance, and accident are often better explanations than conspiracy theories.[30]

Other scholars have attempted to formulate the conditions under which we should believe in conspiracy theories, claiming that in some instances belief is entirely rational.[31] Some scholars argue that authoritative accounts should be discarded and the conspiracy theories entertained when the evidence in favor of the official story would give the impression of having been planted. For example, researchers point to the intact passport belonging to one of the 9/11 hijackers found near the World Trade Center and claim that it is too convenient.[32]

Such standards can be helpful, but they often leave much room for subjectivity, thus rendering them elastic to the point of accommodating any preexisting belief. But, no matter what standards we apply, we should always be forthright and apply those standards consistently.[33]

The Diversity of Conspiracy Theories

Excluded from our definition of conspiracy theory are theories that accuse groups of conspiring for the common good (e.g., scientists working secretly to cure cancer for the betterment of humanity), theories that don't accuse a group of doing harm (e.g., Elvis faked his death), and theories about fiction (e.g., *Grease* is really about Sandy's hallucinations as she slowly drowns). Conspiracy theories vary in many ways, but what they have in common is a group working in secret for their own benefit and against the common good in a way that threatens bedrock ground rules and commits widespread fraud.[34] Let's briefly explore some of this diversity.

The Villains

The conspirators in various theories range from the religious (e.g., Jews, the Catholic Church) to the anti-religious (atheists or Satanists), from left (communists) to right (Koch brothers), and from the well-known (the *New York Times*) to the alternative (fake-news outlets). Almost any group can be accused of conspiring, and over time most groups are accused of conspiring at one time or another. However, groups that are well known and powerful tend to attract more accusations than groups that are unknown and powerless.

The Number of Conspirators

Conspiracy theories are at their core about groups: a group is conspiring to hurt other groups. The size of the group accused of conspiring can range from more than a million (e.g., the Freemasons) to a few dozen (e.g., the Trump campaign). Some conspiracy theories accuse a single person (e.g., George W. Bush destroyed the Twin Towers) but mean to imply that others were involved even if not explicitly named (Bush is not accused of setting explosives in the towers himself).

When Is Conspiring?

Conspiracy theories often address historical events such as the 1941 bombing of Pearl Harbor, the 1963 assassination of President Kennedy, or the 1969 moon landing. Other conspiracy theories examine events that are more contemporary, such as the most recent election; still others posit plots that will occur sometime in the future (e.g., the New World Order is planning to enslave all of humanity within the next ten years). Some conspiracy theories don't address specific events as much as they address continuing circumstances such as inequality.

The Methods

Plots range from voter fraud to dumbing down the population with fluoridated water. Sometimes the methods are rather simple, but in other cases the schemes seem quite elaborate. Consider the chemtrail conspiracy theory, which asserts that powerful groups are spraying chemicals into the air from jet planes to poison us. The problem with this scheme is that it posits a terrible delivery system: putting chemicals into the air that high up guarantees them floating into oceans rather than poisoning anyone.

The Goals

Conspiracy theories inherently assume that the conspirators wish to achieve something. This can range from making illicit profits to depopulating the planet. Sometimes the conspirators' goals have been achieved. Those who believe that President Trump conspired with Russia to rig the 2016 election can point to the fact that Trump won the election. But in other instances, the goals are never achieved: those who believe that school shootings are false flag attacks intended to curtail gun rights cannot point to any meaningful attenuation of gun rights in the United States as a result of these attacks.

One reason there are so many conspiracy theories is that there are no "official" versions in the way there are official accounts of events. There is only one report of the 9/11 Commission, but there are thousands of different variations of 9/11 conspiracy theories. Given that most conspiracy theories attract so little attention, there is no good way of measuring their numbers. In this way, conspiracy theories can be thought of as fan fiction; anyone can make up their own variation.

Conspiracy theories also attract varying amounts of attention. Millions of conspiracy theories have come and gone, but only a select few amass a large following or spark major investigations or much interest from the media. The vast majority of conspiracy theories will arrive with little notice, be discussed briefly at the office water cooler or on the dark corners of social media, and then quietly disappear. For example, in 2016, conspiracy theories suggesting that Barack Obama murdered Supreme Court Justice Antonin Scalia made headlines immediately after the justice's death, but have since been forgotten.[35] It is important to note that, usually, the most contemporaneously relevant conspiracy theories attract our attention; but if we only focus on those, then we may have a biased view of the whole.

Conspiracy Beliefs

Conspiracy beliefs are individuals' acceptance of specific conspiracy theories as likely true. While beliefs are hard to measure directly, polling the public and examining public discourse provide reasonable insight. Polls in the United States suggest that everyone believes in at least one conspiracy theory. Consider that there is an infinite number of conspiracy theories for people to believe in. Most polls only ask respondents about a few conspiracy theories, and usually about only one version of each of those. A recent poll asking about seven conspiracy theories showed that 55 percent of Americans believe in at least one.[36] Other polls suggest that the more conspiracy theories respondents are asked about, the less likely they are to believe in none.

How we measure beliefs is rather important. We need to consider that polling, while the best method for measuring beliefs, also has its shortcomings. Sometimes poll respondents jokingly say they believe in theories they don't really believe in.[37] Sometimes poll respondents say they believe a theory because they want to express a more general belief: for example, some poll respondents said they believed that Hillary Clinton was a demon, but it's unlikely all of those respondents were expressing much more than an intense dislike of her during a contentious election.[38] That said, most people don't lie about their conspiracy beliefs to pollsters.[39] Nonetheless, poll results still leave significant room for interpretation.

How a survey item is worded can affect whether the idea being asked about counts as a conspiracy theory or not. Consider a survey item asking respondents to express agreement with "Vaccines cause autism" and one asking respondents to express agreement with "Pharmaceutical companies and governments are actively working to hide the dangerous effects of vaccines from the public." The latter expresses a conspiracy theory; the former expresses a belief that is often held by anti-vaxx conspiracy theorists but is not necessarily a conspiracy theory in itself.[40]

Beyond the issue of question wording, what level of certainty qualifies as a conspiracy belief? Consider two versions of a survey question asking respondents about the chemtrail conspiracy theory. One version of this question asked respondents to agree or disagree with the theory; 5 percent agreed, 8 percent were not sure, and 87 percent disagreed.[41] A different version asked respondents if the chemtrail conspiracy theory was "completely false," "somewhat false," "somewhat true," "completely true," or if they were "unsure." Nine percent indicated they believed it was "completely true" and 19 percent indicated they believed it was "somewhat true."[42]

When the respondents who had indicated they were unsure were asked to make a "best guess," 10 percent of the total sample indicated the theory was "completely true" and 29 percent indicated it was "somewhat true." The different ways of operationalizing belief lead to estimates that vary by a factor of eight: 5 percent believe the chemtrail conspiracy theory in the first version of the question, while about 40 percent believe it's true in the second. It is not obvious which percentage is the "right" one.

Conspiracy Thinking

Some social scientists have focused less on beliefs in specific conspiracy theories and more on generalized *conspiracy thinking*.[43] Sometimes referred to as "conspiracist ideation," "conspiracy mentality," and "conspiratorial worldview" (among other variations), conspiracy thinking is conceived of as a stable predisposition that to one degree or another drives individuals to accept conspiracy theories. It could be thought of as an ideology or worldview in which the powerful actors that one doesn't like are orchestrating conspiracies.

The focus on conspiracy thinking means paying less attention to the characteristics of specific conspiracy theories and more to the characteristics of individuals. This aligns with traditional theories of public opinion that highlight the importance of predispositions in the reception of information.[44]

A *predisposition* is a tendency to hold a particular attitude, or act in a particular way. People tend to hold many different predispositions, (i.e., political, social, racial, religious, etc.), and these color how people view the world. Two people with different predispositions will likely come to very different conclusions about the exact same information. Partisanship is perhaps the predisposition most studied by political scientists (particularly in the United States). People who identify as Republicans or Democrats don't do so lightheartedly—those identifications can be very strong and heartfelt, and they condition how partisans view the world. For example, Republicans and Democrats view the country's economic performance very differently depending on who is president: right now during the Trump presidency, Republicans believe the economy is doing great (unlike Democrats); when Obama was president (with similar economic performance numbers) Republicans (unlike Democrats) believed the economy was doing poorly and that the positive reports were rigged.[45] We will return to partisanship in later chapters, but the important point here is that predispositions make people more likely to view events and circumstances in a particular way.

The research into conspiracy thinking has been ongoing for less than a decade, and social scientists have yet to discover why some people have higher levels of it than others, but it is certain that some people do exhibit more of it than others. Researcher Michael Shermer suggests the causes could be evolutionary, and therefore an adaptive trait:

> We make two types of errors: a type I error, or false positive, is believing a pattern is real when it is not; a type II error, or false negative, is not believing a pattern is real when it is. If you believe that the rustle in the grass is a dangerous predator when it is just the wind (a type I error), you are more likely to survive than if you believe that the rustle in the grass is just the wind when it is a dangerous predator (a type II error). Because the cost of making a type I error is less than the cost of making a type II error and because there is no time for careful deliberation between patternicities in the split-second world of predator-prey interactions, natural selection would have favored those animals most likely to assume that all patterns are real.

Those humans who assumed the worst were more likely to survive; those humans who assumed the rustle was just the wind were, over time, more likely to become food for predators, and therefore were less likely to reproduce. The humans who survived to produce more humans (like themselves) were those most likely to assume that the rustle was dangerous. While the evolutionary argument makes some sense (assuming you don't reject outright the theory of evolution as a conspiracy among biologists and Satanists), there is yet to be direct evidence showing that conspiracy thinking stems from evolutionary causes.[46]

Along similar lines, some researchers have attempted to find links between conspiracy thinking and biological factors, such as prenatal hormone exposure. However, such research is in its early stages, and no evidence yet indicates a relationship.[47] Similarly, scholars have found evidence that psychological factors, such as delusional thinking styles, are associated with conspiracy thinking and may therefore cause it.[48] Other scholars argue, however, that socialization—the processes that introduce young people into society and form their worldviews—determines what level of conspiracy thinking people will have later in life. For example, a person who is exposed to conspiracy theories or is the victim of real conspiracies during their youth may be more likely to see the world through a conspiracy lens later.[49] Because social scientists have yet to track the development of conspiracy thinking in people over long periods of time, it is currently impossible to know the reasons some people exhibit higher levels of conspiracy thinking than others.

Conspiracy thinking is usually measured in one of two ways. The first is to present survey respondents with a series of specific conspiracy theories and ask how many they believe in.[50] If a respondent believes in many, then he or she has high levels of conspiracy thinking. The second way is to ask questions that do not touch upon specific conspiracy theories but, rather, tap into general worldviews. Such a survey might ask respondents to agree or disagree with statements such as "Much of our lives are being controlled by plots hatched in secret places" or "Big events like wars, the recent recession, and the outcomes of elections are controlled by small groups of people who are working in secret against the rest of us."[51] There is an advantage to this latter strategy in that it seeks to tap conspiracy thinking more directly, rather than through the resultant conspiracy beliefs, which may be driven by factors other than just conspiracy thinking.

Conspiracy Theorist

Conspiracy theorist has varied uses. Its most general use is to indicate a person who believes in any conspiracy theory. The problem is that since everyone believes in at lease one conspiracy theory, the term is meaningless. A more specific use is to refer to someone who believes in a specific conspiracy theory or theories, such as 9/11 conspiracy theorists or JFK assassination conspiracy theorists. Some use the term to refer to those who invent, expand upon, or investigate conspiracy theories. Still others use *conspiracy theorist* to refer to those who use conspiracy theories for personal or political gain. Alex Jones and David Icke, for example, created small empires for themselves and have turned a handsome profit in turn. Politicians and

Photo 2.2   Alex Jones is perhaps the most successful professional conspiracy theorist in the United States.
Jeff Malet Photography / Newscom

activists have advanced political goals using conspiracy theories: Donald Trump, Bernie Sanders, Joe McCarthy, and Charles Choughlin immediately come to mind. In this book, I will limit the use of the term *conspiracy theorist* and use it only when its meaning is quite clear, and again, I use the term with no pejorative intent.

The Post-Truth World?

Fake news, misinformation, and disinformation have become important topics, particularly since the 2016 US presidential election and Brexit referendum. However, it is important to note the difference between conspiracy theories and these other concepts. For example, while not all fake news stories directly promote conspiracy theories, conspiracy theories frequently belie much of the fake-news environment: the premise of much fake news is that its special information is being hidden by the mainstream establishment and can only be accessed through alternative sources.

Many in the news claimed in 2016 that the United States (and the UK) entered a "post-truth" era in 2016. For example:

> It's official: Truth is dead. Facts are passe. . . . Oxford Dictionaries has selected "post-truth" as 2016's international word of the year, after the contentious "Brexit" referendum and an equally divisive U.S. presidential election caused usage of the adjective to skyrocket, according to the Oxford University Press. The dictionary defines "post-truth" as "relating to or denoting circumstances in which objective facts are less influential in shaping public opinion than appeals to emotion and personal belief."[52]

The discussion quickly became hyperbolic: "How did we come to a mass state of altered consciousness, as foreseen by George Orwell in *Nineteen Eighty-Four* (though it took massive blasts of electricity to persuade Winston Smith he was seeing six fingers on O'Brien's hand)? And how did we come to it so quickly?"[53] But such claims did not match the reality. First, misinformation, disinformation, fake news, and conspiracy theories have always been among us. And people were more influenced by emotions and group attachment (rather than facts) long before 2016.[54] None of this is new. Second, many people are concerned about being in a post-truth world precisely because we are very concerned with truth and we value it immensely. If we did not know about truth, then we would not be concerned about living in a post-truth world or even care if we did. Put another way, if no one cared about truth, then we wouldn't be living in a "post-truth" world—we would just call it a "truth" world because we would not care if what we thought was truth was actually true or not. The problem we really face is more perennial: people are not that great at finding truth and often come to very different conclusions about it.

Misinformation

Misinformation is information that is either false on its face or would mislead someone into adopting a false belief; it could be spread intentionally or unintentionally.[55] Conspiracy theories could be false; and for this reason, can be a form of misinformation. But on the other hand, because conspiracy theories could be true, they are not necessarily false and are therefore not necessarily misinformation. Instead, conspiracy theories—because they are at best speculative—could be misleading if they are presented as verified information when in fact they are not.

Disinformation

Information that is spread with the intent to deceive, often in the form of propaganda, is *disinformation*.[56] Governments sometimes run covert campaigns to mislead people for some political purpose. For example, the US government documented efforts by the Russian government to spread disinformation in the months leading up to the 2016 presidential election. And these efforts included "ambitious plans to stoke unrest and even violence inside the US as recently as 2018."[57] Of course, the Russians were not the only or first country to engage in such activities.

Fake News

Fake news became an important topic following the 2016 election and is best defined as "fabricated information that mimics news media content in form" but is not created with the traditional norms attributed to traditional journalistic outlets, such as fact checking and editorial gatekeeping, for "ensuring the accuracy and credibility of information."[58] Fake news can provide misinformation and/or disinformation. It can be created and disseminated for partisan political purposes (e.g., to influence voters), for economic purposes (e.g., to attract clicks), for global political purposes (e.g., to cause unrest in a competing country), or as a hoax (e.g., to trick people for the sake of doing so).

Fake outlets are numerous and often difficult to differentiate from legitimate news because fake-news purveyors—in order to appear authoritative—imitate the form of traditional news outlets. This creates the potential for pieces of fake news to reach millions on social media platforms where there is a lack of gatekeeping, and audiences are left to determine legitimacy for themselves. During the three months prior to the 2016 presidential election, the average American adult was exposed to at least one or a few fake stories.[59] When people find fake news stories on social media, they are likely to believe and share them if those stories comport with what they already believe. For example, researchers followed interactions with a fake post on

Facebook that claimed the Italian government was spraying Viagra into the air; they found that this post was engaged with more by people who had a history of engaging with conspiracy-laden content on the platform.[60] While traditional media sources still have the most reach and influence, the evidence suggests that fake news can influence people at critical junctures when authoritative information is most needed.

It is important to point out that the term *fake news* is often applied to legitimate news sources by political actors. President Trump, for example, frequently refers to CNN as fake news to discredit unfavorable reporting. Traditional news sources make mistakes, occasionally spread misinformation, have multiple biases, and engage in too much opinion and punditry. Sometimes traditional news sources don't do enough to correct these deficiencies. But just because traditional news sources aren't perfect is not an appropriate reason to abandon them, turn to fake news, or take unscrupulous politicians at their word. Traditional news outlets utilize multiple layers of gatekeeping, editing, and fact checking; they attempt to establish a reputation for credibility; and they can be held to account for their mistakes. This is what separates them from less reliable sources.

While the current systems of traditional news gatekeeping are not perfect, they are the best currently available. Similarly, the checks put in place by the scientific method and the peer-review process leave much to be desired, but they make science far more reliable than the alternatives of pseudoscience, superstition, and revelation.

The term *conspiracy theory* is used by some to include a host of other unauthoritative ideas, such as the existence of Bigfoot or aliens. While conspiracy theories can contain elements of pseudoscience, the paranormal, and the supernatural, it is important to keep the distinctions between such concepts clear. The following concepts are sometimes conflated with conspiracy theory.

Pseudoscience

Pseudoscience includes beliefs and practices purported to be based on the scientific method, but are not. There are many forms of pseudoscience, and we encounter it every day, whether online, on television, or in the local crystal shop. *Pseudoscience* and *conspiracy theory* refer to different, but overlapping, concepts. Both tend to rely on selectively chosen evidence to prove their validity, while ignoring all of the evidence that disproves their contentions. Pseudoscientific concepts often appear in conspiracy theories, but they are not a necessary component. Just the same, conspiracy theories can be a part of pseudoscientific claims, but are not necessary. For example, some pseudoscientific claims contend that positive proof is being hidden from the public by a conspiracy to hide the truth.

Cryptozoology

Cryptozoology is the pseudoscientific study of animals; the animals studied by cryptozoologists tend not to be verified as real by biologists. Bigfoot is perhaps the most prominent example in the United States; this mythical creature has spawned numerous cable television shows, including *Finding Bigfoot, Killing Bigfoot,* and *10 Million Dollar Bigfoot Bounty.* Despite the premises of these shows, none of them have brought forward an actual Bigfoot or any tangible evidence thereof. Long-standing groups, such as the Bigfoot Field Researchers Organization, have formed to track sightings and find specimens, but without success. No one has yet to locate a specimen of the creature, even though numerous people claim to have seen one.[61]

Hunters have provided multiple samples of supposed Bigfoot hair, but testing reveals that most belong to bears.[62] And the numerous prints that have been identified as possibly belonging to a Bigfoot have not offered anything conclusive.[63] While numerous people claim to have personally seen such a creature, an analysis of those sightings suggests that they occur in places inhabited by bears, suggesting the eyewitnesses are mistaking bears for Bigfoots.[64]

Some videos and pictures of Bigfoot have been put forward. The most famous visual account is the widely disputed Patterson film, shot in 1967 by Roger Patterson and Bob Gimlin. It shows a large creature with dark fur walking through the northern Californian woods for about a minute. However, attempts to authenticate the film by locating the creature have yet to be successful.[65] Outside the United States, myths speak of similar creatures, such as the Yeti, or Abominable Snowman, who supposedly occupies the Himalayan region.[66] These creatures also have yet to be verified as real.

The sheer number of people who claim to have seen a Bigfoot, even though there is no evidence that such a creature exists, suggests that eyewitness accounts and personal testimonies are not very good evidence. People make mistakes and fall victim to delusions; memory is malleable and prone to confabulation.

Other cryptozoological creatures include the Chupacabra, a small monster that supposedly feasts on goats. Sightings have occurred nearly worldwide, but mostly in Mexico and Latin America.[67] The Loch Ness Monster, or Nessie, is said to live in Loch Ness in the Scottish Highlands. Nessie has been a boon for Scottish tourism since its first publicized sightings in 1933. Since then, numerous photos purport to show a dragon or dinosaur-like creature, but none of these can be verified. A BBC television show in 2003 documented a comprehensive search of the loch using sonar beams and satellite tracking: they did not find any evidence of Nessie.[68]

Bigfoots, Chupacabras, and lake monsters on their own are not conspiracy theories. The mere existence of undiscovered creatures does not meet our definition as there is no expectation that cryptozoological creatures are conspiring against anyone. However, if one posited that the government was covering up the existence of Bigfoot for some nefarious purpose, or that corporations were secretly breeding an army of Chupacabras to take over the world, then that person would be engaging in conspiracy theory. Also, these mythical creatures demonstrate that bad evidence and vivid imaginations can create long-standing beliefs.

Paranormal

Paranormal phenomena are often included in discussions of conspiracy theory but do not meet the definition of conspiracy theory on their own. The paranormal is one "subset of pseudoscience," but what "sets the paranormal apart from other pseudosciences is a reliance on explanations for alleged phenomena that are well outside the bounds of established science," such as extrasensory perception (ESP), telekinesis, ghosts, poltergeists, life after death, reincarnation, faith healing, human auras, and so forth.[69] This contrasts with pseudoscientific explanations for nonparanormal phenomena, which, while still unscientific, seek to explain *observable* phenomena, though poorly.[70]

Many believe that they or someone they know possesses extrasensory perception (ESP). This is often described as the ability to see the future, to see events taking place in other places, or to communicate with others simply by sharing thoughts.[71] Some people believe that their pets have these extraordinary abilities as well.[72] There have been many studies that purportedly show evidence of ESP, but upon further investigation scientists have been unable to replicate any such findings; this likely indicates that such findings are statistical artifacts, or that the researchers who claim to identify evidence of ESP are using poor or biased methods.[73]

Telekinesis involves using one's mind to move or otherwise affect physical objects. This became popularized in the 1970s, most famously by Uri Geller, a man who claimed the ability to bend spoons with his mind.[74] Geller also claimed the ability to locate water and minerals underground and to make broken watches and televisions begin working with psychic powers. However, Geller's abilities seem to be more easily explained by simple parlor tricks (e.g., bending the spoons in advance).[75] Many others have since attempted to cash in on people's fascination with these supposed powers. James Hydrick, for example, claimed the ability to flip telephone book pages and spin pencils.[76] However, when these powers were tested under conditions that would have ruled out the possibility that Hydrick was simply blowing on the pages and pencils, his powers disappeared. The military applications of psychic powers (if they were to exist) have not escaped the American and Russian governments, who both invested in programs intended to deploy telekinesis as a form of statecraft. Despite the millions invested, neither government has ever been able to document any success.[77]

Ghosts are the essence of a dead person that (supposedly) can be detected by the living. A belief in ghosts is a boon to religious beliefs that offer believers' souls eternal life after death. The first problem is that there is no evidence that souls exist in the first place, and no evidence that souls transfer a person's essence after death into some other realm, be it to heaven, hell, or somewhere else. And despite the numerous television shows that send camera crews into creepy buildings to make contact with aggrieved spirits, there is no reason to expect that souls could affect the natural world in any way, much less (as is often alleged on cable TV) inhabit houses, insane asylums, and abandoned hospitals. In fact, those who have tried to define and/or identify the soul have not been able to do so. Just the very idea elicits questions that proponents can't answer.[78] For example, if a person gets Alzheimer's disease or amnesia shortly before their death, does their soul retain their previous memories and personality? If so, how so?

Life after death can be an appealing concept, especially for those who fear their eventual demise, wish to live forever, or can't stomach losing loved ones. People spend millions each year attempting to contact deceased relatives through channelers such as John Edward and the Long Island Medium, Theresa Caputo. But such channelers have not been able to prove their abilities under controlled scientific conditions, and the "contacts" they make with the dead seem to be the product of seasoned guesswork (cold reading) or of previous research (hot reading) rather than any link to the beyond.[79] Also frequent are claims of reincarnation (the dead being born again as someone else), faith healing (diseases being cured with supernatural powers), and out-of-body experiences (people leaving their body after a trauma before returning), but none of these can be substantiated under controlled scientific conditions.[80]

Many conspiracy theories have a supernatural element to them even though supernatural beliefs are not necessarily conspiratorial in nature. By *supernatural*, I mean having to do with non-natural forces such as gods, angels, demons, fate, and karma. The Salem witch trials, for example, mixed supernatural elements into conspiracy theories by accusing women of conspiring with Satan.[81]

But the supernatural has never been observed under controlled conditions and therefore cannot be substantiated: praying for patients receiving medical treatment seems to do more harm than good, if indeed it does anything at all; astrology (using celestial forces to predict human events) fails repeatedly under control conditions; and reported near-death experiences have not yielded any evidence of supernatural realms.[82]

Beliefs in aliens could qualify as supernatural, paranormal, and pseudoscientific, depending on how one conceptualized the aliens. It would be pseudoscientific to believe that aliens have visited Earth and abducted countless people, given that no such accounts can be verified.[83] But one would have science on their side if they claimed that some form of life probably exists somewhere else in the universe.[84] If one claimed that alien visits were being covered up by the government for some nefarious purpose, then one would be engaging in conspiracy theory.

Conclusion

Defining terms is always important, but it is particularly important when discussing conspiracy theories because the terms we use denote the level of legitimacy we attach to those theories. Uses will vary, but in this book *conspiracy* refers to small groups of powerful individuals acting in secret for their own benefit, and against the common good; *conspiracy theory* refers to an unauthoritative accusatory perception that a small group of powerful individuals acted/are acting/will act in secret for their own benefit, and against the common good.

People should believe a conspiracy theory—and label it a conspiracy—when that theory has been endorsed by the appropriate epistemological authorities. Conspiracy theories, when they reach a certain evidentiary threshold, should form the basis of appeals and should be investigated further. But until a conspiracy theory is deemed true by the appropriate epistemological authorities, it should be treated as suspect and properly labeled as a conspiracy theory.

Conspiracy theories are often associated with other unauthoritative accounts, such as paranormal and supernatural ideas. Conspiracy theories can include paranormal and other elements, but paranormal and other ideas are not necessarily conspiracy theories. Conspiracy theories are associated with other dubious ideas, perhaps because these other ideas, like conspiracy theories, are outside of the mainstream and challenge authoritative accounts.

Key Terms

Bigfoot
Chupacabra
cock-up theory
conspiracy
conspiracy belief
conspiracy theorist
conspiracy theory
conspiracy thinking
epistemic authority
epistemology
extrasensory perception (ESP)

fake news
falsifiability
ghosts
misinformation
paranormal
post-truth world
predisposition
pseudoscience
psychopathology
supernatural
telekinesis

Bibliography

Achen, Christopher H., and Larry M. Bartels. *Democracy for Realists: Why Elections Do Not Produce Responsive Government.* Princeton, NJ: Princeton University Press, 2017.

Allcott, Hunt, and Matthew Gentzkow. "Social Media and Fake News in the 2016 Election." *Journal of Economic Perspectives* 31, no. 2 (2017): 211–36.

Baker, Robert A. "The Aliens among Us: Hypnotic Regression Revisited." In *The Hundredth Monkey and Other Paradigms of the Paranormal: A Skeptical Inquirer Collection,* edited by Kendrick Frazier, 54–69. Buffalo, NY: Prometheus Books, 1991.

Baker, Sinead. "The Mystery of MH370 Is about to Be Laid to Rest for Good—Here Are All the Theories, Dead Ends, and Unanswered Questions from the Most Bizarre Airline Disaster of the Century." *Business Insider* (2018). Published electronically July 28, 2018.

Banjo, Shelly. "Facebook, Twitter and the Digital Disinformation Mess." *Washington Post* (2019). Published electronically May 23, 2019.

"BBC 'Proves' Nessie Does Not Exist." BBC News (2003). Published electronically July 27, 2003.

Benson, Herbert, Jeffery A. Dusek, Jane B. Sherwood, Peter Lam, Charles F. Bethea, William Carpenter, Sidney Levitsky, et al. "Study of the Therapeutic Effects of Intercessory Prayer (STEP) in Cardiac Bypass Patients: A Multicenter Randomized Trial of Uncertainty and Certainty of Receiving Intercessory Prayer." *American Heart Journal* 151, no. 4 (January 4, 2006): 934–42.

Berinsky, Adam J. "Telling the Truth about Believing the Lies? Evidence for the Limited Prevalence of Expressive Survey Responding." *Journal of Politics* 80, no. 1 (2018): 2011–224.

Bessi, Alessandro, Mauro Coletto, George Alexandru Davidescu, Antonio Scala, Guido Caldarelli, and Walter Quattrociocchi. "Science vs. Conspiracy: Collective Narratives in the Age of Misinformation." *PLoS ONE* 10, no. 2 (2015): e0118093.

Blackmore, Susan J. *Dying to Live: Near-Death Experiences.* Buffalo, NY: Prometheus Books, 1993.

Bost, P. R. "The Truth Is around Here Somewhere: Integrating the Research on Conspiracy Beliefs." In *Conspiracy Theories and the People Who Believe Them,* edited by Joseph E. Uscinski, 269–82. New York: Oxford University Press, 2018.

Boudry, Maarten, and Johan Braeckman. "Immunizing Strategies and Epistemic Mechanisms." *Philosophia* 39 (2011): 145–61.

Brotherton, Rob, Christopher C. French, and Alan D. Pickering. "Measuring Belief in Conspiracy Theories: The Generic Conspiracist Beliefs Scale." *Frontiers in Psychology* 4, Article 279 (2013).

Buenting, Joel, and Jason Taylor. "Conspiracy Theories and Fortuitous Data." *Philosophy of the Social Sciences* 40, no. 4 (2010): 567–78.

Bullock, John G., Alan S. Gerber, Seth J. Hill, and Gregory A. Huber. "Partisan Bias in Factual Beliefs about Politics." *Quarterly Journal of Political Science* 10 (2015): 519–78.

Carey, John M., Brendan Nyhan, Benjamin Valentino, and Mingnan Liu. "An Inflated View of the Facts? How Preferences and Predispositions Shape Conspiracy Beliefs about the Deflategate Scandal." *Research & Politics* 3, no. 3 (2016): 2053168016668671.

Claassen, Ryan L., and Michael J. Ensley. "Motivated Reasoning and Yard-Sign-Stealing Partisans: Mine Is a Likable Rogue, Yours Is a Degenerate Criminal." *Political Behavior* 38, no. 2 (2016): 317–35.

Clarke, Steve. "Conspiracy Theories and Conspiracy Theorizing." *Philosophy of the Social Sciences* 32, no. 2 (2002): 131–50.

Corsi, Jerome R. *Where's the Birth Certificate?: The Case That Barack Obama Is Not Eligible to Be President.* Washington, DC: WND Books, 2011.

Cox, Archibald. "Watergate and the U.S. Constitution." *British Journal of Law and Society* 2, no. 1 (1975): 1–13.

Daegling, David J. *Bigfoot Exposed: An Anthropologist Examines America's Enduring Legend.* Lanham, MD: AltaMira Press, 2004.

Dagnall, Neil, Kenneth Drinkwater, Andrew Parker, Andrew Denovan, and Megan Parton. "Conspiracy Theory and Cognitive Style: A Worldview." *Frontiers in Psychology* 6 (2015).

Dean, John W. *The Nixon Defense: What He Knew and When He Knew It.* New York: Viking, 2014.

DeHaven-Smith, Lance. *Conspiracy Theory in America.* Austin: University of Texas Press, 2013.

Dennett, Michael. "Evidence for Bigfoot? An Investigation of the Mill Creek 'Sasquatch Prints.'" *Skeptical Inquirer* 13, no. 3 (1989): 264–72.

Dentith, M. R. X. "Conspiracy Theories and Philosophy: Bringing the Epistemology of a Freighted Term into the Social Sciences." In *Conspiracy Theories and the People Who Believe Them*, edited by Joseph E. Uscinski, 94–108. New York: Oxford University Press, 2018.

Dunbar, David, and Brad Reagan. *Debunking 9/11 Myths: Why Conspiracy Theories Can't Stand Up to the Facts.* New York: Sterling, 2006.

Edelson, Jack, Alexander Alduncin, Christopher Krewson, James A. Sieja, and Joseph E. Uscinski. "The Effect of Conspiratorial Thinking and Motivated Reasoning on Belief in Election Fraud." *Political Research Quarterly* 70, no. 4 (2017).

Einstein, Katherine Levine, and David M. Glick. "Do I Think BLS Data Are BS? The Consequences of Conspiracy Theories." *Political Behavior* 37, no. 3 (2014): 1–23.

Engel, Richard, Kate Benyon-Tinker, and Kennett Werner. "Russian Documents Reveal Desire to Sow Racial Discord—and Violence—in the U.S." NBC News (2019). Published electronically May 20, 2019.

Flynn, D. J., Brendan Nyhan, and Jason Reifler. "The Nature and Origins of Misperceptions: Understanding False and Unsupported Beliefs about Politics." *Political Psychology* 38 (2017): 127–50.

Frazier, Kendrick. "Double-Blind Test of Astrology Avoids Bias, Still Refutes the Astrological Hypothesis." In *The Outer Edge: Classic Investigations of the Paranormal*, edited by Barry Karr, Joe Nickell, and Tom Genoni, 40–43. New York: CSICOP, 1996.

———. *Science Confronts the Paranormal.* Buffalo, NY: Prometheus Books, 1986.

Griffin, David Ray. *Debunking 9/11 Debunking: An Answer to* Popular Mechanics *and Other Defenders of the Official Conspiracy Theory.* N.p.: Interlink Books, 2007.

Grimes, David Robert. "On the Viability of Conspiratorial Beliefs." *PloS ONE* 11, no. 1 (2016): e0147905.

Harambam, Jaron, and Stef Aupers. "'I Am Not a Conspiracy Theorist': Relational Identifications in the Dutch Conspiracy Milieu." *Cultural Sociology* 11, no. 1 (2017): 113–29.

Hill, Frances. *A Delusion of Satan: The Full Story of the Salem Witch Trials.* Tantor eBooks, 2014.

Hines, Terence. *Pseudoscience and the Paranormal.* Buffalo, NY: Prometheus Books, 2003.

Hyman, Ray. "Cold Reading: How to Convince Strangers That You Know All about Them [1977]." In *Pseudoscience and Deception: The Smoke and Mirrors of Paranormal Claims,* edited by Bryan Farha. Lanham, MD: University Press of America (2014): 39–56.

Icke, David. *Children of the Matrix: How an Interdimensional Race Has Controlled the World for Thousands of Years—and Still Does.* Wildwood, MO: Bridge of Love Publications USA, 2001.

———. *Human Race Get Off Your Knees: The Lion Sleeps No More.* Isle of Wight: David Icke Books, 2010.

Jenson, Tom. "Democrats and Republicans Differ on Conspiracy Theory Beliefs." *Public Policy Polling* (2013). Published electronically April 2, 2013.

Kean, Thomas. *The 9/11 Commission Report: Final Report of the National Commission on Terrorist Attacks upon the United States.* Washington, DC: Government Printing Office, 2011.

Keeley, Brian. "Of Conspiracy Theories." *Journal of Philosophy* 96, no. 3 (1999): 109–26.

Klofstad, Casey A., Joseph E. Uscinski, Jennifer M. Connolly, and Jonathan P. West. "What Drives People to Believe in Zika Conspiracy Theories?" *Palgrave Communications* 5, no. 1 (2019): 36.

Knight, Peter. "Conspiracy Theories in America: A Historical Overview." In *Conspiracy Theories in American History,* vol. 1, edited by Peter Knight, 1–13. Santa Barbara, CA: ABC-CLIO, 2003.

Latner, Richard. "'Here Are No Newters': Witchcraft and Religious Discord in Salem Village and Andover." *New England Quarterly* 79, no. 1 (2006): 92–122.

Lazer, David M. J., et al. "The Science of Fake News." *Science* 359, no. 6380 (2018): 1094–96.

Levy, Neil. "Radically Socialized Knowledge and Conspiracy Theories." *Episteme* 4, no. 2 (2007): 181–92.

Lilienfeld, Scott O. "New Analyses Raise Doubts about Replicability of ESP Findings." *Skeptical Inquirer* 23 (1999): 9–10.

Lodge, Milton, and Charles S. Taber. *The Rationalizing Voter.* New York: Cambridge University Press, 2013.

Lopez, Jesse, and D. Sunshine Hillygus. "Why So Serious?: Survey Trolls and Misinformation." *SSRN*, March 14, 2018. https://ssrn.com/abstract=3131087 or http://dx.doi.org/10.2139/ssrn.3131087.

Lozier, J. D., P. Aniello, and M. J. Hickerson. "Predicting the Distribution of Sasquatch in Western North America: Anything Goes with Ecological Niche Modelling." *Journal of Biogeography* 36, no. 9 (2009): 1623–27.

Mandik, Pete. "Shit Happens." *Episteme* 4, no. 2 (2007): 205–18.

Manwell, Laurie A. "In Denial of Democracy: Social Psychological Implications for Public Discourse on State Crimes against Democracy Post-9/11." *American Behavioral Scientist* 53, no. 6 (2010): 848–84.

Mays, Vickie M., Courtney N. Coles, and Susan D. Cochran. "Is There a Legacy of the U.S. Public Health Syphilis Study at Tuskegee in HIV/AIDS-Related Beliefs among Heterosexual African Americans and Latinos?" *Ethics & Behavior* 22, no. 6 (2012): 461–71.

McKenzie-McHarg, Andrew. "Conspiracy Theory: The Nineteenth-Century Prehistory of a Twentieth-Century Concept." In *Conspiracy Theories and the People Who Believe Them*, edited by Joseph E. Uscinski, 62–81. New York: Oxford University Press, 2018.

McKenzie-McHarg, Andrew, and Rolf Fredheim. "Cock-Ups and Slap-Downs: A Quantitative Analysis of Conspiracy Rhetoric in the British Parliament 1916–2015." *Historical Methods: A Journal of Quantitative and Interdisciplinary History* 50, no. 3 (2017): 156–69.

Miller, Joanne M., Kyle L. Saunders, and Christina E. Farhart. "Conspiracy Endorsement as Motivated Reasoning: The Moderating Roles of Political Knowledge and Trust." *American Journal of Political Science* 60, no. 4 (2016): 824–44.

Nathan, Debbie, and Michael Snedeker. *Satan's Silence: Ritual Abuse and the Making of a Modern American Witch Hunt*. iUniverse, 2001.

Nickell, Joe. "Bigfoot as Big Myth: Seven Phases of Mythmaking." *Skeptical Inquirer* 41, no. 5 (September/October 2017).

Nickell, Joe, Barry Karr, and Tom Genoni. *The Outer Edge: Classic Investigations of the Paranormal*. Committee for the Scientific Investigation of Claims of the Paranormal, 1996.

Norman, Matthew. "Whoever Wins the US Presidential Election, We've Entered a Post-Truth World—There's No Going Back Now." *The Independent* (2016). Published electronically November 8, 2016.

Oliver, Eric, and Thomas Wood. "Conspiracy Theories and the Paranoid Style(s) of Mass Opinion." *American Journal of Political Science* 58, no. 4 (2014): 952–66.

Olmsted, Kathryn S. *Challenging the Secret Government: The Post-Watergate Investigations of the CIA and FBI*. Chapel Hill: University of North Carolina Press, 2000.

Orr, Martin, and Ginna Husting. "Media Marginalization of Racial Minorities: 'Conspiracy Theorists' in U.S. Ghettos and on the 'Arab Street.'" In *Conspiracy Theories and the People Who Believe Them*, edited by Joseph E. Uscinski, 82–93. New York: Oxford University Press, 2018.

Peck, Michael. "The CIA's Secret Plan to Crush Russia during the Cold War: Super Psychic Powers." *National Interest* (2017). Published electronically March 20, 2017.

Popper, Sir Karl R. *Conjectures and Refutations*. London: Routledge & Kegan Paul, 1972.

———. *The Open Society and Its Enemies. Vol. 2: The High Tide of Profecy: Hegel, Marx, and the Aftermath.* 5th ed. London: Routledge & Kegan Paul, 1966.

"Possible Bigfoot Sighting in Whitehall, NY." WHEC Channel 10 (2018). Published electronically August 13, 2018.

Public Policy Polling. "Clinton's Florida Lead Continues to Grow." (2016). Published electronically October 14, 2016.

Radford, Benjamin. "Bigfoot at 50: Evaluating a Half-Century of Bigfoot Evidence." *Skeptical Inquirer* 26, no. 2 (2002): 29–34.

———. *Tracking the Chupacabra: The Vampire Beast in Fact, Fiction, and Folklore.* Albuquerque: University of New Mexico Press, 2011.

Räikkä, Juha, and Lee Basham. "Conspiracy Theory Phobia." In *Conspiracy Theories and the People Who Believe Them*, edited by Joseph E. Uscinski, 178–86. New York: Oxford University Press, 2018.

Randi, James. *The Magic of Uri Geller.* New York: Ballantine Books, 1975.

———. *The Truth about Uri Geller.* Buffalo, NY: Prometheus Books, 1982.

Regal, Brian. *Pseudoscience: A Critical Encyclopedia.* Westport, CT: ABC-CLIO, 2009.

Richards, Gareth. "Digit Ratio (2d: 4d) and Beliefs in Superstitions, Conspiracy Theories and the Paranormal." *Developmental Psychology Section* (2017): 21.

Sagan, Carl. *The Demon-Haunted World: Science as a Candle in the Dark.* New York: Ballantine Books, 1997.

Sheldrake, Rupert, and Pamela Smart. "Psychic Pets: A Survey in North-West England." *Journal-Society for Psychical Research* 61 (1997): 353–64.

Shermer, Michael. *Why People Believe Weird Things: Pseudoscience, Superstition, and Other Confusions of Our Time.* New York: Macmillan, 2002.

Street, Jon. "Sen. Elizabeth Warren: Middle Class Is Not Defined by Income Level." *CNSNews.com* (2013). Published electronically January 8, 2013.

Sykes, Bryan C., Rhettman A. Mullis, Christophe Hagenmuller, Terry W. Melton, and Michel Sartori. "Genetic Analysis of Hair Samples Attributed to Yeti, Bigfoot and Other Anomalous Primates." *Proceedings of the Royal Society B* 281, no. 1789 (2014): 20140161.

Tingley, Dustin, and Gernot Wagner. "Solar Geoengineering and the Chemtrails Conspiracy on Social Media." *Palgrave Communications* 3, no. 1 (2017): 12.

Uscinski, Joseph E. "The Psychology behind Why People Believe Conspiracy Theories about Scalia's Death." *Washington Post*, February 19, 2016.

van Prooijen, Jan-Willem, and Karen M. Douglas. "Conspiracy Theories as Part of History: The Role of Societal Crisis Situations." *Memory Studies* 10, no. 3 (2017): 323–33.

van Prooijen, Jan-Willem, and Mark van Vugt. "Conspiracy Theories: Evolved Functions and Psychological Mechanisms." *Perspectives on Psychological Science* 13, no. 6 (2018): 770–88.

Walker, Jesse. "What We Mean When We Say 'Conspiracy Theory.'" In *Conspiracy Theories and the People Who Believe Them*, edited by Joseph E. Uscinski, 53–61. New York: Oxford University Press, 2018.

Wang, Amy. "'Post-Truth' Named 2016 Word of the Year by Oxford Dictionaries." *Washington Post* (2019). Published electronically November 16, 2016.

Zaller, John. *The Nature and Origins of Mass Opinion.* Cambridge: Cambridge University Press, 1992.

3

The Popularity of Conspiracy and Anomalous Beliefs

Do you believe that President John F. Kennedy was killed by a lone gunman or by a conspiracy? If you answered the latter, who do you believe orchestrated the conspiracy? The Soviets, Fidel Castro, the Mafia, the CIA, or someone else? Do you believe the moon landing was faked by NASA as part of a Cold War plot? How about vaccines? Do you believe the true dangers of vaccines are being hidden from you by an unscrupulous biomedical industry? Are you afraid to eat genetically modified foods because they are unsafe, and do you believe this fact is actively being hidden from us? Maybe you are afraid to travel around the world in an airplane or boat because someone has convinced you that you will fall off the edge?

I could go on asking about your conspiracy beliefs, but I would run out of space before running out of conspiracy theories. If you answered yes to having a conspiracy belief, then in the most general sense, you are a conspiracy theorist. Now, no need to panic; you are not alone. This chapter uses recent US and worldwide polling data to show just how prevalent and widespread conspiracy beliefs are. In addition to examining the prevalence of conspiracy beliefs, I will describe the prevalence of other *anomalous beliefs*, or beliefs that speak to the existence of paranormal, pseudoscientific, and supernatural phenomenon.

Conspiracy and Anomalous Beliefs

Most of the research measuring conspiracy and other anomalous beliefs uses surveys to poll the public. This involves researchers picking topics to investigate, writing questions to ask, and then distributing a survey to a sample of people. Obviously, if researchers wanted to poll the United States, they could not reach all 320 million people; instead they would attempt to contact a manageable sample of people (between five hundred and twelve hundred, usually) and ensure that those individuals are representative of the population as a whole. The hope is that the results of asking questions to just this group of people would be similar to the results if we asked everyone in the population.

When polling the public, one major consideration is the cost associated with polling each additional respondent (either paying respondents or paying people to contact respondents) and with survey time (paying respondents or surveyors). When looking at the results of a survey, we should understand that the surveys that have been performed are only a small subset of the surveys that could be performed if resources were unlimited.

To best understand public opinion, it is best to gather multiple surveys over time asking about the same topic in both similar and different ways. In other words, survey results are partly due to public opinion (the concept being measured) and partly due to the method of measurement (e.g., the way the survey question is worded and administered). Here are a few important considerations to have in mind when looking at polls of conspiracy beliefs:

When was the survey taken? Belief in a conspiracy theory is likely to wax and wane over time and in relation to contemporaneous events. Asking about 9/11 conspiracy theories, for example, might yield different results depending on whether the poll was taken the week after, the year after, or a decade after the attacks. Particularly with conspiracy theories that address events, we need to be cognizant of the time that has passed.

What is the instrument? By this, I mean what the survey question is, how it is asked, and what answers a respondent could provide. Changing the wording of a survey question or changing the responses a respondent could choose will change the results, sometimes radically. Also, we need to consider whether the question is actually asking about a conspiracy belief. For example, asking respondents if they agree that "the findings of the 9/11 Commission are entirely correct" will likely elicit negative responses from 9/11 conspiracy theorists, but it will also garner negative responses from people who believe that the 9/11 Commission made a few inadvertent errors. In such an instance, it would be better to ask whether respondents agree that "the findings of the 9/11 Commission are part of a purposeful cover-up."

How should we interpret the answer set? Most survey items about conspiracy beliefs ask survey takers to respond on a five-point Likert scale (e.g., from "strongly agree" to "strongly disagree"), to respond either "agree" or "disagree," or to indicate agreement with a "yes" or "no." How should we interpret responses on a five-point scale? Are the conspiracy believers just the ones who respond "strongly agree"? Or should we consider a respondent to be a believer if they respond either "strongly agree" or "agree"? (There is no right or wrong answer, but usually those who strongly agree and agree are combined.) This brings up questions about how to compare polls that have different answer sets.

What events and conditions might affect the results? The circumstances surrounding polls may impact the results. Asking if an election was tainted by fraud shortly after the results are known will likely lead some respondents—on the losing side—to answer affirmatively.[1] But had the election turned out differently, then the losers would be different people, and it would be *those losers* who would then believe in fraud. For example, after Democrats win an election, it is usually the Republicans who cry foul and assert that the outcome was due to fraud, but when Republicans win, it is the Democrats who assert fraud.[2]

During times when conspiracies and conspiracy theories are salient in political discourse, people may be more likely to report belief in conspiracy theories. For example, when Americans were asked about a conspiracy theory involving the faking of unemployment statistics by the Bureau of Labor Statistics (BLS), about 30 percent expressed belief.[3] A few months later in the spring of 2013, several scandals became prominent in the news, each potentially indicating a conspiracy perpetrated by the Obama administration. The researchers asked the same question again and found that belief in the BLS conspiracy theory rose about twenty percentage points. They attributed this sharp increase in reported belief to the priming effect of news: news surrounding other scandals *primed* respondents to be more receptive to this particular conspiracy theory.[4]

People sometimes report that they believe in ideas they never thought very deeply about. For example, when researchers made up, out of whole cloth, a conspiracy theory that "the U.S. government is mandating the switch to compact fluorescent light bulbs because such lights make people more obedient and easier to control," almost 20 percent claimed to have heard it before (which is fascinating in itself), and 11 percent responded that they agreed with it.[5]

Despite its problems, polling is perhaps the best tool for measuring conspiracy beliefs. It is important that we take individual polls with a grain of salt, understand that there are likely multiple reasons for any particular outcome, and track different measures of a conspiracy belief over time.[6]

The Popularity of Kennedy Conspiracy Theories

Perhaps the most consistently popular conspiracy theories in the United States are Kennedy assassination theories. More than 50 percent of Americans have believed in one version of this theory or another for more than fifty years.[7] In some polls, belief in this conspiracy theory has nearly reached 80 percent.[8] These beliefs are similar elsewhere as well: a 2017 poll in France, for example, showed that more than 50 percent of the French believed one version of the Kennedy conspiracy theory.[9]

There are numerous reasons for such high polling numbers. The first has to do with how pollsters ask about JFK assassination conspiracy theories. Most pollsters ask respondents if they believe a conspiracy or cover-up took place; thus, anyone who believes *any* conspiracy theory about the assassination can answer affirmatively. When pollsters follow up by asking about who conspired to kill Kennedy, the opinions divide greatly. Some people believe that the CIA, Fidel Castro, or the Mafia was involved, and many others aren't sure.[10] In short, the standard measure of belief in Kennedy conspiracy theories conflates belief in numerous incompatible conspiracy theories. Second, JFK assassination theories are ubiquitous in the culture. Numerous movies, television shows, and books have been produced attempting to expose the conspiracy—and these collectively create a culture that reproduces these beliefs.[11] Because so many people believe in Kennedy conspiracy theories, young citizens are invariably exposed to them during their formative years, and these beliefs take root.[12]

The Popularity of Space Alien Conspiracy Theories

Since World War II, Americans have had a fascination with aliens and alien visitors. Much of this was sparked by the supposed 1947 crash landing of an alien spaceship in Roswell, New Mexico.[13] As the decades wore on, the tales became elaborate, outlandish, and conspiratorial. While the military has maintained that nothing otherworldly was recovered in the desert, conspiracy theorists claim that the military recovered alien space technology, bodies, and weapons. This shows that it takes little more than some sticks and tin foil on the ground to spark widespread conspiracy theorizing.

When asked in 2013 if they believed "a UFO crashed at Roswell, New Mexico, in 1947, and the US government covered it up, or not," 21 percent of Americans responded affirmatively, and 32 percent were not sure.[14] Belief in government cover-ups regarding aliens tends to be steady across polls, but some polls in the late 1990s showed a spike in belief. For example, this 1997 poll from CNN found:

> While nearly three-quarters of the 1,024 adults questioned for the poll said they had never seen or known anyone who saw a UFO, 54 percent believe intelligent life exists outside Earth. Sixty-four percent of the respondents said that aliens have contacted humans, half said they've abducted humans, and 37 percent said they have contacted the U.S. government.

Photo 3.1 *The X-Files* brought conspiracy theories into popular television in the 1990s. Fox Broadcasting / Photofest © Fox Broadcasting

Those are unusually high numbers and could represent polling error, or a fascination with aliens, possibly driven by the contemporaneous popular television show *The X-Files*. One important point is that when the survey questions are more general, they elicit higher levels of agreement. For example, when asked if any form of life exists anywhere in the universe, belief stands around 60 percent of Americans. If asked a more specific question—for example, if people like ourselves exist elsewhere in the universe—only about 40 percent of Americans agree.[15] Very small, though non-negligible, numbers of people claim to have been abducted or know someone who has been abducted.[16]

Belief in aliens is popular to varying degrees across the world. When asked in 2005 if they believed that extraterrestrials had visited Earth sometime in the past, 24 percent of Americans, 21 percent of Canadians, and 19 percent of Britons answered yes.[17] In a poll of several European countries and Argentina in 2016, respondents were asked to agree or disagree with the statement "Humans have made contact with aliens and this fact has been deliberately hidden from the public." Agreeing were 25 percent of Argentinians, 11 percent of both Portuguese people and Italians, 9 percent of Britons, 8 percent of Poles, and 6 percent of both Swedes and Germans.[18]

The *reptilian elite conspiracy theory* goes further than accusing the government of hiding alien contact; it asserts that interdimensional shape-shifting lizards secretly rule the planet. This theory, pioneered by the UK's David Icke, attracts large audiences to sold-out arenas across the world, but the attraction seems less wide than deep.[19] Despite being named by *Time* magazine as one of the "most enduring" conspiracy theories of all time, the one poll of belief in this theory shows that only 4 percent of Americans agree with it.[20]

Immigration Conspiracy Theories

We switch now from space aliens to human aliens. Immigration attracts numerous conspiracy theories (many of which are tied to xenophobia, racism, and innate concerns over *the other*).[21] A poll of Americans in 2018 showed that 55 percent believe that the government is concealing the true cost of immigration to taxpayers and society, that 41 percent perceive that a conspiracy of silence punishes those who speak out in opposition to immigration, and that 40 percent agree that "in the last 20 years, the US Government has deliberately tried to make American society more ethnically diverse through its immigration policy." There is a strong view among Americans that diversity is a costly and forced project.

Conspiratorial views about immigration are prevalent outside of the United States as well. When asked the same questions in 2018, 58 percent of Britons believed that their government was concealing the true cost of immigration, 59 percent perceived that a conspiracy of silence punishes those who speak out in opposition to immigration, and 51 percent believed that the British government deliberately tried to make British society more ethnically diverse.[22] When asked in 2016 if they agreed that "the Government is deliberately hiding the truth about how many immigrants really live in this country," 42 percent of Germans, 41 percent of Britons, 31 percent of Swedes, 29 percent of Italians, 20 percent of Poles and Argentinians, and 16 percent of Portuguese people agreed. Belief in this theory might seem low in Poland, a state that has in recent years banned many forms of immigration, but because of the bans, there is little reason for Poles to believe that government has much to hide. One theory that has taken hold across parts of Europe is the "white replacement theory"; in it, both governments and corporations are replacing white Europeans with cheaper laborers. In 2017, this theory was endorsed by nearly half of French respondents.[23]

The Popularity of Conspiracy Theories about Science

Many conspiracy theories address scientific findings, suggesting that they are either faked by scientists, controlled by unscrupulous organizations, or part of a political scam. Such conspiracy theories, by thwarting science, thwart progress and endanger lives. Climate change is perhaps the most prominent example. While the veracity of climate change is mostly accepted across Europe, many Americans have been slow to accept the science and instead look to conspiracy theories to explain away the findings of thousands of independent scientists. As many as 37 percent of Americans believe climate change is a hoax.[24] This mass skepticism has kept serious legislation to address climate change from passing in Congress. Climate skepticism has been palpable in Australia as well, where 21 percent believe that "global warming is a hoax perpetrated by scientists."[25]

Just as conspiracy beliefs have stymied legislation to address climate change, conspiracy beliefs have fueled legislation limiting the use of genetically modified (GM) foods. In many parts of the world, conspiracy theories have driven the adoption of destructive anti-GM policies. In Europe, conspiracy theories and financial interests have convinced governments to enact GM importation bans.[26] This has been financially beneficial to European producers, but it has hurt African farmers who would benefit greatly from using GM seeds but cannot sell the GM food to Europe. This policy has cost lives. Had Kenya adopted GM corn in 2006, between "440 and 4,000 lives could theoretically have been saved. Similarly, Uganda had the possibility in 2007 to introduce the black sigatoka–resistant banana, thereby potentially saving between 500 and 5,500 lives over the past decade."[27] Currently, conspiracy theories are challenging the safety of Round-up, an agricultural weed killer, and Golden Rice, a GM rice whose vitamin content can save the lives of the world's poorest children. Despite the evidence attesting to GM crops' safety, conspiracy theorists continue to attack their use.[28]

Outside of food production, African nations put millions of lives at risk because they would not accept donations of GM crops from the United States, even though millions of people were facing extreme hunger.[29] In the United States, Vermont was one of the first states to implement GM labeling regulations. Cost increased and choice decreased as a consequence. As additional states considered bending to conspiracy theories, the federal government stepped in to supersede further state laws with its own set of rules, which, according to the government, do nothing to affect food or environmental safety, but at best appease conspiracy theorists.[30] About 12 percent of Americans signaled agreement with the very specific conspiracy theory that "the global dissemination of genetically modified foods by Monsanto, Inc., is part of a secret program, called Agenda 21, launched by the Rockefeller and Ford Foundations to shrink the world's population"; 46 percent neither agreed nor disagreed.[31] When just asked about the safety of GM foods, "roughly half of Americans believe that foods with GM ingredients are worse for one's health than non-GM foods," despite there being a strong scientific consensus that GM foods are safe.[32]

The 1969 moon landing was one of the greatest achievements of human civilization. Despite the fact that it would be nearly impossible to fake, between 5 and 10 percent of Americans believe it was a hoax.[33] About 16 percent of the French agree.[34] Flat-earthers have existed for millennia, but their numbers have dwindled as evidence of Earth's roundness has solidified. Despite the number of NBA players who have recently sworn off their round-Earth beliefs, only about 4 percent of Americans and 10 percent of the French believe the Earth is flat.[35]

Conspiracy theories attacking accepted health and medical practices are popular as well. A 2014 study by Eric Oliver and Thomas Wood examined belief in medical conspiracy theories in the United States. They found that such theories have high levels of support:

> 37% of the sample agreed that the Food and Drug Administration is intentionally suppressing natural cures for cancer because of drug company pressure; 20% agreed either that corporations were preventing public health officials from releasing data linking cell phones to cancer or that physicians still want to vaccinate children even though they know such vaccines to be dangerous.[36]

Twelve percent of respondents agreed with the conspiracy theory that HIV was being spread by the CIA.[37] In a 2013 survey, about 15 percent of Americans agreed that "the pharmaceutical industry is in league with the medical industry to 'invent' new diseases in order to make money"; 16 percent were unsure.[38]

Two-thirds of Americans agreed in 2018 that "pharmaceutical companies spend less money on developing drugs that cure diseases like cancer and diabetes because there is more money to be made by selling drugs that treat rather than cure diseases."[39] This popular belief, however, makes little sense: scientists have cured numerous diseases over the last century; a cure for cancer or diabetes would be incredibly profitable; and scientists are working on such cures as we speak. That some diseases have yet to be cured doesn't mean that cures are being withheld; it simply means that progress takes time.

Diseases once thought eradicated have experienced a resurgence because of conspiracy theories asserting that the MMR and other vaccines are unsafe.[40] Celebrities have convinced untold numbers of credulous people to not vaccinate their children.[41] President Trump, before entering office, tweeted support for anti-vaxx beliefs. Despite its success at preventing certain types of cancers, unfounded conspiracy theories have driven parents to eschew the HPV vaccine for their daughters.[42] Politicians have not helped on this matter: Michele Bachmann, a former Republican congresswoman and presidential candidate, falsely claimed in a nationally televised debate that HPV vaccination policy was part of a conspiracy and that the vaccine made people "retarded."[43] Although a vaccine to combat the recent outbreaks of Zika in Brazil and the United States has yet to be developed, conspiracy theorists have already decided that it is part of a dark conspiracy to defraud, experiment on, or poison them. These conspiracy theories have outpaced scientific information about the virus.[44] Ten percent of Britons believe "the truth about vaccines is being hidden."[45] About 20 percent of Americans agree that "there is a link between childhood vaccines and autism," and about 35 percent are unsure.[46] These numbers are not massive, but they are enough to prevent society from achieving herd immunity should the conspiracy believers opt not to vaccinate.

Fluoridation of the public water supply is supported by the vast majority of the medical community, and even by dentists who would gain financially from not regulating fluoride in the water supply. For example, the Calgary City Council (Canada) voted to remove fluoride from its local drinking water in 2011; a few years later, tooth decay in children increased significantly in comparison to nearby Edmonton, a city that continued to fluoridate.[47] Despite the evidence of its safety and benefits, fluoride has long been a thorny issue, owing largely to conspiracy theories.

In the 1950s, the fluoride conspiracy theories emanated largely from conservatives and suggested that the government was using fluoridation to institute communism. However, this has changed in recent decades. In Portland, Oregon, for example, left-wing conspiracy theories became fuel for an

Photo 3.2   Many people want to keep fluoride out of tap water.
© iStock / Getty Images Plus / Annemiek1962

intense political battle after the city council voted to begin fluoridating. The opposition came from leftists and included high-profile supporters such as Ralph Nader, the NAACP, and the Sierra Club. Portland eventually voted to overturn the city council's decision.[48]

In 2013, only about 10 percent of Americans believed the government fluoridated the water supply "not for dental health reasons, but for other, more sinister reasons."[49] While fluoride conspiracy theories are not widely held, they can become potent during the local policy-making process. An account from the 1950s shows that scientists and experts were often powerless at the hands of conspiracy theories:

> It would appear the backers of this new aid to dental health made the classic military error of underestimating the enemy. . . . They relied too heavily on the presumed confidence of voters in the AMA, ADA, U.S. Public Health Service, and state and local health authorities who have given fluoridation their blessing. . . . [But] after [fluoride opponents] fire their counterbarrage of speeches, leaflets, mailing pieces and newspaper ads, the poor voter is baffled and uncertain. The strategy of fluoridation's foes is to . . . create doubts in the voters' minds. Once this is accomplished, they know people are likely to vote to maintain the status quo.[50]

Anti-fluoridation attitudes are also evident across the globe. In a study of sixteen European countries using focus groups, researchers found that most of the participants were against water fluoridation, although groups in Greece, Ireland, Poland, and Sweden were more in favor.[51]

When first identified in the 1980s, HIV and AIDS were widely misunderstood. Unfortunately, these diseases—despite the great advancements scientists have made in understanding and combatting them—continue to spark misinformation and misunderstanding. Many Americans either strongly believe or question whether the CIA deliberately infected African Americans with HIV.[52]

In Africa the fear of AIDS has been eclipsed by the fear of medicines for preventing AIDS.[53] The former health minister of South Africa, Manto Tshabalala-Msimang, claimed that the country's AIDS crisis was caused by "a global conspiracy intent on reducing the continent's population."[54] He suggested that those infected with HIV cure it via massage and vitamins because, he contended, the pharmaceuticals were part of a Western plot; as many as three hundred thousand people died prematurely.[55] Across other parts of the globe, similar theories attract varying levels of acceptance: 25 percent of Argentinians believe that "the AIDS virus was created and spread around the world on purpose by a secret group or organization."[56] Thirty percent of the French in 2017 believed that "AIDS was created in a laboratory and tested on Africans."[57] These beliefs have been tied to unsafe sexual practices.[58]

The Popularity of Economic Conspiracy Theories

There are numerous conspiracy theories about economics. Economics is often confusing for laypeople, and for that reason, conspiracy theories are much easier explanations for economic outcomes than more complicated textbook explanations. In a study using respondents from Israel, Switzerland, and the United States, researchers found that when asked about several different economic phenomena, as many respondents adopted a conspiratorial view as they did a "textbook" economics view.[59]

There is a worldwide distrust of corporations and the rich. Further, the public holds views about the economy that run counter to the views of trained economists, they tend to distrust capitalist institutions, and they often blame economic outcomes on small groups of powerful people. For example, when asked how much they trust people "who run large companies," about 70 percent of people from Germany, Great Britain, Italy, Poland, and Portugal responded "not much" or "not at all." Almost 80 percent of Argentinians responded "not much" or "not at all," but only 40 percent of Swedes did.[60] Going from general distrust to accusations of conspiracy, in the United States, about 40 percent believe that corporations "are likely to work in secret against the rest of us." Given these beliefs, it is quite easy for politicians to exploit these sentiments with campaigns built on demonizing corporations and the rich, and arguing that the economy is "rigged."[61]

One might think that this conspiratorial view of big financial organizations and the rich would mean that labor organizations are highly trusted, but they are not. When asked how much they trust "trade union leaders," about 60 percent of Swedes and Britons; almost 70 percent of Germans; more than 80 percent of Poles, Portuguese, and Italians; and 90 percent of Argentinians responded "not much" or "not at all."[62] About 25 percent of Americans responded that unions "are likely to work in secret against the rest of us."[63] Big economic organizations—whether business or labor—appear to spark conspiracy beliefs.

The Popularity of Conspiracy Theories about Government

While I will save the more partisan conspiracy theories for later chapters, polls show that, regardless of who is in charge, conspiracy theories are often aimed at government. When asked in 2016 if they could trust government ministers in their country to tell the truth, more than 80 percent of Argentinians, Italians, Poles, and Portuguese; 70 percent of Germans and Britons, and 60 percent of Swedes answered "not much" or "not at all."[64] Similar numbers from these countries believed that senior leaders of the European Union or the United States could not be trusted to tell the truth either.[65]

Many people worldwide are unsure whether the democracy they live in is real. When asked if they agree that "even though we live in what's called a democracy, a few people will always run things in this country anyway," 70 percent of Portuguese and Argentinians; 60 percent of Italians; 50 percent of Germans, Britons, and Poles; and 33 percent of Swedes answered affirmatively. When Americans were asked if "a secretive power elite with a globalist agenda is conspiring to eventually rule the world through an authoritarian world government, or New World Order, or not," 28 percent answered affirmatively, and an equal number were unsure.[66] Fifteen percent of Americans believe that "media or the government adds secret mind-controlling technology to television broadcast signals," and another 15 percent are unsure.[67] An equal number of Floridians in 2018 believed that the government controlled major weather events like hurricanes.[68] There is great skepticism toward government and corporations, which sometimes manifests as conspiracy beliefs. Some of this skepticism is rightly deserved, but often the conspiracy beliefs go beyond the evidence.

Anomalous Beliefs

We now move away from conspiracy beliefs and show that other anomalous beliefs are quite popular as well. Many people have predicted that the world would come to an end; but the prophesized dates always come and go without Armageddon. In 2011, 27 percent of Americans agreed with the statement "We are currently living in End Times as foretold by Biblical prophecy."[69] Undergirding this, two-thirds of Americans believed in angels and 57 percent believed in Satan.[70] A far smaller number of Britons in 2016 (about 20 percent) believed in angels, and 15 percent believed in the devil.[71]

The supernatural often bleeds into partisan politics. Thirteen percent of Americans in 2013 believed that President Obama was the Antichrist; a 2016 poll of North Carolina showed that 20 percent believed that Hillary Clinton was the devil.[72] In 2017, 36 percent of Americans believed that President Trump was "scarier" than the devil.[73]

In 2017, about 52 percent of Americans believed that "places can be haunted by spirits."[74] Thirteen percent in 2008 believed that there was "currently a ghost or spirit living" in their own home.[75] Fifty-seven percent of Americans believed in the existence of ghosts in 2008 compared to just 30 percent of Britons in 2016.[76] In 2008, 35 percent of Americans reported they had personally experienced the presence of a ghost.[77] About 30 percent of Britons believed in an "afterlife" in 2016, and 20 percent believed in an "everlasting soul."[78] A fifth of Americans in 2017 believed that certain individuals could make contact with the dead, and an equal number of Brits in 2016 believed in past lives or reincarnation.[79]

In 2005, 40 percent of Americans believed in extrasensory perception (ESP); 31 percent believed in "telepathy/communication between minds without using traditional senses," and 26 percent believed in "clairvoyance/ the power of the mind to know the past and predict the future."[80] About 20 percent of Americans in 2017 believed that "fortune tellers and psychics can foresee the future," and 25 percent believed that people can move objects with their minds.[81]

In 2005 a quarter of Americans believed in astrology—that the positions of the planets and the stars can affect people's lives.[82] In 2017, slightly less than 10 percent of Americans believed that tarot cards and palm reading could accurately predict the future; but only 47 percent agreed that most people "who advertise as psychics or mediums are fakes."[83] About 21 percent of Americans in 2005 believed in witches; 30 percent in 2018 believed that people could put "curses" on other people.[84] Large numbers of people believe in these phenomena, but there has never been strong evidence supporting them.[85] The beliefs persist regardless.

Despite the number of cable television shows searching for him, only 16 percent of Americans in 2017 believed that Bigfoot is real; but an astonishing 55 percent believed that "ancient, advanced civilizations, such as Atlantis, once existed."[86] There are other beliefs, which could be considered urban legends, that have attracted interest. *Urban legends* are modern myths or folklore (for example, the idea that eating watermelon seeds will grow a watermelon in your stomach). Since the mid-1960s, an urban legend has claimed that Paul McCartney, the Beatle, died in a car crash and was replaced with a doppelganger. Less than 10 percent of Americans believe this, but it remains well known and is often referred to as a conspiracy theory (even though it isn't).[87]

Conclusion

Representative polls are perhaps the best way to measure the prevalence of conspiracy and anomalous beliefs among the public because they speak to the public's beliefs as a whole and avoid anecdotal accounts. Belief in QAnon and flat Earth theories would seem to be very high, given the amount of news coverage these theories have received in recent years, but polls show that neither of these theories is very popular.[88] *Time* magazine listed the moon landing and lizard-people theories in their "Top Ten," but again, polls show that neither of these theories is widely believed by Americans.[89] In this way, polls are better than anecdotes at telling us about the number of people who believe a particular idea.

On the other hand, polling results need to be contextualized before we draw conclusions. First, poll results may be dependent on the environment in which the polls are taken. Ongoing prominent scandals may lead people to be more likely in polls to express belief in conspiracy theories. Also, the political circumstances (i.e., who is in power) could affect which poll respondents are most likely to express belief in conspiracy theories. Second, because respondents can only respond to questions on the polls that they are asked, the choices made by researchers in choosing which conspiracy theories to ask about are imperative and may cause bias. Third, how questions about conspiracy theories are worded can affect the number of people who express belief and whether those questions are even tapping into conspiracy beliefs. In general, when a survey item asks about a very specific conspiracy theory (e.g., Did Castro kill President Kennedy?), fewer respondents are likely to express belief in it than when the item taps a more general theory (e.g., Was Kennedy killed by a conspiracy?). Fourth, because surveys ask questions that the pollsters are interested in, questionnaires may ask about concepts that that respondents have never thought about deeply. Because of this, some survey questions may elicit non-responses (i.e., flippant responses to ideas that the respondent has thought little about). In other instances, respondents are often willing to express a belief in a conspiracy theory that the researchers made up.[90] Fifth, people sometimes joke around on surveys or want to prove a larger point about a political adversary by agreeing with a conspiracy theory they don't really believe in. Finally, polling is expensive; it's prohibitive to poll people often or to do so everywhere. This is why most polls of conspiracy beliefs are administered in wealthy, open societies. Analyzing text (i.e., letters to the editor, tweets, comments on news articles) may address some of these problems, but because writers are not representative of the population as a whole, the results of any such analyses may speak less to public opinion and more to the intensity exhibited by the subset of people who express their thoughts publicly.

Despite whatever problems there are with polling, the results of the numerous polls presented here suggest that everyone believes at least one conspiracy theory, if not several. Some people believe many conspiracy theories. Some conspiracy theories amass large followings, but most attract few believers. Also, some conspiracy theories are well known as conspiracy theories (e.g., the faked moon landing) but are not widely believed in polls.

Polls show that people in the United States and elsewhere share many anomalous beliefs. These include paranormal (e.g., ESP) and supernatural (e.g., the coming end times) beliefs, among others. It is important to note that conspiracy and other anomalous beliefs were widespread long before the internet or the supposed "post-truth" era.

Key Term

anomalous beliefs

Bibliography

Bailey, Ronald. "New Useless and Costly USDA Bioengineered Food Disclosure Regulations Issued." *Reason* (2018). Published electronically December 27, 2018.

———. "Vermont GMO Labeling Hits Kosher Foods." *Reason* (2016). Published electronically July 11, 2016.

Barkan, Ross. "'Their Greed Has No End': Bernie Sanders Makes a Surprise Appearance in Manhattan." *Observer* (2015). Published electronically October 26, 2015.

Blumgart, Jake. "What's the Matter with Portland?" *Slate*, May 17, 2013.

Bogart, Laura M., and Sheryl Thorburn. "Are HIV/AIDS Conspiracy Beliefs a Barrier to HIV Prevention among African Americans?" *JAIDS Journal of Acquired Immune Deficiency Syndromes* 38, no. 2 (2005): 213–18.

Bogart, Laura M., and Sheryl Thorburn Bird. "Exploring the Relationship of Conspiracy Beliefs about HIV/AIDS to Sexual Behaviors and Attitudes among African-American Adults." *Journal of the National Medical Association* 95, no. 11 (2003): 1057.

Broniatowski, David A., Karen M. Hilyard, and Mark Dredze. "Effective Vaccine Communication during the Disneyland Measles Outbreak." *Vaccine* 34, no. 28 (June 14, 2016): 3225–28.

Butler, Lisa D., Cheryl Koopman, and Philip G. Zimbardo. "The Psychological Impact of Viewing the Film *JFK*: Emotions, Beliefs, and Political Behavioral Intentions." *Political Psychology* 16, no. 2 (1995): 237–57.

Carlson, Darren. "Life on Mars? Over a Third of Americans Say They Believe Life in Some Form Exists on the Red Planet." *Gallup.com* (2001). Published electronically February 27, 2001.

CBS News. "CBS Poll: JFK Conspiracy Lives." *CBSNews.com*, November 20, 1998 (July 25, 2011).

Chigwedere, Pride, George R. Seage III, Sofia Gruskin, Tun-Hou Lee, and M. Essex. "Estimating the Lost Benefits of Antiretroviral Drug Use in South Africa." *JAIDS Journal of Acquired Immune Deficiency Syndromes* 49, no. 4 (2008): 410–15.

CNN. "Poll: U.S. Hiding Knowledge of Aliens." *CNN.com* (1997). Published electronically June 15, 1997. http://articles.cnn.com/1997-06-15/us/9706_15_ufo.poll_1_ufo-aliens-crash-site?_s=PM:US.

"Conspiracy Theories: Separating Fact from Fiction." *Time.com* (2009). Published electronically July 20, 2009.

Craciun, Catrinel, and Adriana Baban. "'Who Will Take the Blame?': Understanding the Reasons Why Romanian Mothers Decline HPV Vaccination for Their Daughters." *Vaccine* 30, no. 48 (2012): 6789–93.

Dahlgreen, Will. "British People More Likely to Believe in Ghosts Than a Creator." *YouGov* (2016). Published electronically March 26, 2016.

Dredze, Mark, David A. Broniatowski, and Karen M. Hilyard. "Zika Vaccine Misconceptions: A Social Media Analysis." *Vaccine* 34, no. 30 (May 20, 2016): 3441–42.

Drobnic Holan, Angie, and Louise Jacobson. "Michele Bachmann Says HPV Vaccine Can Cause Mental Retardation." *Politifact.com* (2011). Published electronically September 16, 2011.

Drochon, Hugo. "Study Shows 60% of Britons Believe in Conspiracy Theories." *The Guardian* (2018). Published electronically November 22, 2018.

————. "Who Believes in Conspiracy Theories in Great Britain and Europe?" In *Conspiracy Theories and the People Who Believe Them*, edited by Joseph E. Uscinski, 337–46. New York: Oxford University Press, 2018.

Dubock, Adrian. "Golden Rice, Part 3: A Thoroughly Studied GMO Crop Approved by Australia, Canada, New Zealand and the US." *Genetic Literacy Project* (2019). Published electronically May 28, 2019.

Edelson, Jack, Alexander Alduncin, Christopher Krewson, James A. Sieja, and Joseph E. Uscinski. "The Effect of Conspiratorial Thinking and Motivated Reasoning on Belief in Election Fraud." *Political Research Quarterly* 70, no. 4 (2017): 933–46.

"8 in 10 French People Believe a Conspiracy Theory: Survey." *France24* (2018). Published electronically January 8, 2018.

Einstein, Katherine Levine, and David M. Glick. "Cynicism, Conspiracies, and Contemporaneous Conditions Moderating Experimental Treatment Effects." Unpublished paper (2015).

————. "Do I Think BLS Data Are BS? The Consequences of Conspiracy Theories." *Political Behavior* 37, no. 3 (2014): 1–23.

English, Cameron. "Quit the Glyphosate Conspiracy Theories." *RealClearScience* (2018). Published electronically January 19, 2018.

Frankovic, Kathy. "Americans Think Ghosts Are More Likely Than Aliens on Earth." *YouGov* (2018).

Frazier, Kendrick. *Science Confronts the Paranormal*. Buffalo, NY: Prometheus Books, 1986.

Funk, Cary, Brian Kennedy, and Meg Hefferon. "Public Perspectives on Food Risks." *Pew Internet* (2018). Published electronically November 10, 2019.

Gaston, Sophia, and Joseph E. Uscinski. "Out of the Shadows: Conspiracy Thinking on Immigration." Henry Jackson Society, 2018. https://henryjacksonsociety.org/wp-content/uploads/2018/12/Out-of-the-Shadows-Conspiracy-thinking-on-immigration.pdf.

Goertzel, Ted. "The Conspiracy Theory Pyramid Scheme." In *Conspiracy Theories and the People Who Believe Them*, edited by Joseph E. Uscinski, 226–42. New York: Oxford University Press, 2018.

Griffin, Marcus, Darren Shickle, and Nicola Moran. "European Citizens' Opinions on Water Fluoridation." *Community Dentistry and Oral Epidemiology* 36, no. 2 (2008): 95–102.

Hill, Kyle. "Why Portland Is Wrong about Water Fluoridation." *Scientific American*, May 22, 2013.

Icke, David. *Children of the Matrix: How an Interdimensional Race Has Controlled the World for Thousands of Years—and Still Does*. Wildwood, MO: Bridge of Love Publications USA, 2001.

Ipsos. "Majority of Americans Believe in Ghosts (57%) and UFOs (52%)." (2008). Published electronically October 31, 2008.

Jenkins, Krista. "The Best Medicine Is Truth." July 31, 2018. http://view2.fdu.edu/publicmind/2018/180731/.

Jenson, Tom. "Democrats and Republicans Differ on Conspiracy Theory Beliefs." *Public Policy Polling* (2013). Published electronically April 2, 2013.

Klass, Philip J. *The Real Roswell Crashed-Saucer Coverup*. Buffalo, NY: Prometheus Books, 1997.

Leiser, David, Nofar Duani, and Pascal Wagner-Egger. "The Conspiratorial Style in Lay Economic Thinking." *PLoS ONE* 12, no. 3 (2017): e0171238.

Lyons, Linda. "Paranormal Beliefs Come (Super)Naturally to Some." *News.gallup .com* (2005). Published electronically November 1, 2005.

MacGregor, Karen. "Conspiracy Theories Fuel Row over AIDS Crisis in South Africa." *Independent.co.uk* (2000).

Markley, Robert. "Alien Assassinations: The X-Files and the Paranoid Structure of History." *Camera Obscura* 14, no. 1–2/40–41 (1997): 75–102.

McHoskey, John W. "Case Closed? On the John F. Kennedy Assassination: Biased Assimilation of Evidence and Attitude Polarization." *Basic and Applied Social Psychology* 17, no. 3 (1995): 1995.

McLaren, Lindsay, Steven Patterson, Salima Thawer, Peter Faris, Deborah McNeil, Melissa Potestio, and Luke Shwart. "Measuring the Short-Term Impact of Fluoridation Cessation on Dental Caries in Grade 2 Children Using Tooth Surface Indices." *Community Dentistry and Oral Epidemiology* 44, no. 3 (2016): 274–82.

Michael, Meron Tesfa. "Africa Bites the Bullet on Genetically Modified Food Aid." *World Press* (2002). Published electronically September 26, 2002

Moore, David. "Three in Four Americans Believe in Paranormal." *Gallup.com* (2005). Published electronically June 16, 2005.

Nattrass, Nicoli. "How Bad Ideas Gain Social Traction." *The Lancet* 380, no. 9839 (2012): 332–33.

Nguyen, Hoang. "Most Flat Earthers Consider Themselves Very Religious." *YouGov* (2018). Published electronically April 2, 2018.

Oliver, Eric, and Thomas Wood. "Conspiracy Theories and the Paranoid Style(s) of Mass Opinion." *American Journal of Political Science* 58, no. 4 (2014): 952–66.

———. "Medical Conspiracy Theories and Health Behaviors in the United States." *JAMA Internal Medicine* 174, no. 5 (2014): 817–18.

"Paranormal America 2017." Chapman University. Published electronically October 11, 2017. https://blogs.chapman.edu/wilkinson/2017/10/11/paranormal -america-2017/.

Pollard, John. "Skinhead Culture: The Ideologies, Mythologies, Religions and Conspiracy Theories of Racist Skinheads." *Patterns of Prejudice* 50, no. 4–5 (October 19, 2016): 398–419.

Public Policy Polling. "Clinton Leads in NC for First Time since March" (2016). Published electronically August 9, 2016.

———. "Support for Impeachment at Record High" (2017). Published electronically October 31, 2017.

Sinclair, Betsy, Steven S. Smith, and Patrick D. Tucker. "'It's Largely a Rigged System': Voter Confidence and the Winner Effect in 2016." *Political Research Quarterly* 71, no. 4 (2018): 1065912918768006.

Smallpage, Steven M., Adam M. Enders, and Joseph E. Uscinski. "The Partisan Contours of Conspiracy Theory Beliefs." *Research & Politics* 4, no. 4 (2017): 2053168017746554.

Street, Andrew P. "Why Do Australians Believe Silly Things?" ABC News (2017). Published electronically September 29, 2017.

Swift, Art. "Majority in U.S. Still Believe JFK Killed in a Conspiracy." *Gallup.com*, November 15, 2013.

Tupy, Marian. "Europe's Anti-GMO Stance Is Killing Africans." *Reason* (2017). Published electronically September 5, 2017.

Uscinski, Joseph E., Karen Douglas, and Stephan Lewandowsky. "Climate Change Conspiracy Theories." *Oxford Research Encyclopedia of Climate Science* (Oxford: Oxford University Press, 2017): 1–43.

Uscinski, Joseph E., and Casey Klofstad. "Commentary: Florida Believes in Conspiracy Theories Too." *Orlando Sentinel* (2018). Published electronically September 6, 2018.

———. "New Poll: The QAnon Conspiracy Movement Is Very Unpopular." *Washington Post* (2018). Published electronically August 30, 2018.

Wesseler, Justus, Richard D. Smart, Jennifer Thomson, and David Zilberman. "Foregone Benefits of Important Food Crop Improvements in Sub-Saharan Africa." *PLoS ONE* 12, no. 7 (2017): e0181353.

YouGov. "Yougov NY Psychics and Mediums" (2017). https://d25d2506sfb94s .cloudfront.net/cumulus_uploads/document/921030f7y9/Copy%20of%20 Results%20for%20YouGov%20NY%20(Psychics%20and%20Mediums)%20 227%2010.30.2017.pdf.

4

The Psychology
and Sociology of
Conspiracy Theories

hat psychological and sociological factors lead people to adopt conspiracy theories? By *psychological* factors, I mean those arising within
an individual's mind, specifically their cognition, personality traits,
and emotional states. By *sociological* factors, I mean those arising from group
membership and responding to group competition.

Psychologists, during the last decade, have led the research into conspiracy beliefs, publishing more studies than scholars from other fields. It
might therefore seem that the reasons for conspiracy beliefs lie within the
individual's psyche. While psychological factors are important to understanding conspiracy beliefs, they are the place to begin rather than end. A
fuller explanation of conspiracy beliefs combines psychological factors with
broader sociological and political dynamics. The latter half of this chapter
addresses the sociological, or group-centered, factors, and the following
chapter addresses political factors.

Psychological Factors

Most of the research into conspiracy beliefs comes from psychologists, and
much of this work has been performed during the last decade. Psychologists
studied other anomalous beliefs for decades prior. A handful of psychological studies were undertaken to better understand conspiracy beliefs in the
1990s, but none of these were part of a larger research agenda until around
2007 when conspiracy theories about 9/11 and Princess Diana's death
became salient enough to warrant study.

There are many ways to study beliefs, but let me provide broad over-
views of the most common research designs: the first is by surveying representative samples of people about their conspiracy beliefs and then also asking

about their other beliefs, characteristics, and demographics. With such data, researchers can then see what factors predict people's conspiracy beliefs.

The second is performed with smaller samples of people in laboratory settings. For example, researchers might invite subjects into a lab setting, randomly pick some of them to receive a treatment that causes them to experience feelings of stress (while the others do not receive that treatment), and then ask each of the participants if they believe in a conspiracy theory. If those who received the treatment were more likely to believe in the conspiracy theory, then it would seem that the "stress" treatment caused participants to adopt that belief. Unlike in the mass-survey setting, the use of randomized treatments in a laboratory setting allows researchers to see which factors cause conspiracy beliefs.

Other studies rely less on asking people questions and more on tracking people's written expressions or social media activity. Some such studies examine how people express conspiracy beliefs in letters to the editor of newspapers, comment sections of online news articles, tweets, and Reddit posts.

The psychology literature focuses on three potential causes of these beliefs: cognitive traits, personality traits, and psychological conditions. This section will focus mainly on conspiracy beliefs but will make reference to the factors that drive anomalous beliefs as well.

Cognitive Traits

Cognition is the mental process of acquiring knowledge and understanding. Every day, each of us is bombarded with billions of data points. Our brains are tasked with making sense of all that information and learning from it. Importantly, each of us has different cognitive traits that lead us to interpret incoming information somewhat differently. Scholars have found that some of these cognitive traits make individuals more or less likely to believe conspiracy theories. Following are a few of the cognitive traits that have been identified as being associated with conspiracy beliefs.

People engage in the *conjunction fallacy* when their reasoning violates the conjunction rule. According to famed economists Amos Tversky and Daniel Kahneman, "perhaps the simplest and the most basic qualitative law of probability is the conjunction rule."[1] Consider this scenario:

> "Linda is 31 years old, single, outspoken and very bright. She majored in philosophy. As a student, she was deeply concerned with issues of discrimination and social justice, and also participated in anti-nuclear demonstrations." Following this description, participants rated the likelihood of a number of statements about Linda, including three key propositions: (i) Linda is an active feminist; (ii) Linda is a bank teller; and (iii) Linda is a bank teller and an active feminist. Thus, participants judge the likelihood of

two singular, constituent propositions (one representative and one unrepresentative) and a conjunction of the two propositions. Participants who select the conjunctive statement as being more likely than either individual constituent statement have fallen victim to the conjunction fallacy; a conjunction cannot be more probable than one of its constituents, because the former is necessarily a more restrictive set of possibilities than the latter.[2]

To put this another way, if you buy two scratch-off lottery tickets, the odds of both of them winning must be lower than just one of them winning, or of neither of them winning. However, people often violate the conjunction rule in their reasoning by believing that two events (whose likelihood are both less than one) are more likely to occur together than individually. People who fall victim to this fallacy have been found more likely to believe in conspiracy theories and in paranormal phenomena.[3]

Some people have a strong *need for cognitive closure* which can be thought of as an intolerance for uncertainty. Some people want answers now! In a study examining participants' beliefs in conspiracy theories surrounding the recent European refugee crisis and a hypothetical plane crash, researchers hypothesized that conspiracy theories, because they "offer simple answers" and "explanations for uncertain situations," should be found "attractive to individuals who are intolerant of uncertainty and seek cognitive closure."[4] The findings showed that participants with a high need for cognitive closure were more likely to adopt the conspiracy theories to explain these events when another explanation was unavailable.[5]

People, perhaps through evolutionary processes, have developed psychological *cheater detectors*, or a willingness to suspect others of cheating. Some people have "overactive" cheater detectors that drive them to suspect others of cheating even when little evidence suggests it.[6] Consider, for example, a scenario in which an expensive house burns down. There is little reason to suspect a conspiracy to set the house ablaze just on the limited information that the fire occurred. But what if someone then discovered that the owners were in serious debt, needed fast cash to stay solvent, and had taken out a large insurance policy on the house only months before it burned down? Studies show that when people are made aware of such motives, they are more likely to believe that the actors with those motives engaged in a conspiracy.[7]

Consider the death of Supreme Court Justice Antonin Scalia in 2016. Scalia's passing gave then-president Barack Obama the opportunity to shift the balance of the court in his favor. Since he had something to gain, many people assumed that Obama had murdered Scalia.[8] However, a more sober view is that an overweight seventy-nine-year-old smoker with diabetes and heart problems can die without being murdered. If we assumed that every time a grandmother passed away, the grandkids receiving the inheritance

Photo 4.1   Many people initially believed that Justice Scalia had been murdered.
Polaris / Newscom

killed her, then every grandchild who inherits money must be a murderer. Such a view is untenable. This feeds into another error of reasoning: *intentionality bias.* Some people work backward from outcomes to motives to actions, assuming that because something happened, someone must have intentionally caused it to happen. People whose reasoning is strongly affected by this bias are prone to believing in conspiracy theories.[9] The problem is that actions don't always turn out as intended, and (conversely) outcomes are not always intentional.

Conspiracy beliefs can also be caused by the way people traverse the information environment. Some researchers, such as Cass Sunstein, argue that belief in conspiracy theories stems from *crippled epistemologies*, "in accordance with which it is rational to hold such theories."[10] The way to understand conspiracy beliefs is, therefore,

> to examine how people acquire information. For most of what they believe that they know, human beings lack personal or direct information; they must rely on what other people think. In some domains, people suffer from a "crippled epistemology," in the sense that they know very few things, and what they know is wrong. Many extremists fall in this category; their extremism stems not from irrationality, but from the fact that they have little (relevant) information, and their extremist views are supported by what little they know. Conspiracy theorizing often has the same feature. Those who believe that Israel was responsible for the attacks of 9/11, or that the Central Intelligence Agency killed President Kennedy, may well be responding quite rationally to the informational signals that they receive.[11]

People often pick information sources that comport with what they already believe rather than with the truth. These choices determine the information that they will receive; their information environments then reinforce (or potentially polarize) their current ideologies. An oft-cited quote from cultural critic Walter Lippman observes that people look to the news the way a drunk looks to a lamppost—not for illumination, but rather for reinforcement. This strategy is not reliable for getting accurate information.

An implication is that many people's expressed opinions are nothing more than the parroting of a trusted elite's opinion. This is often why political arguments end in stalemate—because when opinions are not arrived at through careful reasoning to begin with, they likely cannot be altered with reason and evidence.[12]

When confronted with information that challenges their worldview, many attempt to reason that information away. This is a process called *motivated reasoning*.[13] When engaging in this, people might hold evidence in favor of an opposing position to a higher standard than evidence supporting their own position.[14] Or, they might excuse their or their group's actions but condemn those actions if perpetuated by an opposing group.[15] Motivated reasoning drives people to accept conspiracy theories that demonize their opponents but reject theories that demonize themselves.[16]

Relatedly, people with less capacity for analytic thinking tend to believe conspiracy theories.[17] Thus, it is no surprise that higher levels of education are a consistent predictor of resistance to conspiracy theories.[18] Courses in critical thinking appear to make students especially resistant.[19] I want to stress that the negative relationship between education and conspiracy beliefs is a tendency across the populations, not an ironclad determinant. Some highly educated people believe many conspiracy theories.

Personality Traits

Numerous *personality traits*—patterns of thought and emotion—have been found to be associated with conspiracy beliefs. Let's briefly examine a few of these, beginning with attachment styles—that is, the ways adults view and interact with others. Researchers have identified four distinct styles: secure, anxious, avoidant, and fearful. An adult is said to have an *anxious attachment style* when they become dependent on another person and experience anxiety when separated.[20] People showing signs of having an anxious attachment style have been shown to be more likely to believe in conspiracy theories.[21] Scholars have also shown that the *avoidant attachment style*, "because of its emphasis on self-reliance," is associated with belief in conspiracy theories.[22]

The *need for uniqueness* is a desire people have to feel special. Those with a higher need for uniqueness exhibit higher levels of conspiracy thinking and higher levels of belief in specific conspiracy theories.[23] This is likely because conspiracy theories are often presented as special knowledge, available only to those who are themselves special. High levels of *narcissism*, or an elevated sense of self-love, also predict belief in conspiracy theories; this could be because narcissistic people often have a dim view of others.[24]

People who have a hard time separating fact from fantasy are prone to believing in dubious ideas. Delusions are beliefs that are held rather strongly but contradict the available evidence. *Delusional thinking* indicates an individual's proneness to delusions. *Magical thinking* refers to a style of thinking in which magic is real—for example, that one's thoughts can influence external events.[25] *Schizotypy* refers to a continuum of personality characteristics, which at the high end can indicate psychosis and schizophrenia. *Hallucination proneness* is, at the high end, an inability to tell internally generated sensations from externally generated ones.[26] People prone to hallucinations have been shown to be the most likely to report having alien contact.[27] Each of these traits—delusional thinking, magical thinking, schizotypy, and hallucination proneness—has been found to predict conspiracy and other anomalous beliefs.[28]

Manichean thinking is a tendency toward believing that politics is a battle between good and evil rather than an ongoing negotiation between different groups who desire different outcomes. *Dogmatism* often refers to a tendency to hold beliefs so strongly that adherents cannot rationally discuss or negotiate those beliefs, and therefore cannot bend in the face of evidence or argument. *Authoritarianism* is a trait that predicts obedience to authority and a desire to oppress subordinates.[29] Each of these three traits has been found by researchers to predict conspiracy beliefs.[30]

It is intuitive to see that Manichean thinking would lead to conspiracy beliefs: conspiracy theories posit evil groups working against the innocent public. It is easy to understand why dogmatism would lead people to *cling* to conspiracy beliefs once those beliefs are formed, since dogmatism insulates beliefs from refutation. But it is not clear why dogmatic people would believe conspiracy theories in the first place. Authoritarianism, despite some studies showing its relation to conspiracy beliefs, has a tenuous link to conspiracy beliefs. Given that it leads people to be more subservient to authority, rather than more suspicious of it, we might suspect that authoritarianism would lead people to reject conspiracy theories, since many of those theories challenge authority.

Paranormal ideation (the tendency to believe in paranormal phenomena), *supernatural ideation* (the tendency to believe in supernatural phenomena), and conspiracy beliefs have been shown in multiple settings to correlate with one another.[31] This may be because paranormal, supernatural, and conspiracy beliefs have a common denominator: the willingness to believe ideas that lack strong evidence. Therefore, it is very likely that people who subscribe strongly to these beliefs are people who, as discussed earlier, have an inability to separate fact from fantasy.

Psychological Conditions

By *psychological conditions*, I refer not to disorders, but rather to temporary emotional states that individuals experience. These could manifest as, or be indicative of, a psychopathology, but not necessarily. A long list of conditions has been shown to predict belief in conspiracy theories, ranging from boredom to more severe conditions such as suicidal thinking.[32]

Paranoia is a term that is haphazardly tossed around when describing conspiracy theorists. It has been identified in some studies as predicting conspiracy beliefs, but it is important to understand the distinction between paranoia and conspiracy beliefs.[33] Paranoia refers to individuals' irrational fears that others are out to get them personally; conspiracy theories are about a group that is out to get *us*.[34] Feelings of powerlessness, social exclusion, uncertainty, anxiety, and of lacking control correlate with conspiracy beliefs.[35] People who feel excluded, controlled by others, ineffectual, and uncertain about the future are likely to turn to conspiracy theories either as a way to make sense of their perceived position or as a coping mechanism. We will return to this idea in the following chapters about partisan conspiracy theories.

Criticisms of the Psychological Approach

Researchers have identified dozens of psychological factors that predict belief in conspiracy theories. It has become a cottage industry, with new studies continually detailing how some trait predicts belief in one conspiracy theory or another. While the growing literature shows that individual differences play a large role in determining whether a person will adopt a conspiracy belief or not, some critiques are in order.

First, the factors associated with belief in one conspiracy theory may not be associated with belief in other conspiracy theories. By this, I mean that a psychological trait or condition might lead someone to believe in certain conspiracy theories but, at the same time, reject others. It isn't clear how durable the effect of each psychological factor is across the range of conspiracy theories.

Second, the literature is sometimes contradictory. Authoritarianism, for example, is a significant predictor of conspiracy beliefs in some studies, but not in others.[36] Further, it is not a strong predictor of belief in either the Birther or 9/11 Truth theories, but for reasons that are not entirely clear, authoritarianism predicts believing in both theories simultaneously.[37]

Third, many of the findings may lack external validity, meaning that the factors that affect beliefs in a laboratory or survey environment may not have any effect in the real world. To wit, the psychological literature fails to account for the role of broader factors such as the social and political environments in which media and elites transmit information. Because of this, there has yet to be any serious attempt by psychologists to develop broader scientific theories that could tie all of the factors they have identified together into a coherent framework.

Sociological Factors

Conspiracy theories focus on groups working in secret against other groups (or the whole). The victimized group could be small (e.g., the hardworking citizens of a small town) or large (e.g., all Americans). Sociological approaches to conspiracy theories begin with groups and group conflict. By *groups*, I refer to stable aggregates of individuals who share interests, seek cooperation, and compete for power.[38] Groups can be based upon national, regional, religious, language-based, class, occupational, partisan, racial, and ethnic distinctions. Some groups are more diffuse than others; "women" or "men" as groups are not that cohesive or organized, given their size, diversity, and lack of organization.

The specific circumstances a group finds itself in can determine members' beliefs. For example, some African Americans, given the history of slavery, harassment, and discrimination, are prone to seeing conspiracies that focus on their eradication, sterilization, and subjugation.[39] African American director Spike Lee expresses the historical element behind these conspiracy theories quite well while discussing conspiracy theories suggesting the US government blew up the New Orleans levies to flood black neighborhoods:

> It's not far-fetched . . . a choice had to be made. To save one neighborhood, [you have to] flood another neighborhood. Look if we're in LA, and there is an emergency situation, and we call from Beverly Hills or we call from Compton, which one are the cops coming to first. . . . Do you think that election in 2000 was fair? You don't think that was rigged? If they can rig an election they can do anything! With the history of this country—you ever heard of [the] Tuskegee Experiments? There are many other examples,

if we go down the line, where stuff like this happened to African-American people. I don't put anything past the American Government when it comes to people of color in this country.[40]

As this demonstrates, group membership tends to determine which conspiracy theories people believe in.

Group identification can predict which conspiracy theories members will believe in because such identities provide self-esteem and a sense of belonging. Attacks on one's group can be easily taken as attacks on oneself; competing groups are often viewed as biased, immoral, or ill-intentioned; and what benefits one's own group is often confused with justice.

People can be quick to think and act upon in- and out-group identities, sometimes with horrifying results. Group-centered conspiracy theories can be aided by a collective narcissism and by motivated reasoning, which can lead members to dismiss the bad actions of their own group and concentrate only on the supposed bad actions of opposing groups.[41]

Some group-centered conspiracy theories arise when group members feel their interests are threatened. Christians are more likely than non-Christians to believe that Starbucks is conspiring against Christmas.[42] Christians and Muslims are more likely than Jews to believe in Jewish conspiracy theories.[43] People with New Age beliefs are more likely than Catholics to believe in Da Vinci Code conspiracy theories.[44] Partisans are more likely to

Photo 4.2   Da Vinci Code theories assert that Jesus fathered offspring whose descendants persist. These theories led to the very popular book and movie of the same name.

believe that the opposing party, rather than their own, is conspiring against them.[45] Regional conspiracy theories can manifest when important interests are at stake; for example, prior to the Civil War, many conspiracy theories surrounded slaveholders and abolitionists.[46] Further, group-centered conspiracy theories can give rise to prejudice.[47]

Group members take cues from group leaders, if indeed their group has a visible leadership. Partisan groups are particularly susceptible to cues from party leaders because those leaders reach large audiences through the mainstream media. When party leaders engage in conspiracy theorizing, the press covers it, and that can give the impression that such theories have broad support. But it is important to understand that conspiracy theories coming from partisan leaders tend to not have much reach beyond like-minded partisans who are already disposed to conspiracy theorizing.

Conclusion

Psychologists have identified numerous factors associated with conspiracy and other anomalous beliefs. These fall into three categories: cognitive factors, personality traits, and psychological conditions. While these factors can shed light on which specific individuals are more likely to believe a conspiracy theory when they come into contact with it, they do not address the broader social and political factors that bring people into contact with conspiracy theories in the first place.

Sociological factors, focusing on group competition, drive the selection of conspiracy theories (i.e., which conspiracy theories a person will believe in). Individuals tend to believe the conspiracy theories that accuse competing groups, but are less willing to believe theories that accuse their own group. The implication for group competition is that individuals within groups point fingers at opposing groups but excuse bad acts committed by their own side. This is rarely a good trait.

Key Terms

attachment styles
authoritarianism
cheater detector
cognition
conjunction fallacy
crippled epistemologies
delusional thinking
delusions
dogmatism
hallucination proneness
intentionality bias

magical thinking
Manichean thinking
motivated reasoning
need for cognitive closure
need for uniqueness
paranoia
paranormal ideation
personality traits
schizotypy
supernatural ideation

Bibliography

Aarnio, Kia, and Marjaana Lindeman. "Paranormal Beliefs, Education, and Thinking Styles." *Personality and Individual Differences* 39, no. 7 (November 1, 2005): 1227–36.

Adorno, Theodor W., Else Frenkel-Brunswick, Daniel J. Levinson, and R. Nevitt Sanford. *The Authoritarian Personality.* New York: Harper, 1950.

Bilewicz, Michal, and Ireneusz Krzeminski. "Anti-Semitism in Poland and Ukraine: The Belief in Jewish Control as a Mechanism of Scapegoating." *International Journal of Conflict and Violence* 4, no. 2 (2010): 234–43.

Bost, Preston R., and Stephen G. Prunier. "Rationality in Conspiracy Beliefs: The Role of Perceived Motive." *Psychological Reports: Sociocultural Issues in Psychology* 113, no. 1 (2013): 118–28.

Bronstein, Michael V., Gordon Pennycook, Adam Bear, David G. Rand, and Tyrone D. Cannon. "Belief in Fake News Is Associated with Delusionality, Dogmatism, Religious Fundamentalism, and Reduced Analytic Thinking." *Journal of Applied Research in Memory and Cognition* (October 24, 2018).

Brotherton, Rob, and Silan Eser. "Bored to Fears: Boredom Proneness, Paranoia, and Conspiracy Theories." *Personality and Individual Differences* 80 (2015): 1–5.

Brotherton, Rob, and Christopher C. French. "Belief in Conspiracy Theories and Susceptibility to the Conjunction Fallacy." *Applied Cognitive Psychology* 28, no. 2 (2014): 238–48.

———. "Intention Seekers: Conspiracist Ideation and Biased Attributions of Intentionality." *PloS ONE* 10, no. 5 (2015): e0124125.

Cichocka, Aleksandra, Marta Marchlewska, and Agnieszka Golec de Zavala. "Does Self-Love or Self-Hate Predict Conspiracy Beliefs? Narcissism, Self-Esteem, and the Endorsement of Conspiracy Theories." *Social Psychological and Personality Science* 7, no. 2 (2016): 157–66.

Claassen, Ryan L., and Michael J. Ensley. "Motivated Reasoning and Yard-Sign-Stealing Partisans: Mine Is a Likable Rogue, Yours Is a Degenerate Criminal." *Political Behavior* 38, no. 2 (2016): 317–35.

Comsides, L. "The Logic of Social Exchange: Has Natural Selection Shaped How Humans Reason? Studies with the Wason Selection Task." *Cognition* 31, no. 3 (1989): 187–276.

Dagnall, Neil, Kenneth Drinkwater, Andrew Parker, Andrew Denovan, and Megan Parton. "Conspiracy Theory and Cognitive Style: A Worldview." *Frontiers in Psychology* 6 (2015): 206.

Darwin, Hannah, Nick Neave, and Joni Holmes. "Belief in Conspiracy Theories. The Role of Paranormal Belief, Paranoid Ideation and Schizotypy." *Personality and Individual Differences* 50, no. 8 (2011): 1289–93.

Davis, David Brion. *The Slave Power Conspiracy and the Paranoid Style.* Baton Rouge: Louisiana State University Press, 1969.

Douglas, K. M., Joseph E. Uscinski, R. M. Sutton, Aleksandra Cichocka, Turkay Nefes, Jim Ang, and Farzin Deravi. "Understanding Conspiracy Theories." *Advances in Political Psychology* 6 (2019).

Drinkwater, Ken, Neil Dagnall, and Andrew Parker. "Reality Testing, Conspiracy Theories, and Paranormal Beliefs." *Journal of Parapsychology* 76, no. 1 (2012): 57.

Dyer, Kathleen D., and Raymond E. Hall. "Effect of Critical Thinking Education on Epistemically Unwarranted Beliefs in College Students." *Research in Higher Education* 60, no. 3 (May 1, 2019): 293–314.

Freeman, Daniel, and Richard P. Bentall. "The Concomitants of Conspiracy Concerns." *Social Psychiatry and Psychiatric Epidemiology* 52, no. 5 (2017): 1–10.

French, Christopher C., Julia Santomauro, Victoria Hamilton, Rachel Fox, and Michael A. Thalbourne. "Psychological Aspects of the Alien Contact Experience." *Cortex* 44, no. 10 (November 1, 2008): 1387–95.

Gaudette, Emily. "Starbucks Continues So-Called 'War on Christmas' with Lesbian Positive Ad." *Newsweek* (2017). Published electronically November 21, 2017.

Green, Ricky, and Karen M. Douglas. "Anxious Attachment and Belief in Conspiracy Theories." *Personality and Individual Differences* 125 (April 15, 2018): 30–37.

Grzesiak-Feldman, Monika, and Monika Irzycka. "Right-Wing Authoritarianism and Conspiracy Thinking in a Polish Sample." *Psychological Reports* 105 (2009): 389–93.

Imhoff, Roland, and Pia Lamberty. "How Paranoid Are Conspiracy Believers? Toward a More Fine-Grained Understanding of the Connect and Disconnect between Paranoia and Belief in Conspiracy Theories." *European Journal of Social Psychology* 48, no. 7 (2018).

———. "Too Special to Be Duped: Need for Uniqueness Motivates Conspiracy Beliefs." *European Journal of Social Psychology* 47, no. 6 (2017): 724–34.

Jolley, Daniel, Rose Meleady, and Karen Douglas. "Exposure to Intergroup Conspiracy Theories Promotes Prejudice Which Spreads across Groups." *British Journal of Psychology* (March 13, 2019).

Lee, Spike. "Spike Lee on Real Time with Bill Maher." HBO, 2007.

Leone, Luigi, Mauro Giacomantonio, Riccardo Williams, and Desirée Michetti. "Avoidant Attachment Style and Conspiracy Ideation." *Personality and Individual Differences* 134 (November 1, 2018): 329–36.

Lodge, Milton, and Charles S. Taber. *The Rationalizing Voter.* New York: Cambridge University Press, 2013.

Lord, Charles G., Lee Ross, and Mark R. Lepper. "Biased Assimilation and Attitude Polarization: The Effects of Prior Theories on Subsequently Considered Evidence." *Journal of Personality and Social Psychology* 37, no. 11 (1979): 2098–109.

Marchlewska, Marta, Aleksandra Cichocka, and Małgorzata Kossowska. "Addicted to Answers: Need for Cognitive Closure and the Endorsement of Conspiracy Beliefs." *European Journal of Social Psychology* 48, no. 2 (2018).

Miller, Joanne M., Kyle L. Saunders, and Christina E. Farhart. "Conspiracy Endorsement as Motivated Reasoning: The Moderating Roles of Political Knowledge and Trust." *American Journal of Political Science* 60, no. 4 (2016): 824–44.

Newheiser, Anna-Kaisa, Miguel Farias, and Nicole Tausch. "The Functional Nature of Conspiracy Beliefs: Examining the Underpinnings of Belief in the *Da Vinci Code* Conspiracy." *Personality and Individual Differences* 51, no. 8 (2011): 1007–11.

Nyhan, Brendan. "9/11 and Birther Misperceptions Compared." *Brendan-nyhan .com/blog* (2009).

Nyhan, Brendan, Jason Reifler, and Peter A. Ubel. "The Hazards of Correcting Myths about Health Care Reform." *Medical Care* 51, no. 2 (2013): 127–32.

Oliver, Eric, and Thomas Wood. "Conspiracy Theories and the Paranoid Style(s) of Mass Opinion." *American Journal of Political Science* 58, no. 4 (2014): 952–66.

———. *Enchanted America: How Intuition and Reason Divide Our Politics.* Chicago: University of Chicago Press, 2018.

Richey, Sean. "A Birther and a Truther: The Influence of the Authoritarian Personality on Conspiracy Beliefs." *Politics & Policy* 45, no. 3 (2017): 465–85.

Rogers, Paul, John E. Fisk, and Dawn Wiltshire. "Paranormal Belief and the Conjunction Fallacy: Controlling for Temporal Relatedness and Potential Surprise Differentials in Component Events." *Applied Cognitive Psychology* 25, no. 5 (2011): 692–702.

Smallpage, Steven M., Adam M. Enders, and Joseph E. Uscinski. "The Partisan Contours of Conspiracy Theory Beliefs." *Research & Politics* 4, no. 4 (2017): 2053168017746554.

Soral, Wiktor, Aleksandra Cichocka, Michał Bilewicz, and Marta Marchlewska. "The Collective Conspiracy Mentality in Poland." In *Conspiracy Theories and the People Who Believe Them,* edited by Joseph E. Uscinski, 372–84. New York: Oxford University Press, 2018.

Ståhl, Tomas, and Jan-Willem van Prooijen. "Epistemic Rationality: Skepticism toward Unfounded Beliefs Requires Sufficient Cognitive Ability and Motivation to Be Rational." *Personality and Individual Differences* 122 (2018): 155–63.

Sunstein, Cass, and Adrian Vermeule. "Conspiracy Theories." *SSRN eLibrary* (2008).

Thomas, S. B., and S. C. Quinn. "The Tuskegee Syphilis Study, 1932 to 1972: Implications for HIV Education and AIDS Risk Education Programs in the Black Community." *American Journal of Public Health* 81, no. 11 (November 1, 1991): 1498–505.

Tversky, Amos, and Daniel Kahneman. "Extensional versus Intuitive Reasoning: The Conjunction Fallacy in Probability Judgment." *Psychological Review* 90, no. 4 (1983): 293.

Uscinski, Joseph E. "The Psychology behind Why People Believe Conspiracy Theories about Scalia's Death." *Washington Post*, February 19, 2016.

Uscinski, Joseph E., and Joseph M. Parent. *American Conspiracy Theories.* New York: Oxford University Press, 2014.

van Prooijen, Jan-Willem. "Why Education Predicts Decreased Belief in Conspiracy Theories." *Applied Cognitive Psychology* 31, no. 1 (2017): 50–58.

5

The Politics of Conspiracy Theories

C onspiracy theories are inherently political. They address who has power and what that power is used for when no one is looking. Even the lizard-people conspiracy theories, for example, posit political claims: that important truths are being hidden from the public, that power is exercised by secretive unaccountable actors, and that these actors wish to do us harm. Because conspiracy beliefs are opinions that attempt to make sense of the political world, they are political opinions, not unlike mundane opinions about presidential performance or issue preference. This chapter addresses the political factors affecting how and why people believe, spread, or otherwise act on conspiracy theories. This includes an examination of how opinions form in the mass public, how elites influence the masses, and how political conditions drive conspiracy theories.

Power and Conspiracy Theories

Conspiracy theories accuse powerful people of working together. Those accused of conspiring are either actually powerful or at least thought to be powerful. Power in this sense—political power—is the ability to bring about change, particularly in what other people do. It is therefore natural for conspiracy theories to accuse people who currently hold real political power or who have the means to purchase or manipulate power from behind the scenes. Rarely do we hear about homeless amputees orchestrating massive conspiracies.

That only the powerful (or those thought to be powerful) are accused of conspiring might seem rather commonplace, given that by the time you are reading this book, you likely have already encountered thousands of conspiracy theories that accuse the most dominant groups and individuals. But political philosopher Machiavelli suggested some centuries ago that accusing only the powerful of conspiring might miss the mark. Machiavelli, in writing about political strategy, suggests that we should be on the lookout for conspiracies emanating from the weak because it is the weak, not the strong, who need to conspire in darkness to achieve their ends.[1] The strong can just get what they want with force.

According to this view, accusing the powerful of conspiring overlooks the fact that powerful people can get what they want without having to sneak around in the shadows. For example, many accused President George W. Bush of orchestrating the 9/11 terror attacks as a pretense for going to war. What these conspiracy theorists fail to consider is that the American president has the power to go to war without any real pretense. Consider that in 2018, the White House was directing military activities in seven different countries without formal declarations of war, galvanizing events, or fanfare.[2] During the final year of the Obama administration, the US military dropped more than twenty-six thousand bombs, or "nearly three bombs every hour, 24 hours a day," even though few Americans knew the country was at war or, if they knew, with whom.[3]

That said, powerful people do conspire to get what they want, from time to time. One reason could be that modern democracies attempt to limit power. Watergate occurred not because Richard Nixon had too much power but rather because he was fearful of his political competitors. After the break-in was discovered, the cover-up occurred because Nixon was going to be held accountable for his actions by other branches of government. Iran-Contra occurred because Congress had placed restrictions on sales of arms to Iran, thus limiting the power of the Reagan administration. Shady dealings occurred to circumvent the restrictions. Another reason that the powerful conspire is so that they can hide what they would do anyway, through force. Consider the Tuskegee experiments: the government had no problem injecting syphilis into the eyes and spines of unwitting test subjects; it was just that they wanted to keep their activities secret.[4]

It is important to consider that the weak can do bad things, too: no one group of people is immune from temptation. The weak, poor, and destitute can commit atrocities, and being at the bottom of a power asymmetry does not mean one is innocent. The powerful can of course do more harm than the less powerful, but a lack of power is not a sign of virtue.

Just because a person has power or authority, we should not assume that they are automatically corrupt, and just because a person does not have power or authority, we should not assume that they have only good intentions. Anyone can do bad things. With this said, there seems to be a natural aversion to power, which conspiracy theories take advantage of. Consider, for example, how accusations against corporations are framed: accusers are quick to point out the size, profitability, and success of the

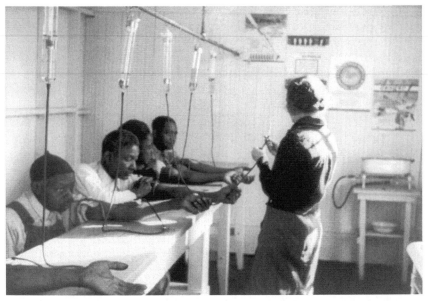

Photo 5.1   African American men receiving intravenous treatment in a Georgia venereal disease clinic during the same decade as the "Tuskegee Study" of African American men with untreated syphilis. The US government later apologized for infecting test subjects with syphilis.
Everett Collection / Newscom

corporations they are accusing, as if those attributes had anything to do with whether those corporations were responsible for some particular harm.[5] Conspiracy theories accusing "big pharma" or "big agriculture," for example, inherently use the size and supposed power of these industries as evidence of their bad intentions.

Some argue that this aversion to power stems from evolution: that early in human history it was particularly wise to be suspicious of powerful outsiders.[6] Suspicious humans were prepared for attacks and therefore more likely to survive and pass on their genes and behaviors. People who were less suspicious were more susceptible to attack and were less able to pass on their genes. Such an evolutionary view could explain (rather than justify) the aversion that people from all over the world have toward the powerful, as well as members of out-groups.[7]

The Locus of Power

Where does power lie? Many conspiracy theories accuse organizations such as the Illuminati, the Freemasons, the Bilderbergers, and Skull & Bones of secretly having and abusing power.[8] Britain's David Icke, a well-known conspiracy theorist, argues that a race of interdimensional reptilian elites interbred with humans thousands of years ago. According to Icke, the lizard-human hybrids are the leaders of every country, political party, royal family, and corporation. This dim view suggests that political and economic elites are not even human. This is not unlike the view of Jewish people that anti-Semites have historically put forward.[9]

Icke begins with the rather mundane assertion (among conspiracy theorists) that a "sinister network of families" secretly controls humanity.

> The Republican and Democratic parties, and their equivalents around the world, are owned by Illuminati bloodlines through the "transnational corporation" structure of the secret society web. . . . The Rothschild Illuminati networks . . . run the government no matter who "wins" an election.[10]

Icke, however, attributes the power of this network to less mundane factors: "non-human" reptilian elites.

> It became clear to me that the Illuminati bloodlines are human-reptilian hybrids. . . . The Rothschilds and the bloodline family network obsessively and incessantly interbreed because they are seeking to retain their "special" genetics which would be quickly diluted by breeding with the general population. . . . The reptilian race covertly controlling human society is from a dimension of reality very close to this one, but beyond visible light and that's why we don't see them. They can move in and out of visible light, however, and there are reptilian "cities" and bases inside the Earth. Some top-secret underground military bases connect with them. The hybrid bloodlines, like the Rothschilds, serve their agenda on the surface and within visible light.[11]

Icke's reptilian elite theory, while not convincing many in public opinion polls, has had a strong cultural impact.[12] He frequently sells out small arenas for daylong events in which the audience is invited to dance away the conspiracy.

Jim Marrs, an American conspiracy theorist famous for his JFK assassination theories, has developed an equally disturbing yet less supernatural view of power. Marrs suggests that secretive elites are currently attempting to reduce the world population:

> We now live in a culture of death and decay that has been imposed upon us by a small group of wealthy elites that publicly espouses involuntary population reduction. We're being killed by chemicals, genetically modified organisms (GMO's), dyes, additives, plastics, tainted water, and polluted air. . . . We are not aware of these things because precious few recognize that we are being psychologically programmed by a mass media controlled by a mere handful of corporate owners. . . . [This] ensures that we cannot protest the population reduction that threatens our very lives.[13]

Of course, there is no evidence that population reduction is taking place (life spans are increasing, as is the population). There is also little evidence suggesting that population reduction would be good for those who remained.

Political activist Lyndon LaRouche was—up until his recent passing—just as concerned about the supposed coming apocalypse, but posited a different set of elite conspirators. LaRouche built a cult following with conspiracy theories focusing on the Queen of England.[14] From LaRouchePAC:

> [T]he 9/11 attacks on Manhattan (and Washington) were run by the British system, and only the Queen, under that system, had the authority to give the go-ahead. But what supplements that case in a most fascinating way, is that Lyndon LaRouche was able in essence to forecast the 9/11 attacks a full eight months before they occurred.[15]

Prior to espousing these conspiracy theories, LaRouche spent the 1980s spreading AIDS conspiracy theories, which were almost successful in urging California to quarantine HIV patients.[16]

Communications professor–turned–conspiracy theorist James Tracy quickly became (in)famous following the shooting at Sandy Hook Elementary School. He accused the media of conspiring to cover up the true circumstances of the shooting. To document his claims, Tracy contributed to the book *No One Died at Sandy Hook*, which begins with the following declaration.[17]

> We are saying that Sandy Hook did not happen as we have been told. We also think the Boston Marathon bombing did not happen as we have been told. We think these events are part of a pattern that stretches at least as far back as the murder of John F. Kennedy, likely farther. These "false flag" events are part of a conspiracy, a vast conspiracy. You have been taught to laugh now. But there is nothing funny here.

Sandy Hook conspiracy theorists have implicated the CIA, FEMA, and other government agencies in the shooting. Some theories suggest that *false flag* events, as they call them, are designed to limit gun rights; others suggest they are simply drills. Several conspiracy theorists took to harassing the parents of the slain Sandy Hook children; this led the parents to organize and push back against online conspiracy theory–driven harassment.

The white replacement, or white genocide, theory asserts that corporations and governments are conspiring to bring inexpensive foreign workers to white-majority countries (Europe, the United States, New Zealand, and Australia) to replace white workers. This theory asserts that, in addition to taking jobs from whites, nonwhite foreigners will displace European culture and, through increased birthrates, outnumber Europeans. This theory is widely believed across Europe; for example, about 50 percent of the French believe it.[18] Brenton Tarrant, the Australian who murdered fifty Muslims at two mosques in Christchurch, New Zealand, provided a manifesto to explain his deadly actions, "The Great Replacement":

> We are experiencing an invasion on a level never seen before in history. Millions of people pouring across our borders, legally. Invited by the state and corporate entities to replace the White people who have failed to reproduce, failed to create the cheap labour, new consumers and tax base that the corporations and states need to thrive. This crisis of mass immigration and sub-replacement fertility is an assault on the European people that, if not combated, will ultimately result in the complete racial and cultural replacement of the European people.[19]

This manifesto was quickly banned by government censors in New Zealand.[20]

It is often noted that conspiracy theories are very similar to populist appeals. *Populism* is a political worldview in which politicians and experts are too disconnected from the regular people, cannot be trusted, and are likely engaged in conspiracies against the people. Populism combines anti-elitism with the rejection of pluralism so that the people have a singular will that only outsiders and enemies can reject.[21] Conspiracy theories fit populist narratives very well because conspiracy theories tend to accuse elites and posit a strong Manichean narrative in which political competitors are enemies of "the people."

Partisan Conspiracy Theorizing

Some people are animated by conspiracy theories that accuse the entirety of the power structure; the conspirators' affiliations matter little. For those conspiracy theorists, like Jim Marrs, partisanship is but a ruse:

> With secretive societies, such as the Council on Foreign Relations, providing leadership for both the Democratic and Republican parties, there has been no significant change in U.S. foreign policy since World War II. The global elite that control both parties sees to it that no one who is not aligned with globalist goals gains the presidency. No effort is spared to keep America in perpetual war, the basis for the elite's global agenda.[22]

It must be utterly exhausting to accuse all powerful people and institutions all the time. Some people temper their conspiracy theorizing by instead impugning specific groups. Many conspiracy theories about government aren't so much about the government in general, but rather about the particular party controlling government.

Many people distrust the government when it is controlled by a competing party but then regain their trust when control is handed to their own party.[23] When their party wins, the outcome is just, when their party loses, the other side cheated. People view the country as being on the right track when their party controls it—but see it as on the wrong track when the opposing party controls it.[24] The circumstances people find themselves in, vis-à-vis their partisanship, affect their opinions in other domains as well. For example, when economic conditions have changed little, the transfer of political control from one party to another leads partisans to flip their outlook, with those who feel they now control government adopting a more positive view and those who feel out of power adopting a more negative view.[25]

When the opposing party is in power, people's sentiments are often expressed as conspiracy theories. As if by clockwork, presidents are regularly accused by· opposing partisans of being foreign agents bent on destroying the United States. Just as Donald Trump has recently been accused of being a Russian asset, Barack Obama was accused of being a secret Muslim bent on undermining American interests, Jimmy Carter was accused of being a Soviet agent, and FDR was often accused of being a communist intent on taking over the United States.[26]

Surveys looking at less specific theories show a similar pattern. A 2012 nationally representative US survey asked respondents, "Which of these groups are likely to work in secret against the rest of us? Check all that apply."[27] Respondents could select from a list of ten groups, as many or as few as they liked. Two options were associated with the Republican Party: "Republicans or other conservative groups" and "Corporations and the rich." Two other options were associated with the Democratic Party: "Democrats or other liberal groups," and "Communists and Socialists." Another option was associated with neither party: "Freemasons or some other fraternal groups." Only 8 percent of Republicans chose "Republicans and other conservative groups," compared to 37 percent of Democratic respondents. Only 26 percent of Republican respondents chose "Corporations and the rich," compared to 57 percent of Democrats. As for groups aligned with the Democratic coalition, 39 percent of Republican respondents chose "Democrats and other liberal groups," but only 6 percent of Democrats did. Approximately 60 percent of Republican respondents chose "Communists and Socialists," while only 20 percent of Democratic respondents did. In sum, partisans are more likely to accuse the opposing party and its coalition of conspiring and less likely to accuse their own party and its coalition of conspiring.

Freemasons and other fraternal groups are not generally considered partisan. Republicans and Democrats were equally likely (around 10 percent each) to choose this option. Compared to the partisan options, very few people expressed concern with the Freemasons. This suggests that partisan conflict is an important driver of conspiracy beliefs, at least in the United States, and that partisans are about equally likely to believe that groups like the Freemasons are part of a conspiracy.

Photo 5.2 The Freemasons, represented by the Masonic square and compass, are one of many groups accused of controlling world events.
© iStock / Getty Images Plus / in8finity

An important question to ask now is how and why partisanship affects conspiracy beliefs. To answer this, we must first consider that conspiracy theories are political, and often partisan, opinions. It becomes fitting, then, to discuss what social scientists have discovered in the last century about how political opinions develop.

Opinion Formation

Following the wars of the early twentieth century, social scientists began to take a strong interest in the public's opinions. A central question was why otherwise good and decent people would support regimes that slaughtered millions. To answer this question, sociologist Paul Lazarsfeld and his team conducted a series of studies across the northeastern United States beginning in the 1930s.[28] By interviewing the same people repeatedly, they intended to observe how media messages could influence the audience's preferences. Lazarsfeld initially assumed that messages in the media could have strong, direct, and intuitive effects on people's opinions, so that, for example, advertisements for political candidates could immediately alter how people intended to vote. If messages in the media had this kind of power, then the propaganda machines employed by the Nazis and other authoritarian governments could potentially explain the public support for those regimes. The idea that media messages could have such strong effects was termed the "hypodermic needle theory."

Lazarsfeld surmised that if the hypodermic needle theory was accurate, his team would observe an ebb and flow of public preferences closely following that of media messages. Instead they found the exact opposite: regardless of the changing media environment, voter preferences, for example, changed little in the months leading up to elections. Media messages did not seem to have much power to change minds (at least directly), and people's preferences were stable over time.[29] Without evidence to support it, researchers retired the hypodermic needle theory and searched for the mechanisms that drove public opinion elsewhere.[30]

In 1960, researchers at the University of Michigan published an exhaustive study of American public opinion, *The American Voter*, which sought to explain the over-time stability of individuals' political opinions.[31] In their account, political opinions arise from socialization processes and, once solidified, are for the most part impervious to external stimuli such as news and advertising. Early-life influences such as parents, schooling, and religion led people to develop *partisan attachments*, which were stable not only over the course of campaigns but over the course of lifetimes.

According to the account in *The American Voter*, partisanship could be thought of as "an immovable mover": partisanship would shape other opinions but would not be much affected by other opinions. This account has been tested repeatedly in the intervening decades, and strong support is consistently found for this conception of partisanship: a socialized group attachment that colors how one sees the political world.

Consider the findings of public opinion scholars Donald Green, Bradley Palmquist, and Eric Schickler, who, writing forty years after *The American Voter*, support its main conclusions and liken party identification to religion:

> Our view, which hearkens back to earlier social-psychological perspectives on partisanship, draws a parallel between party identification and religious identification. Partisan attachments form relatively early in adulthood. . . . When people feel a sense of belonging to a given social group, they absorb the doctrinal positions that the group advocates. However party and religious identifications come about, once they take root in early adulthood, they often persist. Partisan identities are enduring features of citizens' self-conceptions. They do not merely come and go with election cycles and

campaign ephemera. The public's interest in party politics climbs as elections draw near, but partisan self-conceptions remain intact during peaks and lulls in party competition.[32]

Because of the stability introduced by socialization and other social-psychological processes, there is little room for media messages to affect underlying opinions like partisanship. The inability to support the hypodermic needle model, and the findings showing stability in partisanship, gave support to the *minimal effects model* of media influence, which became conventional wisdom for decades.[33]

The minimal effects model relies on two basic claims: first, that audiences have an active psychological resistance to messages that challenge their underlying attachments (including and especially partisanship), and second, that audiences self-select sources of information to meet their demand for gratification and to avoid information sources that challenge their deeply held views. Let's examine each of these.

First, audiences have an active resistance to messages that challenge their partisan attachments or other preferences. Studies find that audiences either ignore or overly scrutinize information with which they disagree and, because of this, give additional weight to information they agree with. This leads to *confirmation bias*, which occurs when people gather and/or consider only evidence that supports a preordained conclusion. Attitude polarization can occur because everyone hears only about how right they are.

Consider the famous study by Charles Lord, Lee Ross, and Mark Lepper, in which undergraduates (some who supported and some who opposed capital punishment) were exposed to one of two "studies" about the death penalty. One of the "studies" in the experiment confirmed and the other disconfirmed the participants' existing beliefs. The study found that both "proponents and opponents of capital punishment rated those results and procedures that confirmed their own beliefs to be the more convincing and probative ones," and as such, "the result of exposing contending factions in a social dispute to an identical body of relevant empirical evidence may be not a narrowing of disagreement but rather an increase in polarization."[34] The reason, they found, was that

> people who hold strong opinions on complex social issues are likely to examine relevant empirical evidence in a biased manner. They are apt to accept "confirming" evidence at face value while subjecting "disconfirming" evidence to critical evaluation, and, as a result, draw undue support for their initial positions from mixed or random empirical findings.[35]

Lord et al.'s finding was tested some years later, but this time with information about the assassination of President Kennedy. The finding was little different:

due to the processes of biased assimilation and attitude polarization, personal theories about the perpetrator(s) of the assassination are essentially immutable, and therefore the debate surrounding JFK's assassination will continue endlessly . . . proponents of both the [official explanation] and conspiracy theories perceive the same body of evidence as supportive of their position . . . [this] leads to attitude polarization rather than to a moderation or reversal of existing attitudes.[36]

People view information differently depending on what they already believe, meaning that new information may not have as much of an effect on beliefs as some claim.

Second, and perhaps more importantly, audiences self-select media sources that meet their demands, while at the same time avoiding news sources that do not. People cannot be influenced by information if they are not exposed to it. When it comes to cable news channels in the United States, for example, most people are not watching. But the people who are watching tend to select the channel that best fits their partisanship, with Republicans watching Fox News, and Democrats watching CNN or MSNBC.[37]

Self-selection operates much the same way with conspiracy theory content: there are of course many venues for people to seek out conspiracy theories, but those venues are mostly used by people who already believe in conspiracy theories, likely because they have a worldview steeped in conspiracy thinking. An Italian study of Facebook shows that people who have a history of interacting positively with conspiracy theories on the platform interacted positively with pages touting made-up conspiracy theories (e.g., pages discussing Viagra chemtrails), and conversely, people who have a history of interacting with science-oriented pages did not interact positively with made-up conspiracy theories. In other words, "polarized users of conspiracy pages are more active in liking and commenting on" conspiracy theories when presented with them.[38]

By positing these two forms of resistance—the audience's predispositions and its choices of content—the minimal effects model suggests that the media's ability to change minds is limited. News messages therefore serve to reinforce existing opinions, but not to change them. Polarization occurs because people only seek out and then consider information that confirms what they already believe, insulating them from reflection and compromise.

This is not to say that new information cannot influence people at all. It can and often does. For example, many studies show that news outlets can set issue priorities for audiences through a process called "agenda setting."[39] In this, audiences rank the issues that the news media reports the most as the most important. While the media cannot tell audiences what to think, it can affect what audiences think about. There are also well-documented *framing* effects.[40] News outlets have numerous ways that they can discuss any given issue—the choices they make can greatly alter how that issue is perceived. For example, a government budget impasse can be reported as a "crisis," a "negotiation," or a "fight." Each of these frames refers to the same events but gives different impressions of it.[41] I note, though, that because people self-select their sources of information, and then resist information that would cause cognitive dissonance, these aforementioned effects may be smaller than some have suspected.[42] On top of this, news outlets (and other purveyors of information) are incentivized to bring in audiences; they do this by carefully targeting their product to the audience's demands. If they do not, they cease to exist.[43]

One way to think about how the media might influence audiences while accounting for the audience's predispositions is put forward by political scientist John Zaller. In writing about opinion formation and information, Zaller begins with the observation that "[citizens] possess a variety of interests, values, and experiences that may greatly affect their willingness to accept—or alternatively, their resolve to resist—persuasive influence."[44] From this, he shows that people tend to take cues from media and political elites whom they trust; for example a Democrat will take cues from Democrat politicians and news sources, and Republicans will take cues from Republican leaders and news sources. Partisanship is therefore a group attachment that determines which elites a person takes cues from, rather than which issues a person believes.

Further, and congruent with *The American Voter*, it is the underlying dispositions (i.e., partisanship) that are "sticky"; other opinions are malleable and easily affected by elite cues. Consider a study in which constituents received flyers with issue positions from their state legislators. Scholars found that "voters often adopted the positions legislators took, even when legislators offered little justification . . . voters did not evaluate their legislators more negatively when representatives took positions these voters had previously opposed . . . regardless of whether legislators provided justifications."[45] The researchers concluded that such "findings are consistent with theories suggesting voters often defer to politicians' policy judgments."[46]

Consider also the campaign for California's Proposition 19 in 2010, which, had it passed, would have legalized marijuana. Having the caricature of a typical Democrat in mind, most people might assume that Democrats would have had unwavering support for this proposition. Instead, when high-profile Democrats in the Obama administration came out in opposition to the proposition, many Democratic voters who had previously supported passage changed their mind. According to political scientist Michael Tesler:

> Democratic voters in California were especially likely to change their support for Prop. 19 from September to October. While Republican opposition to Prop. 19 remained relatively stable, Democratic support declined by nine and seven percentage points in [polls] conducted during the final month

of the campaign. Moreover . . . the drop in Prop. 19 support was particularly pronounced among the most politically interested Democrats. . . . In September 2010, 75 percent of highly-interested Democrats supported the proposition compared with just 60 percent in October. Meanwhile, support from Republicans and less informed Democrats remained rather constant.[47]

Highly interested Democrats—those most likely to take cues from the high-profile Democrats opposing the proposition—were the ones most likely to change their minds.

My favorite example of these effects occurred when Herman Cain, a former CEO of Godfather's Pizza, ran for the Republican presidential nomination in 2012. YouGov's BrandIndex coincidentally was surveying the public repeatedly about Godfather's brand favorability. Republicans and Democrats viewed the pizza chain similarly when the campaign began, but as the country learned that Cain was formerly the CEO, opinions of Godfather's polarized: Republicans viewed the chain more positively while Democrats viewed it more negatively. By the height of Cain's popularity, Republicans and Democrats differed by twenty-five points (on a scale of −100 to 100) in their view of the pizza chain.[48] No matter one's partisanship, it was the same pizza, but people's political loyalties determined how much they said they liked it.

These are the broad strokes of opinion formation and media effects. The media and other sources of information can affect attitudes, but these effects are rarely as large or drastic as sensationalist accounts suggest. Even long, sustained information campaigns—like those taking place during presidential elections—rarely show evidence of widespread opinion change. Instead, campaigns largely get people to vote for whom they were predisposed to vote for anyway.[49]

Partisanship and Conspiracy Beliefs

Opposing partisans can be thought of as opposing players on sports teams competing in a game where the stakes are particularly high. As the saying goes, politics ain't beanbag. Partisanship, like membership on a sports team, stems from a sense of belonging or group attachment, rather than from a judgment on a set of policies.[50] Further, people favor their team over others and believe their team has better intentions and methods.

When partisans believe in conspiracy theories, those theories tend to accuse the opposing party of conspiring. Partisans therefore believe conspiracy theories that the opposing party rejects.[51] In addition, partisans believe in conspiracy theories that not only accuse the opposition but also align with their partisan worldview in other ways. Using data collected from the 1958 party conventions, political scientists Herbert McCloskey and Dennis Chong compared the beliefs of far-left and far-right activists. They found symmetry

in the willingness of activists on each side to accuse the opposite side of conspiring, but found decidedly different reasons for making those accusations:

> Despite the suspicions of both the left and right towards the government,
> their anti-system responses are usually triggered by different issues. In
> responding, for example, to a series of items concerning the influence of
> the wealthy and powerful on the courts, the nation's laws, the newspapers
> and the political parties, the far left was the most willing of the ideological
> groups to condemn these institutions as pawns of the rich. None of this is
> surprising, of course, since hostility to capitalist elites and the establishment
> has long been a dominant feature of radical-left politics. But the radical
> right is also disenchanted with these institutions, though for different rea-
> sons. Its anger is detonated, not by the institutions' alleged association with
> wealth or "business," but by their supposed susceptibility to the influence
> of an entrenched liberal establishment. In their view, government offices,
> the press, the foundations and other powerful institutions are overflowing
> with technocrats and academics trained at liberal colleges and universities.
> These universities are also the "farm system" that stocks the judiciary and
> various other professions.[52]

Numerous polls show that partisans are equally willing to believe in conspiracy theories; it's just that they believe in different ones for different reasons.[53] Partisan conspiracy theories are both a regular part and a reflection of
partisan conflict.[54]

The One Percent

Many, particularly on the political left, do not want to accept that their side
is as likely to believe in conspiracy theories as the opposing side. Many of the
objections devolve into arguments about what counts as a conspiracy theory
and what does not.[55] Therefore, when determining what is and what is not
a conspiracy theory, we should be forthright with our definitions and apply
them consistently. Doing so will most likely show significant conspiracy theorizing on both sides of the partisan aisle.

When I started researching conspiracy theories more than a decade ago
with my coauthor Joseph Parent, we noticed that our colleagues had focused
their work rather narrowly, on conspiracy theories believed by Republicans,
but seemed blind to conspiracy theories on the left.

> Since the beginning, that is since Richard Hofstadter, the claim has been
> that there is partisan asymmetry because the right is more authoritarian,
> anti-intellectual, and tribal. Although there are differences between the Left
> and Right, scholars and the media should be circumspect about overdraw-
> ing them in this instance. We believe the notion of asymmetry has persisted
> because academics and journalists align largely with the Left. This pushes

these two institutions to disproportionately dwell on conspiracy theories held by the right but overlook conspiracy theories closer to home. Hofstadter himself was a leftist with Marxist sympathies—it is perfectly understandable why he picked up a pen in the wake of the Red Scare. When we presented parts of [*American Conspiracy Theories*] at an academic conference panel in 2013, the other academics presented papers addressing the theories that Obama was born in a foreign country, was a secret Muslim, and that he faked Bureau of Labor Statistics data. All are valuable contributions, but the audience could be forgiven for thinking Republicans were more susceptible to conspiracy theories than Democrats. In political science at least, much of the recent study of conspiratorial beliefs has defended accusations against actors on the left, especially since Obama's election in 2008. Searching through the conference archives of the American Political Science Association (2002–2013) and Midwest Political Science Association (2004–2013), we found many papers studying conspiratorial beliefs on the right and nearly none on the left. The cumulative effect is that our knowledge generating and knowledge disseminating institutions make the right look chock full of cranks and the left look sensible and savvy. There is no conspiracy here; ideology drives the worldviews of professors and journalists just like it does everyone else. But that does not make it just.[56]

While this has changed drastically during the last few years, there still remains a tendency for scholars and journalists to assume that Republicans are particularly prone to conspiracy beliefs.

As an example of a conspiracy theory on the left that is often excused, consider Vermont senator and 2016 Democratic presidential candidate Bernie Sanders's claim—central to nearly all his speeches—that the one percent of the wealthiest Americans "rigged" the US economic and political systems. Many prominent politicians make similar claims in the United States and elsewhere (see Massachusetts senator Elizabeth Warren [D] or the UK's Labour Party leader Jeremy Corbyn).[57] Many on the left are reluctant to accept the one-percent theory as conspiracy theory; they argue instead that the claim is either true, or excusable because it's just a fiery critique of income inequality. I want to explore this theory in depth because it is ubiquitous in popular political rhetoric.

In chapter 2, I defined *conspiracy theory* as an unsubstantiated allegation claiming that a small, powerful group is working in secret, for their own benefit, against the common good, and in a way that undermines bedrock ground rules. If we apply this definition evenhandedly, then the one-percent rhetoric clearly counts. In Sanders's own words, a group, the "one percent," has surreptitiously taken over ("rigged") the economy and the political process. The group's motive, a greed that knows "no end," is making it a struggle for everyone else "to survive."[58] He claims that the entire system was "designed by the wealthiest people in this country to benefit the wealthiest people in this country at the expense of everybody else" and that "heads they win, tails you lose."[59] This rhetoric is first and foremost a cheap attempt at scapegoating some for the problems of others. Sanders clearly accuses a group of working in secret for their own benefit, against the common good and in a way that violates bedrock ground rules. The only question remaining is whether Sanders's rhetoric refers to a *conspiracy*, meaning that Sanders is simply sharing authoritative information about an actual conspiracy taking place, or if he is proffering a *conspiracy theory*, meaning that his claim potentially could be true or false but is unsubstantiated.

Many people in the United States (and other Western countries) believe that the one-percent theory does not count as conspiracy theory; they are convinced the one percent does in fact control the economy, the government, or both. But this belief has not been established as true by the epistemic authorities who study the economy or politics. Economists classify theories positing economic control by a small group as conspiracy theory.[60] Political scientists called these theories into question decades ago. Thus, I am aware of no legitimate economics or politics textbooks that present as fact the one-percent theory.

Consider the critique of such theories by preeminent political scientist Robert Dahl:

> A great many people seem to believe that "they" run things: the old families, the bankers, the City Hall machine, or the party boss behind the scene. This kind of view evidently has a powerful and many-sided appeal. It is simple, compelling, dramatic, "realistic." It gives one standing as an inside-dopester. For individuals with a strong strain of frustrated idealism, it has just the right touch of hard-boiled cynicism. Finally, the hypothesis has one very great advantage over many alternative explanations: It can be cast in a form that makes it virtually impossible to disprove. . . . If the overt leaders of a community do not appear to constitute a ruling elite, then the theory can be saved by arguing that behind the overt leaders there is a set of covert leaders who do. If subsequent evidence shows that this covert group does not make a ruling elite, then the theory can be saved by arguing that behind the first covert group there is another, and so on.[61]

Dahl dismisses such theories due to their unfalsifiability:

> Now whatever else it may be, a theory that cannot even in principle be controverted by empirical evidence is not a scientific theory. The least that we can demand of any ruling elite theory that purports to be more than a metaphysical or polemical doctrine is, first, that the burden of proof be on the proponents of the theory and not on its critics; and, second, that there be clear criteria according to which the theory could be disproved.[62]

Dahl goes on to create a standard for judging theories such as those purported by Bernie Sanders. Dahl argues that in order for reasonable people to accept such theories, those positing them should (1) be able to provide a clearly defined group of elites, (2) show that the preferences of that group diverge from those outside the group, and (3) show that those elites "regularly prevail" in most instances.[63] There are reasonable debates to have along such lines, about how much political power the rich have over the poor, and about why economic inequalities come about and what to do about them. And some scholars have made good-faith efforts to meet these criteria. For example, an analysis by political scientists Martin Gilens and Benjamin Page suggests that wealthy Americans are more likely to get their preferred policies when they disagree with middle-class Americans.[64] But it is far from settled science that the wealthy control the government in the way Sanders's rhetoric would suggest. Political scientist Peter Enns cautions about making strong conclusions on this front: "even on those issues for which the preferences of the wealthy and those in the middle diverge, policy ends up about where we would expect if policymakers represented the middle class and ignored the affluent."[65]

Consider also the practical implications of Sanders's one-percent theory. Is it possible for a small group to take over the entirety of the United States' diffuse political system in order to rig its $20 trillion economy under cover of darkness? No doubt some wealthy, powerful people have at times rigged portions of certain markets, but these efforts are often either done in the open, are exposed, or are not long successful. Long-term rigging of the entire economy—which includes trillions and trillions of transactions every year—does not seem possible. A reasonable take is that the American economy is just too big to be rigged by a small clandestine group.

Further, if the economy were rigged by those at the top, we would expect that the same companies and people would be continually successful. But we don't find that. It might seem as though the rich and successful are perpetually rich and successful, but it's just an illusion. The fact is that today's economic juggernauts are often tomorrow's losers, but because the losers disappear, we only see the juggernauts. Consider the fates of former industry leaders Kodak, MySpace, Toys R Us, TiVo, Radio Shack, Circuit City, Sears, Bear Stearns, Enron, Hostess, America Online, Blockbuster, Quiznos, and Atari. How come being economically powerful did not help them stay in business? How come *they* couldn't rig the system?

The US government, much like the economy, is sprawling, diffuse, and decentralized. Is it really possible for a small group to control all or even most of it? Given that different parts of the government are often working at cross-purposes, it seems unlikely that one group is controlling it for some directed purpose.

As to the one percent, who are they, exactly? Is Sanders referring to the one percent of the wealthiest individuals, the one percent of income earners in a given year, or some other group? Is he using the "one percent" moniker to describe a group in the United States, or the world? If he was doing the latter, his rhetoric might be less appealing to his followers since the vast majority of them would qualify as the world's one percent. For example, an income between thirty and fifty thousand dollars a year would put one into the global one percent of annual incomes, "so if you're an accountant, a registered nurse or even an elementary school teacher, congratulations. The average wage for any of these careers falls well within the top 1 percent worldwide."[66]

Beyond this, there is an inconsistency to Sanders's rhetoric. For example, he accused the one percent of both free-market gambling and running a rigged system.[67] It can't be both! The contradiction shows that Sanders is not making an argument from evidence, but rather from a willingness to scapegoat. This, ironically, is how Adolf Hitler attuned his anti-Semitic conspiracy theories to his audiences: Hitler tarred the Jews as rapacious money capitalists *and* as subversive communists.[68] Such accusations are incompatible, but if a politician is looking to attract the conspiracy-minded with scapegoating, then frequently demonizing a group with wide-ranging accusations is a winning strategy. That the claims are contradictory doesn't really matter, since such details don't concern those who prefer conspiracy theories to anything else.[69]

When Sanders claims that the entire system is "designed by the wealthiest people in this country to benefit the wealthiest people in this country at the expense of everybody else," the logic becomes circular. It's akin to saying that a successful person cheated to get where they are, and the evidence of cheating is that the person is successful. Imagine claiming that a track event (e.g., a fifty-yard sprint) was rigged by fast people because only the fastest people win.

Consider Warren's argument that "after making a killing on the economy they've rigged, they don't pay taxes on that accumulated wealth."[70] To her, the lack of an estate tax in the United States is evidence that the rich rigged the system to not have an estate tax. It's like saying that because there is no special tax on professors, it must be true that professors rigged the tax system to avoid paying the special professor tax.

It is important to further note that inequality has ebbed and flowed during Sanders's political career, but his tune stays the same.[71] Beyond his one-percent theory, Sanders has a long history of making pseudo-scientific claims, such as that cancer is caused by women's sexual repression and that too many choices of deodorant are causing American children to starve.[72]

To conclude this section, just because the villains in Sanders's one-percent conspiracy theories happen to be rich does not excuse the fact that these theories are indeed conspiracy theories and seek to scapegoat some people for others' lots in life. There are reasonable conversations to have about inequality, the tax system, and the functioning of democracy; but the one-percent theory is not one of them. My purpose in this section is not to steer you away from a concern about income inequality or to suggest a certain kind of economic philosophy, but rather to show that some claims about these sensitive topics, while impassioned and persuasive, may also be unreasonable when considered more fully.

Symmetry

A balanced approach shows that Republicans and Democrats display nearly equal levels of conspiracy thinking and beliefs in specific conspiracy theories.[73] Some people reject the idea of symmetry and sometimes rationalize this by moving the goalposts to claim that the left's conspiracy theories are less "bizarre," or that "important" people on the left don't traffic in conspiracy theories.[74] To address the first claim, surveys suggest that Republicans and Democrats believe bizarre conspiracy theories, for example, about the Freemasons and the Zika virus about equally.[75] Also, recent conspiracy theories that would seem to indicate the widespread existence of "bizarre" conspiracy beliefs on the right, such as the QAnon conspiracy theory, are neither well known on the right nor supported much more by the right than by the left.[76]

As for the claim that "important" Democrats engage in conspiracy theorizing less than "important" Republicans, there isn't much systematic data to support it. Donald Trump, the current Republican president, of course, engages in constant conspiracy theorizing, but that is but one person and anecdotal (and claims about asymmetry were being made long before Trump's presidency). Until scholars measure conspiracy theorizing by political elites in a more systematic way, we should not make claims of asymmetry on this point.

Conspiracy Thinking

Individuals' partisan attachments are a strong predictor of *which* conspiracy theories they believe in, but not all partisans believe in particular partisan conspiracy theories. Not every Republican believes that President Obama is a secret Muslim or faked his birth certificate, and not every Democrat believes that President George W. Bush stole the 2000 election, faked the 9/11 attacks, or went to war in Iraq for oil. Individual levels of conspiracy thinking within partisan groups explains why.

To quickly review, conspiracy thinking is the degree to which people view events and circumstance as the product of conspiracies.[77] Conspiracy thinking exists along a continuum, with extremely conspiracy-minded people (those believing that conspiracies are responsible for nearly everything) on one end, and the extremely not-conspiracy-minded people (those believing conspiracies are responsible for nearly nothing) on the other. Most Americans are somewhere in between. It is important to avoid giving any negative connotation: neither the people with high levels nor the ones with low levels of conspiracy thinking are necessarily better than the other group. Just as people with high levels are more likely to believe in dubious ideas, people with low levels are likely to reject the existence of real conspiracies.[78] Both tendencies can be problematic.

When a person with high levels of conspiracy thinking receives information that an event may have been the product of a conspiracy perpetrated by a disliked party, he or she will likely concur with that conspiracy theory.[79] A person with lower levels of conspiracy thinking will be harder to convince.[80]

Many journalists offhandedly refer to partisan conspiracy theories as "far-right" or "far-left." But this is an imprecise way to think about partisan conspiracy beliefs. Conspiracy beliefs are driven by conspiracy thinking, which is separate from partisanship. Partisanship will determine which particular partisan conspiracy theories a person will believe in, but conspiracy beliefs are not necessarily dependent upon the strength of an individual's partisanship. Self-identifying independents may believe in more conspiracy theories than their partisan counterparts.[81]

A Republican (Democrat) with high levels of conspiracy thinking is likely to believe in conspiracy theories that accuse Democrats (Republicans). Although people will direct their conspiracy theories at the political outgroup, it will be mostly the people predisposed to see conspiracies who will do so. Individuals with low levels of conspiracy thinking will not believe in many conspiracy theories, regardless of their partisanship (see figure 5.1).

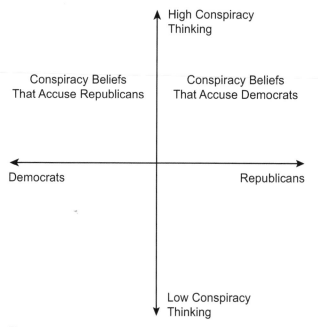

Figure 5.1 A Two-Dimensional Model of Conspiracy Beliefs

A large segment of the US population is disposed toward believing conspiracy theories. But partisan conspiracy theories are likely to convince only one side of the partisan divide and mostly those partisans with high levels of conspiracy thinking. This puts a ceiling on partisan conspiracy theories of about 25 percent. This is, incidentally, where both the Birther and 9/11 Truth theories maxed out in surveys for several years.[82] Belief in 9/11 Truth theories has increased recently, likely due to Donald Trump's rhetoric, which has given conspiracy-minded Republicans permission to believe in 9/11 conspiracy theories.[83]

That said, only in rare cases will a conspiracy theory appeal to a majority of the country in a bipartisan fashion. Kennedy assassination theories are the most prominent. Between 60 and 80 percent of Americans believe in one form of this theory, many more than either the Birther or Truther theories. There are two reasons for this. First, Kennedy conspiracy theories are nonpartisan in the aggregate. The majority of survey questions asked about Kennedy assassination conspiracy theories do not present respondents with partisan cues; for example, "Do you believe that Lee Harvey Oswald acted alone in killing President Kennedy, or was there some larger conspiracy at work?"[84] Americans of any partisan persuasion can answer yes to this question because it does not pin blame on an actor of their own team. Of course, when pollsters ask a follow-up question about who was behind the assassination, answers vary greatly.[85] It isn't that there is a single Kennedy assassination conspiracy theory, but rather many that are bundled together. This is why the number of people who believe this "omnibus" theory is so high. Second, unlike other conspiracy theories, Kennedy theories have seeped into mainstream discourse.[86] The anniversary of Kennedy's assassination each year seems to focus as much on the conspiracy theories as anything else. To conclude this section, conspiracy theories can

Photo 5.3 The model of rifle used to assassinate President Kennedy.
© iStock / Getty Images Plus / JerryBKeane

gain majority support, but only if they are general enough to appeal to nearly everyone who will accept conspiracy theories.

Conspiracy Theories Are for Losers

A person's conspiracy beliefs are determined by their level of conspiracy thinking and by their other attachments. Because individuals' underlying dispositions are largely stable, we should expect that the salience of conspiracy theories in the public sphere would be stable over time. But this does not appear to be the case: salient conspiracy theories come and go. The explanation therefore does not lie in dispositions, but rather in situations: conspiracy theories are more likely to resonate in American society when out-of-power groups use them to attack in-power groups. Joseph Parent and I summed up this argument with the following:

> We argue the targets and timing of resonant conspiracy theories follow a strategic logic, based on foreign threat and domestic power. In this way, conspiracy theories are used by vulnerable groups to manage perceived dangers: they are early warning systems that keep watch over the most sensitive areas and prepare solutions to potential attacks. At bottom, conspiracy theories are a form of threat perception, and fears are fundamentally driven by shifts in relative power. Because defeat and exclusion are their biggest inducements, *conspiracy theories are for losers* (speaking descriptively—not pejoratively).[87]

Referring to them as "losers," even descriptively, did nothing to ingratiate Parent and me to conspiracy theorists, but our claim was based on two important empirical observations.

The first was that after elections, losers tended to feel aggrieved and often resorted to conspiracy theories to explain their losses. Believing in and sharing conspiracy theories therefore provides "a way for groups falling in the pecking order to revamp and recoup from losses, close ranks, staunch losses, overcome collective action problems, and sensitize minds to vulnerabilities."[88] Rather than accept responsibility for their defeat, or give credit to the winning side, it is easier for some to blame their loss on trickery. Polls consistently show this effect:

> After Mitt Romney's defeat in 2012, 49 percent of Republicans believed that the Democrat-leaning activist group, ACORN, had stolen the election for Barack Obama (only 6 percent of Democrats believed this). It did not matter much that ACORN no longer existed in 2012. Such numbers could give the impression that Republicans are prone to belief in election fraud; however, instances where Democrats lose elections show parity. Following the contentious presidential election of 2000, 31 percent of Democrats believed that George W. Bush had stolen the election (only 3 percent of Republicans agreed), and 30 percent of Democrats stated that they would not accept

George W. Bush as a "legitimate president." After the unexpected Republican victory in 2016, 50 percent of Democrats believed the outcome was due to Russians tampering with vote tallies (there is currently no evidence to support this claim). To further demonstrate how both parties explain losses with accusations of fraud, a 2013 national poll asked respondents about fraud in the 2004 and 2008 elections. A total of 37 percent of Democrats believed the statement, "President Bush's supporters committed significant voter fraud in order to win Ohio in 2004," was probably true, while only 9 percent of Republicans agreed. This reverses in a question about President Obama's victory in 2012: 36 percent of Republicans believed it was probably true that "President Obama's supporters committed significant voter fraud in the 2012 presidential election," while only 4 percent of Democrats agreed. Significant portions of both parties cry foul after they lose, and in near equal numbers. Thus, the public's opinions stand in stark contrast to a scholarly consensus that election fraud is negligible, and suggest that opinions about fraud depend heavily on situational factors.[89]

Going into American elections, both sides of the aisle are equally suspicious that the other side will cheat to win; but after the winner is announced, conspiracy theories alleging fraud are largely confined to the losing side.

A second observation supporting the "losers" argument comes from a study of letters to the editor of the *New York Times*. This analysis involved reading one hundred twenty thousand letters to the editor of the *New York Times* from 1890 to 2010 (a random sample of about one thousand letters per year). The letters that advocated or refuted a conspiracy theory were picked out and then coded based upon who was being accused of conspiring. The findings showed that the groups accused by conspiracy theories ebbed and flowed over time, depending on who held power at the time. The proportion of conspiracy-theory letters each year accusing the party occupying the White House and their coalition of conspiring was higher than the proportion of letters accusing out-of-power groups.

> During Republican administrations, conspiracy theories targeting the Right and capitalists average 34 percent, while conspiracy theories targeting the Left and communists average only 11 percent. During Democratic administrations, *mutatis mutandis*, conspiracy theories aimed at the Right and capitalists drop 25 points to 9 percent while conspiracy theories aimed at the Left and communists more than double to 27 percent. Who controls the White House invites conspiracy theories. For illustrations, compare consecutive years when executive power changes party. In 1968, Democrat Lyndon Johnson was president and accusations against the Left and communists were 17 percent of total conspiracy talk while accusations against the Right and capitalists were zero. Republican Richard Nixon won the 1968 presidential election and took office in January 1969. That year accusations of conspiracy against the Left and communists dropped from 17 percent to zero percent while accusations against the Right and capital-

ists increased from zero to 25 percent. A similar pattern crops up after the 2008 presidential election. When Barack Obama took office from George W. Bush, accusations against the Right and capitalists dropped by 40 percentage points while accusations against the Left and communists increased by 10 percentage points between 2008 and 2009.[90]

The letters to the editor data demonstrates the larger pattern driving what Americans have experienced during the last few decades. During the Clinton administration, prominent conspiracy theories focused on Clinton's real estate dealings, the death of White House attorney Vince Foster, and the cover-up of sexual harassment and other illegalities. When George W. Bush came to power, these conspiracy theories became inert. The prominent conspiracy theories then villainized George W. Bush, Dick Cheney, Halliburton, Blackwater, and other members of the Republican coalition. Many of these theories suggested that 9/11 was an inside job, or that the country went to war in Iraq for oil. As soon as Barack Obama won the presidency, these conspiracy theories became politically sterile, and the new prominent conspiracy theories addressed Obama's citizenship and his ties to Muslim and communist extremists. Fears centering on Obama subsided once Republicans controlled the House, Senate, and White House. When Donald Trump unexpectedly entered the presidency, the popular conspiracy theories suggested that Trump had conspired with Russia to rig the election, that he was a longtime Soviet agent, and that he was compromised by embarrassing tapes showing him being urinated on by Russian prostitutes. Democrats' lowly status made them feel anxious and out of control, and therefore prone to conspiracy theorizing.

An often overlooked part of the conspiracy-theories-are-for-losers argument is that shifts in domestic power are not the only driver of conspiracy theorizing. Foreign threat and major wars exert a significant influence on Americans' willingness to openly engage in conspiracy theories about foreigners and foreign powers. For example, during years of acute threat (declared wars and the Cold War) the proportion of foreign conspiracy theories in the letters to the editor data increases by an average of 17 percentage points, from 28 to 45 percent. As outside dangers loom large, conspiracy theorists focus their attention away from domestic threats and toward outside threats.[91]

None of this is to say that beliefs will change with shifts in power, but rather that losers will be more concerned with their perceived enemies when those enemies have power. This leads to conspiracy theories emanating from the out-party taking precedence over conspiracy theories emanating from the in-party because "defeated subgroups have strong incentives to be especially vigilant and vigorous."[92] The incentives ride on partisans' backs and influence them subconsciously. Whether partisans realize it or not, conspiracy theories must conform to the present distribution of power in order to resonate. Consider the Clinton administration's claim that "a vast right-wing conspiracy" was the source of President Clinton's troubles, or President Obama's claim that he was the victim of shadowy billionaires: neither of these conspiracy theories resonated well, and the former became a 1990s punch line.

The conspiracy-theories-are-for-losers argument is demonstrated quite well by Nobel Prize–winning economist and left-leaning *New York Times* columnist Paul Krugman. During the Bush administration, Krugman argued in favor of conspiracy theories, likely because his side was out of power and was engaging in conspiracy theorizing quite prominently: "The truth is that many of the people who throw around terms like 'loopy conspiracy theories' are lazy bullies, they try to suggest that anyone who asks those questions is crazy."[93] When power switched hands and Democrats were back in power, Krugman was less enthused by conspiracy theories (since the most prominent conspiracy theories were accusing his side of conspiring). He sought to wash his side's hands of them: "conspiracy theories are supported by a lot of influential people on the right, but not on the left."[94] When Republican Donald Trump won the presidential election in 2016, Krugman again resorted to conspiracy theories to explain his side's lowly status: "It looks more and more as if we had an election swung, in effect, by a faction of our own security sector in alliance with Putin."[95] Of course, this claim has never been substantiated. Circumstances affect how people view the world and whether they engage in outward conspiracy theorizing, and if this can happen to a Nobel Prize winner, it can happen to anyone.

Conclusion

Conspiracy theories address the use and abuse of power. For that reason, conspiracy theories are political opinions that can be understood much like other political opinions. An individual's predispositions (e.g., their partisanship and levels of conspiracy thinking) predict whether the individual will believe in conspiracy theories and, if so, which partisan conspiracy theories they will believe in. Relative changes in power and threat lead some conspiracy theories to become more salient in public discourse than others. Conspiracy theories accusing those in power resonate far better than the ones that accuse those who are out of power.

Key Terms

agenda setting
confirmation bias
false flag event
framing

hypodermic needle theory
minimal effects model
partisan attachments
populism

Bibliography

Arceneaux, Kevin, Martin Johnson, and Chad Murphy. "Polarized Political Communication, Oppositional Media Hostility, and Selective Exposure." *Journal of Politics* 74, no. 1 (2012): 174–86.

Barkan, Ross. "'Their Greed Has No End': Bernie Sanders Makes a Surprise Appearance in Manhattan." *Observer* (2015). Published electronically October 26, 2015.

Baum, Matthew A. "Partisan Media and Attitude Polarization." In *Regulatory Breakdown: The Crisis of Confidence in U.S. Regulation*, edited by Cary Coglianese, 118–42. Philadelphia: University of Pennsylvania Press, 2012.

Benjamin, Medea. "America Dropped 26,171 Bombs in 2016. What a Bloody End to Obama's Reign." *The Guardian* (2017). Published electronically January 9, 2017.

Berelson, Bernard, Paul Lazarsfeld, and William McPhee. *Voting: A Study of Opinion Formation in a Presidential Campaign*. Chicago: University of Chicago Press, 1954.

Bessi, Alessandro, Mauro Coletto, George Alexandru Davidescu, Antonio Scala, Guido Caldarelli, and Walter Quattrociocchi. "Science vs. Conspiracy: Collective Narratives in the Age of Misinformation." *PLoS ONE* 10, no. 2 (2015): e0118093.

Bineham, Jeffery L. "A Historical Account of the Hypodermic Model in Mass Communication." *Communication Monographs* 55, no. 3 (1988): 230–46.

Bost, P. R. "The Truth Is around Here Somewhere: Integrating the Research on Conspiracy Beliefs." In *Conspiracy Theories and the People Who Believe Them*, edited by Joseph E. Uscinski, 269–82. New York: Oxford University Press, 2018.

Broockman, David E., and Daniel M. Butler. "The Causal Effects of Elite Position-Taking on Voter Attitudes: Field Experiments with Elite Communication." *American Journal of Political Science* 61, no. 1 (2017): 208–21.

Brotherton, Rob, Christopher C. French, and Alan D. Pickering. "Measuring Belief in Conspiracy Theories: The Generic Conspiracist Beliefs Scale." *Frontiers in Psychology* 4, Article 279 (2013).

Bryan, Bob. "Krugman: It's Looking More and More Like the Election Was Swung by the FBI in Virtual 'Alliance with Putin.'" *Business Insider* (2016). Published electronically November 17, 2016.

Campbell, Angus, Philip Converse, Warren Miller, and Donald E. Stokes. *The American Voter*, unabridged edition. Chicago: The University of Chicago Press, 1960.

Clark, Cory, Brittany Liu, Bo Winegard, and Peter Ditto. "Tribalism Is Human Nature." *Current Directions in Psychological Science* (August 20, 2019).

Dahl, Robert A. "A Critique of the Ruling Elite Model." *American Political Science Review* 52, no. 2 (1958): 463–69.

Daly, Christopher. "For Vermont's Sanders, Victory Followed Long Path." *Washington Post* (1990). Published electronically November 11, 1990.

Dunning, Brian. *Conspiracies Declassified: The Skeptoid Guide to the Truth behind the Theories*. Avon, MA: Adams Media, 2018.

Dwyer, Paula. "Everything Is 'Rigged.'" *Chicago Tribune* (2016). Published electronically February 4, 2016.

Edelson, Jack, Alexander Alduncin, Christopher Krewson, James A. Sieja, and Joseph E. Uscinski. "The Effect of Conspiratorial Thinking and Motivated Reasoning on Belief in Election Fraud." *Political Research Quarterly* 70, no. 4 (2017): 933–46.

"8 in 10 French People Believe a Conspiracy Theory: Survey." *France24* (2018). Published electronically January 8, 2018.

Enns, Peter K. "Relative Policy Support and Coincidental Representation." *Perspectives on Politics* 13, no. 4 (2015): 1053–64.

Fetzer, Jim, and Mike Palecek, eds. *Nobody Died at Sandy Hook*. US: Moon Rock Books, 2015.

Finkel, Steven E. "Reexamining the 'Minimal Effects' Model in Recent Presidential Campaigns." *Journal of Politics* 55, no. 1 (1993): 1–21.

Frizell, Sam. "Bernie Sanders' Long History with Alternative Medicine." *Time.com* (2016). Published electronically March 6, 2016.

Gelman, Andrew, and Gary King. "Why Are American Presidential Election Polls So Variable When Votes Are So Predictable?" *British Journal of Political Science* 23, no. 4 (1993): 409–51.

Gershtenson, Joseph, Jeffrey Ladewig, and Dennis L. Plane. "Parties, Institutional Control, and Trust in Government." *Social Science Quarterly* 87, no. 4 (2006): 882–902.

Gilens, Martin, and Benjamin I. Page. "Testing Theories of American Politics: Elites, Interest Groups, and Average Citizens." *Perspectives on Politics* 12, no. 3 (2014): 564–81.

Gordon, Sarah Ann. *Hitler, Germans, and the "Jewish Question."* Princeton, NJ: Princeton University Press, 1984.

Green, Donald P., Bradley Palmquist, and Eric Schickler. *Partisan Hearts and Minds: Political Parties and the Social Identities of Voters*. New Haven, CT: Yale University Press, 2002.

Icke, David. *Human Race Get Off Your Knees: The Lion Sleeps No More*. Isle of Wight: David Icke Books, 2010.

Jasperson, Amy E., Dhavan V. Shah, Mark Watts, Ronald J. Faber, and David P. Fan. "Framing and the Public Agenda: Media Effects on the Importance of the Federal Budget Deficit." *Political Communication* 15, no. 2 (1998): 205–24.

Jenson, Tom. "Democrats and Republicans Differ on Conspiracy Theory Beliefs." *Public Policy Polling* (2013). Published electronically April 2, 2013.

Karp, Paul. "Conspiracy Theorist David Icke Hits Back after Australia Revokes Visa." *The Guardian*, February 20, 2019. https://www.theguardian.com/news/2019/feb/20/conspiracy-theorist-david-icke-hits-back-after-australia-revokes-visa.

Katz, E., and Paul Lazarsfeld. *Personal Influence, the Part Played by People in the Flow of Mass Communications*. New York: The Free Press, 1955.

Klofstad, Casey, Joseph E. Uscinski, Jennifer Connolly, and Jon West. "What Drives People to Believe in Zika Conspiracy Theories?" *Palgrave Communications* 5, no. 36 (2019).

Krugman, Paul. "Attack of the Crazy Centrists." *Washington Post* (2014). Published electronically August 23, 2014.

———. "Who's Crazy Now?" *New York Times* (2006). Published electronically May 8, 2006.

Kurt, Daniel. "Are You in the Top One Percent of the World?" *Investopedia* (2019). Published electronically February 9, 2019.

Lazarsfeld, Paul, Bernard Berelson, and Hazel Gaudet. *The People's Choice*. New York: Columbia University Press, 1944.

Leiser, David, Nofar Duani, and Pascal Wagner-Egger. "The Conspiratorial Style in Lay Economic Thinking." *PLoS ONE* 12, no. 3 (2017): e0171238.

Liataud, Alexa. "White House Acknowledges the U.S. Is at War in Seven Countries." *Vice News* (2018). Published electronically March 15, 2018.

Lord, Charles G., Lee Ross, and Mark R. Lepper. "Biased Assimilation and Attitude Polarization: The Effects of Prior Theories on Subsequently Considered Evidence." *Journal of Personality and Social Psychology* 37, no. 11 (1979): 2098–109.

Lowry, Rich. "Bernie's Conspiracy Theory." *National Review* (2015). Published electronically October 30, 2015.

Machiavelli, Niccolo. *Discourses on Livy*. Translated by Harvey Mansfield and Nathan Tarcov. Chicago: University of Chicago Press, 1996.

Marrs, Jim. *Population Control: How Corporate Owners Are Killing Us*. New York: William Morrow, 2015.

Marzilli, Ted. "Cain's Candidacy Splits Pizza Scores." *YouGov: BrandIndex* (2011). Published electronically November 15, 2011.

McCarthy, Justin. "Highest GOP Satisfaction with U.S. Direction since 2007." *Gallup.com* (2018). Published electronically January 15, 2018.

McClosky, Herbert, and Dennis Chong. "Similarities and Differences between Left-Wing and Right-Wing Radicals." *British Journal of Political Science* 15, no. 3 (1985): 329–63.

McCombs, Maxwell E., and Donald L. Shaw. "The Agenda-Setting Function of Mass Media." *Public Opinion Quarterly* 36, no. 2 (1972): 176–87.

McHoskey, John W. "Case Closed? On the John F. Kennedy Assassination: Biased Assimilation of Evidence and Attitude Polarization." *Basic and Applied Social Psychology* 17, no. 3 (1995): 1995.

Müller, Jan-Werner. *What Is Populism?* London: Penguin UK, 2017.

Nyhan, Brendan. "9/11 and Birther Misperceptions Compared." *Brendan-nyhan.com/blog* (2009).

Oliver, Eric, and Thomas Wood. "Conspiracy Theories and the Paranoid Style(s) of Mass Opinion." *American Journal of Political Science* 58, no. 4 (2014): 952–66.

Pickard, James. "Corbyn Lashes Out at Financial Sector 'Speculators and Gamblers.'" *Financial Times* (2017). Published electronically November 30, 2017.

Prignano, Christina. "Here's How People Are Reacting to Elizabeth Warren's 'Wealth Tax' Proposal." *Boston Globe* (2019). Published electronically January 30, 2019.

Rosenberg, Paul. "QAnon, Tampa and Donald Trump: Not All Conspiracy Theories Are the Same." *Salon.com* (2018). Published electronically August 18th, 2018.

Rosenblatt, Joel. "Champagne Remark May Cost Lawyer $289 Million Bayer Award." *Bloomberg* (2018). Published electronically October 11, 2018.

Saad, Lydia. "Americans Say Economy Is 'Most Important Thing Going Well.'" *Gallup.com* (2018). Published electronically July 19, 2018.

Sabato, Larry J. *The Kennedy Half-Century: The Presidency, Assassination, and Lasting Legacy of John F. Kennedy*. New York: Bloomsbury Publishing USA, 2013.

Sanders, Bernie. "Gambling on Wall Street." *Politico.com* (2009). Published electronically July 21, 2009.

Scheufele, Dietram A., and David Tewksbury. "Framing, Agenda Setting, and Priming: The Evolution of Three Media Effects Models." *Journal of Communication* 57, no. 1 (2007): 9–20.

Shapiro, Dina. "The Risk of Disease Stigma: Threat and Support for Coercive Public Heath Policy." APSA Pre-Conference on Political Communication of Risk. Seattle, WA, 2011.

Smallpage, Steven M., Adam M. Enders, and Joseph E. Uscinski. "The Partisan Contours of Conspiracy Theory Beliefs." *Research & Politics* 4, no. 4 (2017): 2053168017746554.

Swift, Art. "Majority in U.S. Still Believe JFK Killed in a Conspiracy." *Gallup.com*, November 15, 2013.

Tankersley, Jim. "Sorry, Bernie Sanders. Deodorant Isn't Starving America's Children." *Washington Post* (2015). Published electronically May 26, 2015.

Tarrant, Brenton. "The Great Replacement." Unpublished manifesto, 2019.

Tesler, Michael. "How Democrats Derailed Marijuana Legalization in California." *Washington Post—The Monkey Cage* (2014). Published electronically November 10, 2014.

Thomas, S. B., and S. C. Quinn. "The Tuskegee Syphilis Study, 1932 to 1972: Implications for HIV Education and AIDS Risk Education Programs in the Black Community." *American Journal of Public Health* 81, no. 11 (November 1, 1991): 1498–505.

Uscinski, Joseph E. *The People's News: Media, Politics, and the Demands of Capitalism.* New York: New York University Press, 2014.

Uscinski, Joseph E., and Casey Klofstad. "New Poll: The QAnon Conspiracy Movement Is Very Unpopular." *Washington Post* (2018). Published electronically August 30, 2018.

Uscinski, Joseph E., Casey Klofstad, and Matthew Atkinson. "Why Do People Believe in Conspiracy Theories? The Role of Informational Cues and Predispositions." *Political Research Quarterly* 69, no. 1 (2016): 57–71.

Uscinski, Joseph E., and Joseph M. Parent. *American Conspiracy Theories.* New York: Oxford University Press, 2014.

van Prooijen, Jan-Willem, and Mark van Vugt. "Conspiracy Theories: Evolved Functions and Psychological Mechanisms." *Perspectives on Psychological Science* 13, no. 6 (2018): 770–88.

Weigel, David. "Trump's Foes Say He's a 9/11 Truther. Truthers Would Disagree." *Washington Post* (2016). Published electronically February 16, 2016.

Williams, Jennifer, Alex Ward, Jen Kirby, and Amanda Sakuma. "Christchurch Mosque Shooting: What We Know So Far." *Vox.com* (2019). Published electronically March 18, 2019.

Wood, Michael, Karen Douglas, and Robbie Sutton. "Dead and Alive: Beliefs in Contradictory Conspiracy Theories." *Social Psychological and Personality Science* 3, no. 6 (January 25, 2012): 767–73.

Wood, Michael J. "Some Dare Call It Conspiracy: Labeling Something a Conspiracy Theory Does Not Reduce Belief in It." *Political Psychology* 37, no. 5 (2016): 695–705.

Zaller, John. *The Nature and Origins of Mass Opinion.* Cambridge: Cambridge University Press, 1992.

6

President Trump, the Internet, Conspiracy, and Conspiracy Theory

The 2016 US presidential election differed from other recent presidential elections in that conspiracy theories became the grounds on which the campaigns were argued. Candidates either accused the others of engaging in far-reaching conspiracies, or accused them of propagating dubious conspiracy theories. Substantive policy proposals were an afterthought. The election's aftermath has seen a continuing wave of conspiracy accusations, some of which threaten speech and press freedoms and could destabilize foreign policy. Just as important, the United States has a president who justifies policy positions and government action with conspiracy theories.[1]

This chapter addresses President Trump's conspiracy theories as well as the Trump-Russia conspiracy theories that have been levied at him. The concept of conspiracy theory politics is introduced to explain Trump's strategic use of conspiracy theories during his run for the presidency. The consequences of conspiracy theory politics are then discussed. Next, the chapter discusses why the internet is undeserving of many of the criticisms it has received. The problem with the internet, like all communication technologies, I argue, is the people who use it. This book ends with suggestions for dulling the negative impacts of conspiracy theories at the societal level, and for adopting better beliefs at the individual level. The chapter begins with the tragic story of Randy Weaver to demonstrate how conspiracies and conspiracy theories can mix into a toxic cocktail.

Ruby Ridge

I begin this chapter by discussing the 1992 siege at Ruby Ridge because it demonstrates the complexities that develop when conspiracies and conspiracy theories intertwine. Sometimes, as in this case, conspiracy theories become a catalyst that drives those accused of conspiring to engage in actual conspiracies. There were groups in the northwest United States engaging in illegal activities including violence. The government took action to address this, as it should have. And that is where things got messy . . .

Randy Weaver had a worldview steeped in white separatism, end-times fantasies, and antigovernment conspiracy theories. In the 1980s, he moved his family to a remote plot of land in Idaho to start a simple life in near seclusion. At the time, militias and white supremacist movements had been committing various crimes and were thought to be stockpiling weapons. Weaver occasionally attended Aryan Nation meetings.[2] The government, concerned about these groups, inserted an undercover agent to befriend Weaver and gain his cooperation. The agent, known as Gus Magisono, supposedly convinced Weaver to (illegally) saw off a shotgun for him. Magisono was eventually outed as an informant and attempted to convince Weaver to become an informant as well. Weaver refused.[3]

Weaver was charged with the sale of illegal firearms to Magisono and ordered to appear in court. But the summons sent to Weaver was incorrect, and Weaver missed the appearance. Government agents then surveilled Weaver for several months. Eventually, agents approached Weaver's cabin to get a closer look. The armed agents—disguised in camouflage—were detected by Weaver's dogs. A gun battle ensued in which the agents—who did not identify themselves—shot and killed Weaver's fourteen-year-old son and dog.[4] This incident then led to an eleven-day siege involving four hundred government agents and heavy military equipment. Both Weaver and Weaver's friend, Kevin Harris, were shot and injured. Weaver's wife, Vicki, was shot in the head by a government sniper and killed instantly while holding her ten-month-old baby. Government agents, after killing Vicki, taunted the family by naming their base of operations "Camp Vicki."[5] Agents also ran over Weaver's dead dog with a tank-like vehicle several times.[6]

Weaver eventually surrendered. His family was awarded $3.1 million in compensation, and many believe that he could have pursued a much greater amount. In the ensuing investigation, it became clear that the "FBI had violated the Weavers' constitutional rights."[7] Further, it is strongly suspected that federal agents lied and destroyed incriminating evidence.[8]

Jesse Walker, a journalist who covers conspiracy theories, noted how Weaver's conspiracy beliefs sparked the government to concoct, and eventually act on, their own conspiracy beliefs about Weaver. Government agents then conspired against Weaver.

> It isn't hard to find examples of marginal groups whose paranoia about the government drove them to violence. The tale of the Weavers shows how the government's paranoia about marginal groups can drive *it* to violence, too. The feds looked at a family with fringy views and perceived a threat,

and as a result a woman, a boy, a dog, and one of the government's own agents were killed. It wouldn't be the last time something like that happened. A year later in Waco, the Branch Davidians' paranoia would be no match for the paranoia of the Davidians' enemies [the government].[9]

Agents conspired against Weaver by entrapping and later spying on him. The government's ensuing actions convinced Weaver that his conspiracy beliefs about the government were correct. The government killed Weaver's wife, son, and dog under questionable circumstances, with illegal and unconstitutional tactics. Agents acted on incorrect conspiracy-driven beliefs about the Weavers during the siege. Agents later conspired to cover up their activities.[10] It is not clear that government agents were ever held accountable for their actions; in fact, similarly dubious tactics were employed by the same government agencies a year later in Waco, Texas.

Authorities can believe in and act on conspiracy theories; they can also conspire to do harm. Unsympathetic actors, including conspiracy theorists, can be targeted by authorities' conspiracy theories, and be the victim of their conspiracies. Conspiracy theories can bend people's behavior in deleterious ways and become self-fulfilling prophecies.

Donald Trump Runs for President

When Donald Trump entered the race for the Republican nomination for president, he had no formal political experience and was not clearly a Republican.[11] While Trump had widespread name recognition due to his wealth and celebrity status, his only foray into politics prior to his run for president involved accusing President Obama of having faked his birth certificate. Trump's campaign rhetoric included numerous racist, sexist, and xenophobic comments, but more than anything else, it highlighted numerous conspiracy theories.[12]

Among his many conspiracy theories were claims that Syrian refugees were ISIS operatives, that Mexico was sending murderers and rapists to attack Americans, and that President Obama was secretly aligned with Muslim terrorists.[13] These conspiracy theories are particularly dangerous because they scapegoat vulnerable populations, leaving them open to attack by those who would act on Trump's theories. Perhaps his most bizarre conspiracy theory was that Senator Ted Cruz's father took part in the assassination of President John F. Kennedy in 1963.[14] Such an outlandish claim would have disqualified any other candidate, but Trump's endorsement of numerous conspiracy theories never appeared to hurt his campaign's prospects. Through the entire campaign, Trump claimed that the election would be rigged.[15] Even months after his unlikely victory, Trump continued to assert that the election had been sullied by millions of illegal voters.[16]

While some of Trump's conspiracy theories appeared to be nothing more than stream-of-consciousness ramblings,[17] they wove a succinct and overarching populist narrative in which political elites had sold out the interests of regular Americans to foreign interests. This narrative has continued to fuel his presidency.

Trump's success with conspiracy theories exemplifies *conspiracy theory politics*.[18] This style of political rhetoric undermines dominant institutions and modes of thinking, is usually used by outsiders and those out of power, and can make the political playing field more hospitable to outsiders. As political scientists Matthew Atkinson and Darin DeWitt explain,

> Trump, as a disruptive candidate, could not compete on the party establishment's playing field. Trump had never held office and espoused policy views that transcended the mainstream party alignment. He was not the preferred candidate of Republican elites, and he received relatively few endorsements. To be successful, he's had to construct a rhetorical style that mobilized support outside of the party's mainstream.
>
> Trump's solution is what we call "conspiracy theory politics." High-profile politicians who advocate conspiracy theories are typically jeered by the mainstream media and the party establishments. But Trump was not interested in the conventional path to power. Instead, he used conspiracy theories to practice the politics of disruption, and succeeded in building a coalition of support among myriad unconventional ideological groups located outside the traditional political party networks.
>
> Trump's use of conspiracy theory politics proved to be a particularly ingenious form of populism. By focusing his populist appeals on conspiracy rhetoric—rather than substantive policy—Trump galvanized the broad support needed to overcome the party establishment. His conspiracy rhetoric boiled down to a single unifying claim: Political elites have abandoned the interests of regular Americans in favor of foreign interests. For Trump, the political system was corrupt and the establishment could not be trusted. It followed, then, that only a disruptor could stop the corruption.
>
> Trump's conspiracy theories delivered an unconventional political appeal that effectively engaged groups outside of the party's mainstream. By using conspiracy theories, Trump succeeded in mobilizing a group of people for whom his utter lack of knowledge and experience was a virtue and for whom Jeb Bush's experience and party support were viewed as defects.[19]

Trump's conspiracy theories ingratiated him to conspiracy-minded Republicans—that is, Republicans who would not be excited about establishment candidates but would be enthused by an antiestablishment outsider. Polls taken during the 2016 primaries showed that Republicans who supported Trump, as opposed to other more mainstream Republican candidates, were more likely to believe in various conspiracy theories.[20]

To further consider how conspiracy theory politics works, consider the debate over climate change. The evidence in favor of anthropogenic climate change has only strengthened since it was first brought to the public's attention in the 1980s. Now, about 97 percent of climate scientists agree that the climate is changing due to human activity.[21]

Climate change conspiracy theorists originally claimed that there was no scientific agreement on climate change. When confronted with the 97 percent consensus, they claimed that the figure was faked.[22] When studies showed that their denialism was due to conspiracy thinking, climate change deniers claimed that those studies were faked, too.[23] Over time, the climate change conspiracy theories have broadened to accuse more and more of the establishment, each time becoming more implausible.

In terms of conspiracy theory politics, conspiracy theories were the only tool available to the deniers, who did not have more or better scientists, or more or better data, to make their case. Conspiracy theories changed the playing field in favor of climate change deniers: The debate shifted from "What should we do about climate change?" to "Are the scientists part of a hoax?" The conspiracy theories put climate scientists on the defensive trying to answer charges of conspiracy; this has effectively stalled meaningful solutions.[24]

Conspiracy theory politics can also be useful for individuals who are under attack. Consider the charges of sexual harassment against film producer Harvey Weinstein, the harassment charges against former Fox News host Bill O'Reilly, or the charges of sexual misconduct against Alabama Senate candidate Judge Roy Moore. To fight back against the accusations, each claimed that the charges against them were part of a conspiracy.[25] The tactic is meant to shift the debate away from the allegations and toward some larger agenda that their accusers are supposedly a part of.

Trump was not the only candidate in 2016 to make conspiracy theories a major part of their campaign. Bernie Sanders, mentioned in the previous chapter, used the word "rigged" frequently, cried foul when he lost, and campaigned on the idea that the "one percent" rigged the entire political and economic system.[26] Both Sanders and Donald Trump received 40 percent of their respective party's primary votes, but Trump was able to triumph because twenty other Republican candidates split the remaining votes. We can see conspiracy theory politics in the Brexit vote as well. Numerous conspiracy theories were used to motivate "Leave" voters (e.g., that the true number of immigrants was being hidden); thus, it is no surprise that Britons who voted to leave the EU were more likely than those who voted to stay to believe in conspiracy theories.[27]

Trump-Russia Conspiracy Theories

Hillary Clinton, after defeating Bernie Sanders in the Democratic primary, ran a mainstream campaign, but employed conspiracy theories on occasion to battle Trump. While Clinton argued that Donald Trump was unfit to be president because he was a conspiracy theorist, she also claimed that Trump was a part of a powerful Russian conspiracy.[28] "There's something he's hiding; we'll guess, we'll keep guessing at what it might be," she said during the presidential debates.[29]

Clinton's accusations of coordination between Trump and Russia remained politically salient for nearly three years after they arose and became a rallying cry for Democrats. This should come as no surprise, given that Clinton accused Trump of collusion with Russia during the campaign and that Democrats lost the White House and Congress. As discussed in the previous chapter, being on the losing end of a power asymmetry makes people prone to conspiracy theorizing, and elite partisan cues drive the specifics of those theories.[30]

Interestingly, it wasn't just that Democrats believed that Trump was part of a Russian conspiracy; government insiders apparently believed it as early as 2015. Currently, there is an inquiry into the origins of the Trump-Russia

Photo 6.1 Donald Trump, shown with Vladimir Putin, is accused of conspiring with Russian agents to rig the 2016 election.
Dmitry Azarov / Kommersant Photo / Polaris / Newscom

conspiracy theory: how it got started, who in the government acted on it by wiretapping Trump's associates, and if the government "spied" on Trump during the campaign.[31] It remains unclear exactly what the intentions and methods of these operations were, and further investigations are ongoing. I note that accusations of government "spying" against the Trump campaign are themselves properly labeled conspiracy theories as of this writing. Regardless, the Trump-Russia conspiracy theories gave way to the Mueller investigation, which wielded substantial power over the fate of the nation. Further, the Trump-Russia conspiracy theories strained the United States–Russia relationship because they encouraged Trump to take actions against Russia to prove that he was not a Russian agent.

Following Trump's victory, the left-leaning media (e.g., MSNBC) fixated on Trump-Russia conspiracy theories. The narrative played into their audience's ideology and fears and performed the function of absolving them of any blame for their party's defeat in 2016. *Rolling Stone* journalist Matt Taibbi was one of a handful of Trump-Russia skeptics on the left:

> The 2016 campaign season brought to the surface awesome levels of political discontent. After the election, instead of wondering where that anger came from, most of the press quickly pivoted to a new tale about a Russian plot to attack our Democracy. This conveyed the impression that the election season we'd just lived through had been an aberration, thrown off the rails by an extraordinary espionage conspiracy between Trump and a cabal of evil foreigners.
>
> This narrative contradicted everything I'd seen traveling across America in my two years of covering the campaign. The overwhelming theme of that race, long before anyone even thought about Russia, was voter rage at the entire political system. The anger wasn't just on the Republican side, where Trump humiliated the Republicans' chosen $150 million contender, Jeb Bush (who got three delegates, or $50 million per delegate). It was also evident on the Democratic side, where a self-proclaimed "Democratic Socialist" with little money and close to no institutional support became a surprise contender.
>
> Because of a series of press misdiagnoses before the Russiagate stories even began, much of the American public was unprepared for news of a Trump win. A cloak-and-dagger election-fixing conspiracy therefore seemed more likely than it might have otherwise to large parts of the domestic news audience, because they hadn't been prepared for anything else that would make sense. This was particularly true of upscale, urban, blue-leaning news consumers, who were not told to take the possibility of a Trump White House seriously.
>
> Priority number-one of the political class after a vulgar, out-of-work game-show host conquered the White House should have been a long period of ruthless self-examination. [The Trump-Russia conspiracy theory] delayed that for at least two years.[32]

This turn to conspiracy theories occurred on social media as well, as *The Atlantic* reported:

> The Trump era has given rise to a vast alternative left-wing media infrastructure that operates largely out of the view of casual news consumers, but commands a massive audience and growing influence in liberal America. There are polemical podcasters and partisan click farms; wild-eyed conspiracists and cynical fabulists. Some traffic heavily in rumor and wage campaigns of misinformation; others are merely aggregators and commentators who have carved out a corner of the web for themselves. But taken together, they form a media universe where partisan hysteria is too easily stoked, and fake news can travel at the speed of light. . . .
>
> In past political epochs, popular conspiracy theories spread via pamphlets left on windshields, or chain emails forwarded thousands of times. These days, the tinfoil-hat crowd gathers on Twitter. People like [Louise] Mensch, Claude Taylor, Andrea Chalupa, Eric Garland, and Leah McElrath feed their followers a steady diet of highly provocative speculation, rumor, and innuendo that makes it sound as if Trump's presidency—and, really, the entire Republican Party—is perpetually on the verge of a spectacular meltdown.
>
> The most prolific of the conspiracy-mongers tend to focus on the Russia scandal, weaving a narrative so sensationalistic and complex that it could pass for a Netflix political drama. Theirs is a world where it is acceptable to allege that hundreds of American politicians, journalists, and government officials are actually secret Russian agents; that Andrew Breitbart was murdered by Vladimir Putin; that the Kremlin has "kompromat" on *everyone,* and oh-by-the-way a presidency-ending sex tape is going to drop any day now.[33]

Democrats' turn toward conspiracy theories incentivized news outlets to chase sensationalist and dystopian headlines. Responding to their incentives, some outlets printed stories without proper vetting, some of which contained outright falsehoods. As journalist Glenn Greenwald points out, the errors were not the result of sloppiness but rather of a concerted effort to play to a certain point of view:

> Note that all of these "errors" go only in one direction: namely, exaggerating the grave threat posed by Moscow and the Trump circle's connection to it. It's inevitable that media outlets will make mistakes on complex stories. If that's being done in good faith, one would expect the errors would be roughly 50/50 in terms of the agenda served by the false stories. That is most definitely not the case here.[34]

Mistakes in news reporting were numerous and included assertions that Russia-funded news channel RT had taken over C-SPAN, that Russians hacked into the US electricity grid, that many mainstream political websites were outlets for Russian propaganda, that former Trump aide Anthony Scaramucci was under investigation for involvement with a Russian hedge fund, that Trump was communicating to a Russian bank through a secret internet server, and that former Trump advisor Paul Manafort had visited Julian Assange prior to the release of illegally obtained WikiLeaks documents.[35] The list could go on. While some of these reports were eventually corrected, some have yet to be.

On March 24, 2019, after more than two years of investigation and open speculation, Attorney General William Barr released an initial summary of the Mueller report; he released a slightly redacted version of the full report a month later. To some, the report destroyed the Trump-Russia conspiracy theories and called for a reckoning in the Democratic establishment and in the media:

> The key fact is this: Mueller—contrary to weeks of false media claims—did not merely issue a narrow, cramped, legalistic finding that there was insufficient evidence to indict Trump associates for conspiring with Russia and then proving their guilt beyond a reasonable doubt. That would have been devastating enough to those who spent the last two years or more misleading people to believe that conspiracy convictions of Trump's closest aides and family members were inevitable. But his mandate was much broader than that: to state what did or did not happen.
>
> That's precisely what he did: Mueller, in addition to concluding that evidence was insufficient to charge any American with crimes relating to Russian election interference, also stated emphatically in numerous instances that there was no evidence—not merely that there was insufficient evidence to obtain a criminal conviction—that key prongs of this three-year-old conspiracy theory actually happened. . . .
>
> With regard to Facebook ads and Twitter posts . . . , Mueller could not have been more blunt: "The investigation *did not identify evidence* that any U.S. persons knowingly or intentionally coordinated with [Russia's] interference operation" (emphasis added). Note that this exoneration includes not only Trump campaign officials but all Americans.[36]

Mueller's finding that no American conspired with Russia put into perspective how fantastical some of the mainstream coverage of the Trump-Russia conspiracy theories had become. Profit motives were to be found in much of the Trump-Russia coverage.

> The worst-kept secret in the liberal media ecosystem is that Donald Trump is great for business. Rebranded for the resistance, liberal newspapers gobbled up thousands of new subscribers. . . . On television, left-leaning stations, at long last, competed with Fox in the ratings game, fueled by a never-ending Trump obsession.
>
> With Trump has come Russia: two years of conspiracy-mongering about whether the president, a failed real estate mogul and reality TV star consumed with dubious deal-making, conspired with the Russian government to influence the outcome of the 2016 election. Robert Mueller's

determination that no evidence exists to prove Trump and Russian col-
luded to fix the election has exposed, once again, the venality of A-list
political punditry. At the top of the heap is none other than MSNBC's
Rachel Maddow.

Maddow, of course, was not alone. *The New Yorker* once ran a cover in
Russian, a stunt that will age as terribly as all cold war-era red-baiting has to
our 21st-century eyes.[37]

Conspiracy beliefs survive despite evidence to the contrary, and many in the
media have been unwilling to give up theirs in the face of authoritative evidence. *New York Magazine* columnist Jonathan Chait suggested, prior to the
release of the Mueller report, that Trump had been a Russian asset since the
1980s.[38] Discussing an upcoming meeting between Trump and Putin, Chait
wrote "Will Trump Be Meeting with His Counterpart—or His Handler?"[39]
One would think that Mueller's findings would have stymied such wild-eyed
and dangerous speculations, but no. Following the release of Mueller's findings, Chait doubled down: "I wrote an article suggesting Trump was compromised by Russia. I was right."[40]

Despite Mueller's findings that no American conspired with Russia to
rig the election, conspiracy theorists have continued to claim that they were
right all along. Now, they have expanded their conspiracy theories to assert
an even larger cover-up involving Robert Mueller or Attorney General Barr.
Hundreds of self-contradicting Trump-Russia conspiracy theories were put
forward before Mueller's findings were released; those theories' predictions
have gone unfulfilled.[41] Like other conspiracy theorists, Trump-Russia conspiracy theorists play tennis without a net.

The Trump-Russia episode screams irony. It is ironic, given that Democratic elites, responding to Trump's claims that the election would be
rigged, claimed that election rigging could not possibly take place.[42] But
after their defeat, they quickly blamed their loss on an elaborate scheme to
rig the election. It is odd as well that Russia has become such a boogey-
man for Democrats, given that in 2012 President Obama and other Democrats jeered Republican presidential candidate Mitt Romney for thinking
that Russia posed a threat.[43] But most importantly, Democrats spent eight
years chastising Republicans for their conspiracy theories about President
Obama. As soon as Trump became president, many of those same Democrats seemed to lose any sense of self-awareness and descended into a
conspiracy-fueled delirium.

In other ways, the Trump-Russia conspiracy theories smack of Karma:
Trump began his foray into politics in 2011 suggesting that Barack Obama
was a foreign usurper with a phony birth certificate. Just as Obama had to
spend time, effort, and precious political capital fighting off such accusations,
Trump had to spend the first two years of his presidency doing the same.

Of course, Trump-Russia conspiracy theories were not the only prominent conspiracy theories following Trump's victory. Trump and his supporters have fought the accusations of Russian collusion with their own conspiracy theories: that Mueller's investigation was rigged, that Obama wiretapped Trump Tower during the campaign, that Clinton and the FBI conspired against the Trump campaign, and that the deep state allowed Clinton to escape responsibility for her poor handling of classified emails.

It might seem odd, given that they won in 2016, that Trump supporters have trafficked in so many conspiracy theories. It is important to remember, however, that Trump built his coalition by appealing more to populist conspiracy beliefs than to partisanship. He and his supporters have used conspiracy theories to fight what they have seen as an unfair conspiracy against them.[44]

In this environment, each new conspiracy theory breeds more. And ongoing investigations have uncovered or suggested the existence of shady activities, subterfuge, or outright conspiracy by numerous actors. Did fears of an outsider winning the White House drive government agents to conspire against then-candidate Donald Trump? Were the Trump-Russia conspiracy theories part of a plan by Clinton and other actors to discredit the Trump campaign? Was the Mueller investigation a vast overreaction to a conspiracy theory? Did the Trump-Russia conspiracy theories lead Trump to commit actual crimes, such as obstruction of justice? The growing number of opposing conspiracy theories has made truth nearly impossible to decipher.

Political scientists Matthew Atkinson and Darin DeWitt put forward the concept of conspiracy theory politics. They view conspiracy theories as a disruptive tool that can change the political playing field in favor of outsiders and upstarts. But this view is a non-normative one; it does not address the negative side effects that arise when unscrupulous politicians or a profit-driven media use conspiracy theories to manipulate people.

Political theorist Alfred Moore delves into the consequences of conspiracy theory politics, noting the effects it has on how people interact with information: people begin to distrust legitimate sources, relying more and more on less and less. People turn primarily to partisan or alternative sources, and they vehemently reject information sources with which they do not agree.[45] One cannot make meaningful decisions in a democracy awash in conspiracy theories, and one cannot compromise with opponents if one believes those opponents are engaged in a vast conspiracy. Despite whatever electoral advantages come from conspiracy theory politics, there is a much larger price to pay.

As this book heads to press, Trump's attempts to get foreign governments to investigate his political enemies has sparked an impeachment inquiry. Both Republicans and Democrats are accusing the opposing side of engaging in conspiracies, and both believe the opposing party is guilty. Time will tell how this plays out.

Moral Panic and Financial Incentives

Many countries, including the United States, have been concerned about the role of social media in politics during the last few years. The election of Donald Trump, the Brexit vote, and the swing toward populism across the world have been blamed on the internet, and social media in particular. What is the effect of new communication technologies on the spread of conspiracy theories? Is there a need for governments to regulate social media to protect democracy?

In the United States, renewed concern over the internet seems to have been driven by a confluence of moral panics. These include a fear of manipulation by fake news, an obsession with pornography and prostitution disguised as concern for children and human trafficking, and the fear of social media radicalization.[46] These moral panics have led to calls for the regulation, censorship, and in some cases, outright government takeover of social media platforms so they can better serve "society's interests."[47]

The trend toward regulating social media is the same across Europe, where governments in Britain and France are considering employing social media regulators, and Germany has classified Facebook as a monopoly requiring government regulation. In more extreme circumstances, the Christchurch shooting in New Zealand led to censorship of documents associated with the shooter, and a bombing in Sri Lanka led to a social media blackout to prevent conspiracy theories from spreading about the incident. It is not clear that giving the government the power to "regulate" social media, or speech more generally, would benefit society or simply be used by the powerful to eliminate critical speech. Social media platforms make great scapegoats for bitter partisans and moral crusaders, but there is little reason to believe that social media platforms can do what they are accused of. There is little evidence that fake news on social media flipped the 2016 election from Hillary Clinton to Donald Trump.[48] In fact, many see the apparent cooperation between big government and big tech as nothing more than an attempt by government officials to exert control over the information environment by handing market protections to existing social media giants:

> By now, you probably know that YouTube is pure evil . . . get ready for major political and regulatory action against Google, which has owned the video platform since 2006, and is now the target of a Department of Justice antitrust investigation and a congressional investigation along the same lines. . . .
>
> These days, whether you're a right-wing free-marketer or a left-wing democratic socialist, whether you're Tucker Carlson or Sen. Elizabeth Warren

(D–Mass.), you probably worry more about Big Tech than Islamic terrorism and agree that all or most of the so-called FAANG companies (Facebook, Amazon, Apple, Netflix, and Google) need to be broken up, hemmed in, or regulated as public utilities. Hell, even the leaders of those companies are calling for regulation. A month ago, Google's CEO Sundar Pichai took to the op-ed pages of *The New York Times* to plead with Congress to pass "comprehensive privacy legislation" similar to the European Union's General Data Protection Regulation (GDPR) that would cover all online businesses. Ironically—or maybe strategically—Pichai didn't mention that a year after the GDPR's implementation, Google's marketshare had grown.[49]

A broader issue to be aware of as governments attempt to regulate the internet is that government officials as well as many interests would love nothing more than to ban content and control platforms. As much as the companies being regulated might outwardly claim to despise it, they benefit immensely because regulations provide them with monopoly protections that set a high bar for competitors to enter the market. Consequently, what seem like attempts at curbing the power of big tech companies are really just policies designed to increase their market position.

Is the Internet to Blame?

Have the internet and social media platforms become cesspools of conspiracy theories, pseudoscience, hate speech, racism, and extremism? Are they to blame for a new era of conspiracy theorizing? It is very easy to conclude that the internet causes people to believe strange things, including conspiracy theories. After all, strange things are easy to find on the internet. A Google search for the term "conspiracy theory" returns 92.4 million results; "9/11 conspiracy" garners 16.9 million, and "Reptilian Elites" provides more than a hundred thousand.[50] It is easy to agree with journalists who claim that "when you start looking for conspiracy theories online, they seem to be everywhere."[51]

However, it is hard to take some criticisms of the internet seriously. Like all other forms of communication, it is blamed for nearly every social ill (real or imagined). Blaming the internet has become a trope so common in modern reporting that it can't help but be mocked.

> Is social media making us less social? Is it making us dumber? How about lonely? Is social media making us lazy? Is it making us depressed? Stop me if you've heard this one before: A new technology becomes widely adopted. People start to see new types of behavior. The technology is immediately held responsible. Without Facebook, I would be happier. Without Twitter, I would be more productive.[52]

Blaming new technologies for any and every perceived problem is not a new phenomenon. Cable television, broadcast television, radio, newspapers, the printing press, and even paper faced criticisms from contemporary social commentators looking to connect a complex social problem to a simple cause. Such criticisms don't account for human agency; they seem to assume that people are lemmings that cannot resist influence. Further, they rely on a form of nostalgia that allows them to think that long-standing social problems are new.

The charges levied at the internet include: *The internet gets people to believe the wrong stuff, the internet makes people vote the wrong way, the internet leads people to commit violence based on wrong information.* The following sections sum up the major problems with such claims and give strong reason to be skeptical of the internet's influence over the masses. This should, hopefully, give pause to anyone supporting internet regulation.

The Internet Requires Positive Action

For the internet to convince a person of a conspiracy theory, that person has to *go to* the internet and *seek out and access* conspiracy theories. Conspiracy theories certainly have their allure, and there are plenty of conspiracy theories out there for people to consume. But conspiracy theory websites are not highly trafficked, compared to more mainstream outlets in the United States. The main 9/11 Truth website, 911Truth.org, ranks as the 387,197th most trafficked; Alex Jones's Info-Wars website comes in at 1,068th. For comparison, the *New York Times* website comes in at 29th.[53]

Looking at web traffic, we find that people go on the internet to access news, pornography, vacation photos, and cat videos far more often than they go looking for conspiracy theories. Most internet use has little to do with conspiracy theories, and conspiracy theory websites are largely ignored. There is of course easy access to conspiracy theories, but we need to be aware that just because content is available doesn't mean that anyone is looking at it.[54]

Human Biases Still Operate on the Internet

People who reject conspiracy theories do not go to the internet looking for them, nor are they likely to believe them once encountered. The people who access conspiracy theories on the web tend to be predisposed toward conspiracy beliefs and are likely seeking gratification for those preexisting beliefs.[55] As discussed in previous chapters, it is not easy to convince people of ideas that do not match their existing predispositions. This means that regardless of the content, minds aren't going to change that much.

To wit, and as I addressed in chapter 1, there is little evidence showing that conspiracy beliefs have increased since the advent of the internet. It does appear to be true that politicians are engaging in conspiracy theorizing more, particularly in the United States, but is that a good reason to put politicians in charge of policing conspiracy theories on the web? A better solution might be to elect politicians who don't traffic in conspiracy theories.

Authoritative Information Is More Powerful on the Internet

The available evidence suggests that the internet may not be as hospitable to conspiracy theories as some assume. There are many websites alleging conspiracy theories, but unless people are already inclined to seek them out, they will never find them. So, for most people, exposure to a conspiracy theory is only likely to occur on mainstream sites. How do mainstream news sites treat conspiracy theories?

The short answer is: not well. An examination of a year's worth of news stories and blog posts on Google's search engine showed that of three thousand stories referencing conspiracy theories, 63 percent framed the conspiracy theory negatively, with pejoratives such as "fantasy" or "bizarre." Seventeen percent framed the conspiracy theory more neutrally, and only 19 percent addressed it positively. If one were to seek out news on the internet, one would likely get negative portrayals of conspiracy theories.[56]

Furthermore, the internet has built-in mechanisms for self-correction. When conspiracy theories emerge on the internet, many people act to immediately call them into question, and often to shame them. Just as conspiracy theorists post their theories, anti-conspiracy theorists are quick to post evidence refuting them. This process may happen so quickly on the internet that conspiracy theories now no longer have time to fully develop before they face refutation.[57]

On top of this, conspiracy theories don't spread in the way some people assume. Often, social media is accused of spreading conspiracy theories in a snowball fashion, with a conspiracy theory picking up size and speed as more and more people see, indiscriminately believe, and spread it further. But conspiracy theories don't work this way: people are finicky about what they follow on social media and what they choose to believe and then share. No doubt, conspiracy theories do spread: they spread off- and online. But, they do not convince everyone in their path, and polls show that very few conspiracy theories gain much traction. Most conspiracy theories die in the night. The big problems occur when elite politicians and mainstream media adopt them.

What Can Be Done?

Even though most conspiracy theories are harmless, some theories and theorists take healthy skepticism to an unhealthy degree. Violence is sometimes the result. Democracy can be hindered by persistent allegations of conspiracy: if people are convinced that their opponent is conspiring against them, negotiation may prove impossible. Knowing their costs, some have called for banning conspiracy theories.[58]

Such a view, however, forgets that conspiracy theories are not necessarily false: they could be true or false. The problem with conspiracy theories is that they have not been verified as likely true by the appropriate authorities. Should governments or tech companies ban or bury conspiracy theories, they may be suppressing vital ideas that might be found to be true if investigated further. Also, even if many of them turn out to be false, conspiracy theories may help uncover truth by calling for further investigation.

Governments and news outlets blame the supposed increase of conspiracy theorizing on social media and are slowly considering banning content. But there are two ironies: (1) conspiracy theories have been a part of the human experience seemingly forever, and (2) government officials and traditional news outlets traffic in conspiracy theories when it suits them.

Considering all of the dubious information available in the world today, it would be rather piecemeal to ban just a handful of conspiracy theories on a handful of social media sites. If we are going to be puritanical (or at least evenhanded) about truth and call for bans of certain content, then millions of hours of content and millions of news stories are going to disappear because they will not reach whatever arbitrary bar for "truth" we set. If we

Photo 6.2 Mark Zuckerberg and other social media giants are being pressured to more closely moderate content.
Stephen Lam / Reuters / Newscom

are going to ban content that is dubious, then programs and stories about not only conspiracy theories but also aliens, Bigfoot, ghosts, alternative medicines, beauty products, horoscopes, psychics, and religion will all be on the chopping block. And why stop at social media? Why not ban books, television shows, and news outlets?

People like dubious content; there is a market for it. As Michael Shermer points out, there is bias in the media that seems to favor, at times, dubious content:

> Spurious accounts that snare the gullible are readily available. Skeptical treatments are much harder to find. Skepticism does not sell well. A bright and curious person who relies entirely on popular culture to be informed about something . . . is hundreds or thousands of times more likely to come upon a fable treated uncritically than a sober and balanced assessment.[59]

But at the same time, it is extremely difficult to determine what counts as conspiracy theory in real time for the millions of ideas that traverse media every day. Asking tech (or other media) companies to identify conspiracy theories and other dubious ideas would put them in the position of making millions of subjective decisions about what is true and what is not every hour. And they would be making these decisions under pressure from governments who may have a stake in many of these decisions.

Throughout the discussion, the fact that government is one of the biggest purveyors of both conspiracy theories and actual conspiracies has been missed. If policy makers were to have a more open and transparent government that did not engage in conspiracies, and if politicians did not spread conspiracy theories as a means of manipulating the public, then people might feel less need for conspiracy theories in the first place. It would be nice if governments and politicians cleaned up their act, but as with conspiracy theories, it's much easier to scapegoat.

Conclusion

Conspiracy theories are a part of the human condition. Everyone believes at least one, but given the number of conspiracy theories, it is more likely that everyone believes a few. Some people have a worldview defined by them. Conspiracy theories are just another reminder that people disagree about many things, including truth. These disagreements have always existed and always will. We have to live with conspiracy theories and with the people who believe them. The only way to do this is to have compassion and tolerance for others, and to hold our own beliefs to high standards. It would be no small victory if more people were self-aware of their prejudices.

Education should always be a priority: teaching people to be critical thinkers will lead to better beliefs. Also, people should respect expertise, even when their opinions are at odds with the experts. Political transparency and accountability may ease the worst excesses of conspiracy theories, but they cannot eliminate them. People also need to elect officials who do not engage in conspiracy theorizing or in conspiracies.

Bibliography

Atkinson, Matthew D., and Darin DeWitt. "The Politics of Disruption: Social Choice Theory and Conspiracy Theory Politics." In *Conspiracy Theories and the People Who Believe Them*, edited by Joseph E. Uscinski, 122–34. New York: Oxford University Press, 2018.

Atkinson, Matthew D., Darin DeWitt, and Joseph E. Uscinski. "How Conspiracy Theories Helped Power Trump's Disruptive Politics." *Vox.com*, May 2, 2017.

Barkan, Ross. "Will Rachel Maddow Face a Reckoning over Her Trump-Russia Coverage?" *The Guardian* (2019). Published electronically March 28, 2019.

Bendery, Jennifer. "Roy Moore Is Fueling a Crazy Conspiracy Theory about George Soros." *Huffington Post* (2017). Published electronically December 5, 2017.

Berman, Ari. "The Democratic Primary Wasn't Rigged." *The Nation* (2016). Published electronically June 16, 2016.

Bessi, Alessandro, Mauro Coletto, George Alexandru Davidescu, Antonio Scala, Guido Caldarelli, and Walter Quattrociocchi. "Science vs. Conspiracy: Collective Narratives in the Age of Misinformation." *PLoS ONE* 10, no. 2 (2015): e0118093.

Bock, Alan W. "Ambush at Ruby Ridge." *Reason*, 1993. http://reason.com/archives/1993/10/01/ambush-at-ruby-ridge.

Borchers, Callum. "How on Earth Is the Media Supposed to Cover Trump's Wacky JFK-Cruz Conspiracy Theory?" *Washington Post* (2016). Published electronically May 3, 2016.

Cassino, Dan. "Fairleigh Dickinson University's Publicmind Poll Finds Trump Supporters More Conspiracy-Minded Than Other Republicans." News release, May 4, 2016.

Chait, Jonathan. "I Wrote an Article Suggesting Trump Was Compromised by Russia. I Was Right." *New York Magazine* (2019). Published electronically April 2, 2019.

———. "Will Trump Be Meeting with His Counterpart—or His Handler?" (2018). Published electronically July 2018.

Clarke, Steve. "Conspiracy Theories and the Internet: Controlled Demolition and Arrested Development." *Episteme* 4, no. 2 (2007): 167–80.

Coppins, McKay. "How the Left Lost Its Mind." *The Atlantic* (2017). Published electronically July 2, 2017.

DelReal, Jose A. "Here Are 10 More Conspiracy Theories Embraced by Donald Trump." *Washington Post* (2016). Published electronically September 16, 2016.

Drochon, Hugo. "Study Shows 60% of Britons Believe in Conspiracy Theories." *The Guardian* (2018). Published electronically November 22, 2018.

Drucker, David. "Romney Was Right about Russia." *CNN.com* (2017). Published electronically July 31, 2017.

Dwyer, Paula. "Everything Is 'Rigged.'" *Chicago Tribune* (2016). Published electronically February 4, 2016.

Ehrenfreund, Max. "What Is Hillary Clinton Trying to Say with This Ad about Donald Trump and Putin?" *Washington Post* (2016). Published electronically August 7, 2016.

Fandos, Nicholas, and Adam Goldman. "Barr Asserts Intelligence Agencies Spied on the Trump Campaign." *New York Times* (2019). Published electronically April 10, 2019.

Gillespie, Nick. "Are Google and YouTube Evil? No, but Don't Let That Get in the Way of Your Feelings." *Reason* (2019). Published electronically June 10, 2019.

Greenwald, Glenn. "Beyond Buzzfeed: The 10 Worst, Most Embarrassing U.S. Media Failures on the Trump-Russia Story." *The Intercept* (2019). Published electronically January 20, 2019.

———. "Robert Mueller Did Not Merely Reject the Trump-Russia Conspiracy Theories. He Obliterated Them." *The Intercept* (2019). Published electronically April 18, 2019.

Jacobsen, Annie. "The United States of Conspiracy: Why, More and More, Americans Cling to Crazy Theories." *NYDailyNews.com*, August 7, 2011. http://articles.nydailynews.com/2011-08-07/news/29878465_1_conspiracy-theories-bavarian-illuminati-nefarious-business.

Keller, Jared. "'The Internet Made Me Do It': Stop Blaming Social Media for Our Behavioral Problems." *Pacific Standard* (2017). Published electronically June 14, 2017.

Klein, Ezra. "Facebook Is a Capitalism Problem, Not a Mark Zuckerberg Problem." *Vox.com* (2019). Published electronically May 10, 2019.

LaFrance, Adrienne. "Going Online in the Age of Conspiracy Theories: A Video Claiming *Back to the Future* Predicted 9/11 Is the Latest in a Long and Often Bizarre Tradition of Questioning Key Moments in History." *The Atlantic*, October 21, 2015.

Lei, Richard, and George Lardner Jr. "Seige Guided by Hastily Revised Rules of Engagement." *Washington Post* (1995). Published electronically September 4, 1995.

Lewandowsky, Stephan, John Cook, Klaus Oberauer, Scott Brophy, Elisabeth A. Lloyd, and Michael Marriott. "Recurrent Fury: Conspiratorial Discourse in the Blogosphere Triggered by Research on the Role of Conspiracist Ideation in Climate Denial." *Journal of Social and Political Psychology* 3, no. 1 (2015): 142–78.

Lewandowsky, Stephan, Naomi Oreskes, James S. Risbey, Ben R. Newell, and Michael Smithson. "Seepage: Climate Change Denial and Its Effect on the Scientific Community." *Global Environmental Change* 33 (2015): 1–13.

Maddus, Gene. "Harvey Weinstein Hired Investigators to Spy on Accusers, *New Yorker* Reports." *Variety*, November 6, 2017.

Mathis-Lilley, Ben. "Watch Hillary Shred Trump on Releasing His Taxes." *Slate* (2016). Published electronically September 26, 2016.

Moore, Alfred. "On the Democratic Problem of Conspiracy Theory Politics." In *Conspiracy Theories and the People Who Believe Them*, edited by Joseph E. Uscinski. New York: Oxford University Press, 2018.

Nyhan, Brendan. "Fake News and Bots May Be Worrisome, but Their Political Power Is Overblown." *New York Times* (2018). Published electronically February 13, 2018.

Oliver, J. Eric, and Wendy M. Rahn. "Rise of the Trumpenvolk: Populism in the 2016 Election." *The ANNALS of the American Academy of Political and Social Science* 667, no. 1 (2016): 189–206.

Oreskes, Naomi. "The Scientific Consensus on Climate Change." *Science* 306, no. 5702 (2004): 1686–86.

Rosenblum, Nancy L., and Russell Muirhead. *A Lot of People Are Saying: The New Conspiracism and the Assault on Democracy.* Princeton, NJ: Princeton University Press, 2019.

Sagan, Carl. *The Demon-Haunted World: Science as a Candle in the Dark.* New York: Ballantine Books, 1997.

Shackford, Scott. "Backpage Founder's 93 Charges Lack Actual Sex-Trafficking Claims." *Reason* (2018). Published electronically April 9, 2018.

Shelbourne, Mallory. "Trump Claims Voter Fraud without Evidence, Says 'I Won the Popular Vote.'" *The Hill* (2016). Published electronically November 27, 2016.

Simon, Arthur M., and Joseph E. Uscinski. "Prior Experience Predicts Presidential Performance." *Presidential Studies Quarterly* 42, no. 3 (2012): 514–48.

Stewart, Charles, III. "Donald Trump's 'Rigged Election' Talk Is Changing Minds. Democrats' Minds, That Is." *Washington Post* (2016). Published electronically October 19, 2016.

Sunstein, Cass R. *Conspiracy Theories and Other Dangerous Ideas.* New York: Simon & Schuster, 2014.

Taibbi, Matt. "Taibbi: On Russiagate and Our Refusal to Face Why Trump Won" *Rolling Stone* (2019). Published electronically March 29, 2019.

Tani, Maxwell. "The Conspiracy Candidate? 13 Outlandish Theories Donald Trump Has Floated on the Campaign Trail." *Busness Insider* (2016). Published electronically September 16, 2016.

Uscinski, Joseph E. "Down the Rabbit Hole We Go!" In *Conspiracy Theories and the People Who Believe Them*, edited by Joseph E. Uscinski, 1–32. New York: Oxford University Press, 2018.

———. "If Trump's Rhetoric around Conspiracy Theories Follows Him to the White House, It Could Lead to the Violation of Rights on a Massive Scale." *Impact of American Politics & Policy Blog* (2016).

———. "Lots of Americans Agree with Donald Trump about 'Rigged Elections.'" *Washington Post* (2016). Published electronically August 8, 2016.

Uscinski, Joseph E., Karen Douglas, and Stephan Lewandowsky. "Climate Change Conspiracy Theories." *Oxford Research Encyclopedia of Climate Science.* Oxford: Oxford University Press, 2017, 1–43.

Uscinski, Joseph E., and Joseph M. Parent. *American Conspiracy Theories.* New York: Oxford University Press, 2014.

Walker, Jesse. "Ruby Ridge Is History, but the Mindset That Led to Ruby Ridge Is Thriving." *Reason* (2012). Published electronically August 22, 2016.

Wilstein, Matt. "Bill O'Reilly Lashes Out at Critics in Conspiracy-Laden Glenn Beck Interview." *The Daily Beast* (2017). Published electronically October 23, 2017.

Notes

Chapter 1: Why Study Conspiracy Theories?

1   NASA, "Apollo 11 Mission Overview." NASA.gov. May 15, 2019. https://www
    .nasa.gov/mission_pages/apollo/missions/apollo11.html.
2   Brian Dunning, *Conspiracies Declassified: The Skeptoid Guide to the Truth behind
    the Theories* (Avon, MA: Adams Media, 2018), 172.
3   Alan Burdick, "Looking for Life on a Flat Earth," *New Yorker* (2018).
4   David Icke, *Human Race Get Off Your Knees: The Lion Sleeps No More* (Isle of
    Wight: David Icke Books, 2010).
5   Sean Martin, "UFO Hunters Discover Alien Base on Google Moon Maps—
    Bizarre Pyramid Found," *Express* (2018).
6   Jacob Stolworthy, "Stanley Kubrick's Daughter Debunks Moon Landing Con-
    spiracy Theory," *Independent* (2016).
7   C. Krauss, "28 Years after Kennedy's Assassination, Conspiracy Theories Refuse
    to Die," *New York Times*, January 5, 1992; John W. McHoskey, "Case Closed?
    On the John F. Kennedy Assassination: Biased Assimilation of Evidence and Atti-
    tude Polarization," *Basic and Applied Social Psychology* 17, no. 3 (1995); Larry
    J. Sabato, *The Kennedy Half-Century: The Presidency, Assassination, and Lasting
    Legacy of John F. Kennedy* (New York: Bloomsbury Publishing USA, 2013); Lisa
    D. Butler, Cheryl Koopman, and Philip G. Zimbardo, "The Psychological Impact
    of Viewing the Film *JFK*: Emotions, Beliefs, and Political Behavioral Intentions,"
    Political Psychology 16, no. 2 (1995).
8   Philip Shenon, "Files Will Shed Light on a JFK Shooting Conspiracy—but Not
    the One You Think," *The Guardian* (2017).
9   Niraj Chokshi, "False Flags, True Believers and Trolls: Understanding Conspiracy
    Theories after Tragedies," *Washington Post*, December 4, 2015.
10 Ari Berman, "The Democratic Primary Wasn't Rigged," *The Nation* (2016); Jack
    Edelson et al., "The Effect of Conspiratorial Thinking and Motivated Reasoning
    on Belief in Election Fraud," *Political Research Quarterly* 70, no. 4 (2017).
11 "MH370 Conspiracy Theories: What Really Happened to the Missing Malaysia
    Airlines Flight?" *The Week* (2018).

12 Thomas Hargrove, "Third of Americans Suspect 9/11 Government Conspiracy," *Scripps News*, August 1, 2006.

13 "Kenneka Jenkins' Death Photos 'Raise More Questions,' Lawyer Says as Police Close Case," *Chicago Tribune*, 2017.

14 Christopher N. Osher, "Bike Agenda Spins Cities toward U.N. Control, Maes Warns," *Denverpost.com*, August 4, 2010; Patrick T. Hurley and Peter A. Walker, "Whose Vision? Conspiracy Theory and Land-Use Planning in Nevada County, California," *Environment and Planning* 36 (2004).

15 Catherine Carstairs and Rachel Elder, "Expertise, Health, and Popular Opinion: Debating Water Fluoridation, 1945–80," *Canadian Historical Review* 89, no. 3 (2008); Elizabeth Chuck, "Science Says Fluoride in Water Is Good for Kids. So Why Are These Towns Banning It?" NBC News (2018).

16 "8 in 10 French People Believe a Conspiracy Theory: Survey," *France24* (2018).

17 Dara Lind, "The Conspiracy Theory That Led to the Pittsburgh Synagogue Shooting, Explained," *Vox.com* (2018).

18 Peter Knight, ed. *Conspiracy Theories in American History*, 2 vols. (Santa Barbara, CA: ABC-CLIO, 2003); Hugo Drochon, "Who Believes in Conspiracy Theories in Great Britain and Europe?" in *Conspiracy Theories and the People Who Believe Them*, ed. Joseph E. Uscinski (New York: Oxford University Press, 2018).

19 Dunning, *Conspiracies Declassified.*

20 Kathleen Gray, "Bernie Sanders: Election Is about Survival of Middle Class," *Detroit Free Press* (2016); Rich Lowry, "Bernie's Conspiracy Theory," *National Review* (2015).

21 James Pickard, "Corbyn Lashes Out at Financial Sector 'Speculators and Gamblers,'" *Financial Times* (2017).

22 Peter Knight, *Conspiracy Culture: From the Kennedy Assassination to the* X-Files (London: Routledge, 2000), 129

23 Jennifer Crocker et al., "Belief in U.S. Government Conspiracies against Blacks among Black and White College Students: Powerlessness or System Blame?" *Personality and Social Psychology Bulletin* 25, no. 8 (1999); Louis Farrakhan and Henry Louis Gates Jr., "Farrakhan Speaks," *Transition*, no. 70 (1996).

24 Burdick, "Looking for Life on a Flat Earth."

25 Joseph E. Uscinski, Karen Douglas, and Stephan Lewandowsky, "Climate Change Conspiracy Theories," *Oxford Research Encyclopedia of Climate Science* (Oxford: Oxford University Press, 2017).

26 Ted Goertzel, "The Conspiracy Theory Pyramid Scheme," in *Conspiracy Theories and the People Who Believe Them*, ed. Joseph E. Uscinski (New York: Oxford University Press, 2018). Robert M. Hollingworth et al., "The Safety of Genetically Modified Foods Produced through Biotechnology," *Toxological Sciences* 71 (2003).

27 Amy Harmon, "A Lonely Quest for Facts on Genetically Modified Crops," *New York Times*, January 4, 2014; Keith Kloor, "GMO Opponents Are the Climate Skeptics of the Left," *Slate.com*, September 26, 2012; Jim Marrs, *Population Control: How Corporate Owners Are Killing Us* (New York: William Morrow, 2015).

28 David A. Broniatowski, Karen M. Hilyard, and Mark Dredze, "Effective Vaccine Communication during the Disneyland Measles Outbreak," *Vaccine* 34, no. 28 (2016).

29 Goertzel, "The Conspiracy Theory Pyramid Scheme."

30 Edzard Ernst and Angelo Fasce, "Dismantling the Rhetoric of Alternative Medicine: Smokescreens, Errors, Conspiracies, and Follies," *Mètode Science Studies Journal-Annual Review*, no. 8 (2017).

31 "Conspira-Sea Cruise," Legendary World Travel, http://www.divinetravels.com/ConspiraSeaCruise.html.

32 Joseph E. Uscinski and Joseph M. Parent, *American Conspiracy Theories* (New York: Oxford University Press, 2014).

33 Kathryn S. Olmsted, *Real Enemies: Conspiracy Theories and American Democracy, World War I to 9/11* (New York: Oxford University Press, 2008).

34 Uscinski and Parent, *American Conspiracy Theories.*

35 Drochon, "Who Believes in Conspiracy Theories?"

36 BBC Trending, "EU Referendum: 'Use Pens' Plea of Voting Fraud 'Conspiracy Theorists,'" *BBC Trending* (2016).

37 "Turkey Academic Jailed after Raids on Professors and Activists," *Aljazeera.com* (2018); Carlotta Gall, "Turkey Orders New Election for Istanbul Mayor, in Setback for Opposition," *New York Times* (2019).

38 Justin Miller, "How Greg Abbott Got Played by the Russians during His Jade Helm Freakout," *Texas Observer* (2018).

39 Ronald Bailey, "Vermont GMO Labeling Hits Kosher Foods," *Reason* (2016).

40 Marian Tupy, "Europe's Anti-GMO Stance Is Killing Africans," *Reason* (2017).

41 Lindsay McLaren et al., "Measuring the Short-Term Impact of Fluoridation Cessation on Dental Caries in Grade 2 Children Using Tooth Surface Indices," *Community Dentistry and Oral Epidemiology* 44, no. 3 (2016).

42 Uscinski, Douglas, and Lewandowsky, "Climate Change Conspiracy Theories."

43 Elizabeth Nolan Brown, "This Is How Sex-Trafficking Panic Gets Made: Reason Roundup," *Reason* (2018).

44 Scott Shackford, "Backpage Founder's 93 Charges Lack Actual Sex-Trafficking Claims," *Reason* (2018).

45 Cecilia Kang, "Fake News Onslaught Targets Pizzeria as Nest of Child-Trafficking," *New York Times* (2016).

46 Tay Wiles, "Conspiracy Theories Inspire Vigilante Justice in Tucson," *High Country News* (2018); Brown, "This Is How Sex-Trafficking Panic Gets Made"; Stephanie Ebbert, "In Wayland, Suburban Dog-Walking Moms Target Sex Trafficking," *Boston Globe* (2019); Elizabeth Nolan Brown, "Nabbing Robert Kraft Helped Florida Prosecutors Get Headlines. Now Kraft and Other Orchids of Asia Customers Are Fighting Back" (2019); Kim LaCapria, "Hickory (NC) Walmart Human Trafficking Warning," *Snopes.com* (2015).

47 Elizabeth Nolan Brown, "Patriots Owner Robert Kraft's Bust Is Being Billed as a Human Trafficking Bust, but It Looks More Like Ordinary Prostitution," *Reason.com* (2019).

48 Frances Hill, *A Delusion of Satan: The Full Story of the Salem Witch Trials* (Tantor eBooks, 2014); Richard Latner, "'Here Are No Newters': Witchcraft and Religious Discord in Salem Village and Andover," *New England Quarterly* 79, no. 1 (2006); Peter T. Leeson and Jacob W. Russ, "Witch Trials," *Economic Journal* 128, no. 613 (2018).

49 James L. Gibson, "Political Intolerance and Political Repression during the McCarthy Red Scare," *American Political Science Review* 82, no. 2 (1988).

50 Daniel Jolley and Karen Douglas, "The Effects of Anti-Vaccine Conspiracy Theories on Vaccination Intentions," *PLoS ONE* 9, no. 2 (2014); Sander van der Linden, "The Conspiracy-Effect: Exposure to Conspiracy Theories (about Global Warming) Decreases Pro-Social Behavior and Science Acceptance," *Personality and Individual Differences* 87 (2015).

51 Karen M. Douglas and Ana C. Leite, "Suspicion in the Workplace: Organizational Conspiracy Theories and Work-Related Outcomes," *British Journal of Psychology* 108, no. 3 (2017).

52 Eric Oliver and Thomas Wood, "Medical Conspiracy Theories and Health Behaviors in the United States," *JAMA Internal Medicine* 174, no. 5 (2014).

53 Uscinski and Parent, *American Conspiracy Theories*; Karen Douglas and Robbie Sutton, "Does It Take One to Know One? Endorsement of Conspiracy Theories Is Influenced by Personal Willingness to Conspire," *British Journal of Social Psychology* 50, no. 3 (2011).

54 Colin Klein, Peter Clutton, and Adam G. Dunn, "Pathways to Conspiracy: The Social and Linguistic Precursors of Involvement in Reddit's Conspiracy Theory Forum" (2018), psyarxiv.com/8vesf.

55 Brian Morton, "The Guns of Spring," *City Paper Baltimore* (2009); Dale Russakoff and Serge F. Kovaleski, "An Ordinary Boy's Extraordinary Rage," *Washington Post* (1995).

56 Matthew Haag and Maya Salam, "Gunman in 'Pizzagate' Shooting Is Sentenced to 4 Years in Prison," *New York Times* (2017).

57 Kevin Johnson et al., "'It's Time to Destroy Trump & Co.': Scalise Shooter Raged on Facebook," *USA Today* (2017).

58 Wiles, "Conspiracy Theories Inspire Vigilante Justice."

59 Avi Selk, "Falsely Accused of Satanic Horrors, a Couple Spent 21 Years in Prison. Now They're Owed Millions," *Washington Post* (2017); Jeffrey S. Victor, "Moral Panics and the Social Construction of Deviant Behavior: A Theory and Application to the Case of Ritual Child Abuse," *Sociological Perspectives* 41, no. 3 (1998).

60 Michael Butter and Peter Knight, "The History of Conspiracy Theory Research: A Review and Commentary," in *Conspiracy Theories and the People Who Believe Them*, ed. Joseph E. Uscinski (New York: Oxford University Press, 2018).

61 Richard Hofstadter, *The Paranoid Style in American Politics, and Other Essays* (Cambridge, MA: Harvard University Press, 1964).

62 Knight, *Conspiracy Culture*.

63 Brian Keeley, "Of Conspiracy Theories," in *Conspiracy Theories: The Philosophical Debate*, ed. David Coady (Burlington, VT: Ashgate, 2006).

64 Hamid Dabashi, "Living in a Conspiracy Theory in Trump's America," *Aljazeera.com* (2018).

65 Andrew Rosenthal, "No Comment Necessary: Conspiracy Nation," *New York Times* (2013).

66 Annie Jacobsen, "The United States of Conspiracy: Why, More and More, Americans Cling to Crazy Theories," *NYDailyNews.com*, August 7, 2011, http://articles.nydailynews.com/2011-08-07/news/29878465_1_conspiracy-theories-bavarian-illuminati-nefarious-business.

67 David Aaronovitch, *Voodoo Histories: The Role of Conspiracy Theory in Shaping Modern History* (New York: Riverhead Books, 2010).

68 Darrin M. McMahon, "Conspiracies So Vast: Conspiracy Theory Was Born in the Age of Enlightenment and Has Metastasized in the Age of the Internet. Why Wont It Go Away?" *Boston Globe*, February 1, 2004.

69 Charles Krauthammer, "A Rash of Conspiracy Theories," *Washington Post*, July 5, 1991; Kenn Thomas, "Clinton Era Conspiracies! Was Gennifer Flowers on the Grassy Knoll? Probably Not, but Here Are Some Other Bizarre Theories for a New Political Age," *Washington Post*, January 16, 1994.

70 "The Warren Commission Report," *New York Times*, September 28, 1964; Georgie Anne Geyer, "The Rewriting of History to Fit Our Age of Conspiracy," *Los Angeles Times*, 1977.

71 Paul Musgrave, "Conspiracy Theories Are for Losers. QAnon Is No Exception," *Washington Post* (2018).

72 "8 in 10 French People Believe a Conspiracy Theory: Survey," *France24* (2018); Drochon, "Who Believes in Conspiracy Theories?"; Adam M. Enders and Steven M. Smallpage, "Polls, Plots, and Party Politics: Conspiracy Theories in Contemporary America," in *Conspiracy Theories and the People Who Believe Them*, ed. Joseph E. Uscinski, 298–318 (New York: Oxford University Press, 2018).

73 Brendan Nyhan, "9/11 and Birther Misperceptions Compared," *Brendan-nyhan.com/blog* (2009).

74 For example, Isaac Stanley-Becker, "'We Are Q': A Deranged Conspiracy Cult Leaps from the Internet to the Crowd at Trump's 'Maga' Tour," *Washington Post* (2018).

75 Lauren Cox and ABC News Medical Unit, "What's behind Internet Conspiracy Empires?" ABC News (2008).

76 Ibid.

77 Ibid.

78 Hofstadter, *The Paranoid Style in American Politics*.

79 Uscinski and Parent, *American Conspiracy Theories*.

80 Adrian Furnham, "Commercial Conspiracy Theories: A Pilot Study," *Frontiers in Psychology* 4 (2013).

81 Steven M. Smallpage, Adam M. Enders, and Joseph E. Uscinski, "The Partisan Contours of Conspiracy Theory Beliefs," *Research & Politics* 4, no. 4 (2017).

82 Martin Orr and Ginna Husting, "Media Marginalization of Racial Minorities: 'Conspiracy Theorists' in U.S. Ghettos and on the 'Arab Street,'" in *Conspiracy Theories and the People Who Believe Them*, ed. Joseph E. Uscinski (New York: Oxford University Press, 2018).

Chapter 2: What Is a Conspiracy Theory?

1 Jon Street, "Sen. Elizabeth Warren: Middle Class Is Not Defined by Income Level," *CNSNews.com* (2013).

2 Martin Orr and Ginna Husting, "Media Marginalization of Racial Minorities: 'Conspiracy Theorists' in U.S. Ghettos and on the 'Arab Street,'" in *Conspiracy Theories and the People Who Believe Them*, ed. Joseph E. Uscinski (New York: Oxford University Press, 2018).

3 Jaron Harambam and Stef Aupers, "'I Am Not a Conspiracy Theorist': Relational Identifications in the Dutch Conspiracy Milieu," *Cultural Sociology* 11, no. 1 (2017).

4 Laurie A. Manwell, "In Denial of Democracy: Social Psychological Implications for Public Discourse on State Crimes against Democracy Post-9/11," *American Behavioral Scientist* 53, no. 6 (2010).

5 Jesse Walker, "What We Mean When We Say 'Conspiracy Theory,'" in *Conspiracy Theories and the People Who Believe Them*, ed. Joseph E. Uscinski (New York: Oxford University Press, 2018).

6 John W. Dean, *The Nixon Defense: What He Knew and When He Knew It* (New York: Viking, 2014).

7 Vickie M. Mays, Courtney N. Coles, and Susan D. Cochran, "Is There a Legacy of the U.S. Public Health Syphilis Study at Tuskegee in HIV/AIDS-Related Beliefs among Heterosexual African Americans and Latinos?" *Ethics & Behavior* 22, no. 6 (2012).

8 Neil Levy, "Radically Socialized Knowledge and Conspiracy Theories," *Episteme* 4, no. 2 (2007).

9 Archibald Cox, "Watergate and the U.S. Constitution," *British Journal of Law and Society* 2, no. 1 (1975).

10 Kathryn S. Olmsted, *Challenging the Secret Government: The Post-Watergate Investigations of the CIA and FBI* (Chapel Hill: University of North Carolina Press, 2000).

11 Thomas Kean, *The 9/11 Commission Report: Final Report of the National Commission on Terrorist Attacks upon the United States* (Washington, DC: Government Printing Office, 2011); David Dunbar and Brad Reagan, *Debunking 9/11 Myths: Why Conspiracy Theories Can't Stand up to the Facts* (New York: Sterling, 2006).

12 David Ray Griffin, *Debunking 9/11 Debunking: An Answer to Popular Mechanics and Other Defenders of the Official Conspiracy Theory* (N.p.: Interlink Books, 2007).

13 Sinead Baker, "The Mystery of MH370 Is about to Be Laid to Rest for Good—Here Are All the Theories, Dead Ends, and Unanswered Questions from the Most Bizarre Airline Disaster of the Century," *Business Insider* (2018).

14 David Icke, *Children of the Matrix: How an Interdimensional Race Has Controlled the World for Thousands of Years—and Still Does* (Wildwood, MO: Bridge of Love Publications USA, 2001); Icke, *Human Race Get Off Your Knees: The Lion Sleeps No More* (Isle of Wight: David Icke Books, 2010).

15 Jack Edelson et al., "The Effect of Conspiratorial Thinking and Motivated Reasoning on Belief in Election Fraud," *Political Research Quarterly* 70, no. 4 (2017).

16 Ryan L. Claassen and Michael J. Ensley, "Motivated Reasoning and Yard-Sign-Stealing Partisans: Mine Is a Likable Rogue, Yours Is a Degenerate Criminal," *Political Behavior* 38, no. 2 (2016).

17 John M. Carey et al., "An Inflated View of the Facts? How Preferences and Predispositions Shape Conspiracy Beliefs about the Deflategate Scandal," *Research & Politics* 3, no. 3 (2016).

18 Milton Lodge and Charles S. Taber, *The Rationalizing Voter* (New York: Cambridge University Press, 2013).

19 John G. Bullock et al., "Partisan Bias in Factual Beliefs about Politics," *Quarterly Journal of Political Science* 10 (2015).

20 Lance DeHaven-Smith, *Conspiracy Theory in America* (Austin: University of Texas Press, 2013).

21 Andrew McKenzie-McHarg, "Conspiracy Theory: The Nineteenth-Century Prehistory of a Twentieth-Century Concept," in *Conspiracy Theories and the*

People Who Believe Them, ed. Joseph E. Uscinski (New York: Oxford University Press, 2018).

22 Sir Karl R. Popper, *Conjectures and Refutations* (London: Routledge & Kegan Paul, 1972).

23 Dunbar and Reagan, *Debunking 9/11 Myths*.

24 Maarten Boudry and Johan Braeckman, "Immunizing Strategies and Epistemic Mechanisms," *Philosophia* 39 (2011).

25 Jerome R. Corsi, *Where's the Birth Certificate?: The Case That Barack Obama Is Not Eligible to Be President* (Washington, DC: WND Books, 2011).

26 Sir Karl R. Popper, *The Open Society and Its Enemies, Vol. 2: The High Tide of Prophecy: Hegel, Marx, and the Aftermath*, 5th ed. (London: Routledge & Kegan Paul, 1966); Levy, "Radically Socialized Knowledge"; Steve Clarke, "Conspiracy Theories and Conspiracy Theorizing," *Philosophy of the Social Sciences* 32, no. 2 (2002).

27 Brian Keeley, "Of Conspiracy Theories," *Journal of Philosophy* 96, no. 3 (1999).

28 David Robert Grimes, "On the Viability of Conspiratorial Beliefs," *PloS ONE* 11, no. 1 (2016).

29 Pete Mandik, "Shit Happens," *Episteme* 4, no. 2 (2007).

30 Andrew McKenzie-McHarg and Rolf Fredheim, "Cock-Ups and Slap-Downs: A Quantitative Analysis of Conspiracy Rhetoric in the British Parliament 1916–2015," *Historical Methods: A Journal of Quantitative and Interdisciplinary History* 50, no. 3 (2017).

31 M. R. X. Dentith, "Conspiracy Theories and Philosophy: Bringing the Epistemology of a Freighted Term into the Social Sciences," in *Conspiracy Theories and the People Who Believe Them*, ed. Joseph E. Uscinski (New York: Oxford University Press, 2018); Juha Räikkä and Lee Basham, "Conspiracy Theory Phobia," in *Conspiracy Theories and the People Who Believe Them*, ed. Joseph E. Uscinski (New York: Oxford University Press, 2018).

32 Joel Buenting and Jason Taylor, "Conspiracy Theories and Fortuitous Data," *Philosophy of the Social Sciences* 40, no. 4 (2010).

33 Walker, "What We Mean"; P. R. Bost, "The Truth Is around Here Somewhere: Integrating the Research on Conspiracy Beliefs," in *Conspiracy Theories and the People Who Believe Them*, ed. Joseph E. Uscinski, 269–82. New York: Oxford University Press, 2018.

34 Peter Knight, "Conspiracy Theories in America: A Historical Overview," in *Conspiracy Theories in American History*, vol. 1, ed. Peter Knight (Santa Barbara, CA: ABC-CLIO, 2003).

35 Joseph E. Uscinski, "The Psychology behind Why People Believe Conspiracy Theories about Scalia's Death," *Washington Post*, February 19, 2016.

36 Eric Oliver and Thomas Wood, "Conspiracy Theories and the Paranoid Style(s) of Mass Opinion," *American Journal of Political Science* 58, no. 4 (2014).

37 Jesse Lopez and D. Sunshine Hillygus, "Why So Serious?: Survey Trolls and Misinformation," *SSRN* (2018).

38 Public Policy Polling, "Clinton's Florida Lead Continues to Grow" (2016).

39 Adam J. Berinsky, "Telling the Truth about Believing the Lies? Evidence for the Limited Prevalence of Expressive Survey Responding," *Journal of Politics* 80, no. 1 (2018).

40 Walker, "What We Mean."

[41] Tom Jenson, "Democrats and Republicans Differ on Conspiracy Theory Beliefs," Public Policy Polling (2013).

[42] Dustin Tingley and Gernot Wagner, "Solar Geoengineering and the Chemtrails Conspiracy on Social Media," *Palgrave Communications* 3, no. 1 (2017).

[43] Rob Brotherton, Christopher C. French, and Alan D. Pickering, "Measuring Belief in Conspiracy Theories: The Generic Conspiracist Beliefs Scale," *Frontiers in Psychology* 4, Article 279 (2013).

[44] John Zaller, *The Nature and Origins of Mass Opinion* (Cambridge: Cambridge University Press, 1992).

[45] Katherine Levine Einstein and David M. Glick, "Do I Think BLS Data Are BS? The Consequences of Conspiracy Theories," *Political Behavior* 37, no. 3 (2014).

[46] Jan-Willem van Prooijen and Mark van Vugt, "Conspiracy Theories: Evolved Functions and Psychological Mechanisms," *Perspectives on Psychological Science* 13, no. 6 (2018).

[47] Gareth Richards, "Digit Ratio (2d: 4d) and Beliefs in Superstitions, Conspiracy Theories and the Paranormal," *Developmental Psychology Section* (2017).

[48] Neil Dagnall et al., "Conspiracy Theory and Cognitive Style: A Worldview," *Frontiers in Psychology* 6 (2015).

[49] Jan-Willem van Prooijen and Karen M. Douglas, "Conspiracy Theories as Part of History: The Role of Societal Crisis Situations," *Memory Studies* 10, no. 3 (2017).

[50] Joanne M. Miller, Kyle L. Saunders, and Christina E. Farhart, "Conspiracy Endorsement as Motivated Reasoning: The Moderating Roles of Political Knowledge and Trust," *American Journal of Political Science* 60, no. 4 (2016).

[51] Casey A. Klofstad et al., "What Drives People to Believe in Zika Conspiracy Theories?" *Palgrave Communications* 5, no. 1 (2019).

[52] Amy Wang, "'Post-Truth' Named 2016 Word of the Year by Oxford Dictionaries," *Washington Post* (2019).

[53] Matthew Norman, "Whoever Wins the US Presidential Election, We've Entered a Post-Truth World—There's No Going Back Now," *The Independent* (2016).

[54] Christopher H. Achen and Larry M. Bartels, *Democracy for Realists: Why Elections Do Not Produce Responsive Government* (Princeton, NJ: Princeton University Press, 2017).

[55] D. J. Flynn, Brendan Nyhan, and Jason Reifler, "The Nature and Origins of Misperceptions: Understanding False and Unsupported Beliefs about Politics," *Political Psychology* 38 (2017).

[56] Shelly Banjo, "Facebook, Twitter and the Digital Disinformation Mess," *Washington Post* (2019).

[57] Richard Engel, Kate Benyon-Tinker, and Kennett Werner, "Russian Documents Reveal Desire to Sow Racial Discord—and Violence—in the U.S.," *NBC News* (2019).

[58] David M. J. Lazer et al., "The Science of Fake News," *Science* 359, no. 6380 (2018).

[59] Hunt Allcott and Matthew Gentzkow, "Social Media and Fake News in the 2016 Election," *Journal of Economic Perspectives* 31, no. 2 (2017).

[60] Alessandro Bessi et al., "Science vs. Conspiracy: Collective Narratives in the Age of Misinformation," *PLoS ONE* 10, no. 2 (2015).

[61] "Possible Bigfoot Sighting in Whitehall, NY," WHEC Channel 10 (2018).

62 Bryan C. Sykes et al., "Genetic Analysis of Hair Samples Attributed to Yeti, Bigfoot and Other Anomalous Primates," *Proceedings of the Royal Society B* 281, no. 1789 (2014); Benjamin Radford, "Bigfoot at 50: Evaluating a Half-Century of Bigfoot Evidence," *Skeptical Inquirer* 26, no. 2 (2002).

63 Michael Dennett, "Evidence for Bigfoot? An Investigation of the Mill Creek 'Sasquatch Prints,'" *Skeptical Inquirer* 13, no. 3 (1989).

64 J. D. Lozier, P. Aniello, and M. J. Hickerson, "Predicting the Distribution of Sasquatch in Western North America: Anything Goes with Ecological Niche Modelling," *Journal of Biogeography* 36, no. 9 (2009).

65 David J. Daegling, *Bigfoot Exposed: An Anthropologist Examines America's Enduring Legend* (Lanham, MD: AltaMira, 2004).

66 Joe Nickell, "Bigfoot as Big Myth: Seven Phases of Mythmaking," *Skeptical Inquirer* 41, no. 5 (2016).

67 Benjamin Radford, *Tracking the Chupacabra: The Vampire Beast in Fact, Fiction, and Folklore* (Albuquerque: University of New Mexico Press, 2011).

68 "BBC 'Proves' Nessie Does Not Exist," BBC News (2003).

69 Terence Hines, *Pseudoscience and the Paranormal* (Buffalo, NY: Prometheus Books, 2003), 20.

70 Ibid.

71 Joe Nickell, Barry Karr, and Tom Genoni, *The Outer Edge: Classic Investigations of the Paranormal*. Committee for the Scientific Investigation of Claims of the Paranormal, 1996.

72 Rupert Sheldrake and Pamela Smart, "Psychic Pets: A Survey in North-West England," *Journal-Society for Psychical Research* 61 (1997).

73 Scott O. Lilienfeld, "New Analyses Raise Doubts about Replicability of ESP Findings," *Skeptical Inquirer* 23 (1999).

74 James Randi, *The Magic of Uri Geller* (New York: Ballantine Books, 1975).

75 James Randi, *The Truth about Uri Geller* (Buffalo, NY: Prometheus Books, 1982).

76 Brian Regal, *Pseudoscience: A Critical Encyclopedia* (ABC-CLIO, 2009).

77 Michael Peck, "The CIA's Secret Plan to Crush Russia during the Cold War: Super Psychic Powers," *National Interest* (2017).

78 Michael Shermer, *Why People Believe Weird Things: Pseudoscience, Superstition, and Other Confusions of Our Time* (New York: Macmillan, 2002).

79 Ray Hyman, "Cold Reading: How to Convince Strangers That You Know All about Them [1977]," in *Pseudoscience and Deception: The Smoke and Mirrors of Paranormal Claims*, ed. Bryan Farha (Lanham, MD: University Press of America, 2014).

80 Kendrick Frazier, *Science Confronts the Paranormal* (Buffalo, NY: Prometheus Books, 1986).

81 Frances Hill, *A Delusion of Satan: The Full Story of the Salem Witch Trials* (Tantor eBooks, 2014); Richard Latner, "'Here Are No Newters': Witchcraft and Religious Discord in Salem Village and Andover," *New England Quarterly* 79, no. 1 (2006); Debbie Nathan and Michael Snedeker, *Satan's Silence: Ritual Abuse and the Making of a Modern American Witch Hunt* (iUniverse, 2001).

82 Herbert Benson et al., "Study of the Therapeutic Effects of Intercessory Prayer (STEP) in Cardiac Bypass Patients: A Multicenter Randomized Trial of Uncertainty and Certainty of Receiving Intercessory Prayer," *American Heart Journal*

151, no. 4 (2006); Susan J. Blackmore, *Dying to Live: Near-Death Experiences* (Buffalo, NY: Prometheus Books, 1993); Kendrick Frazier, "Double-Blind Test of Astrology Avoids Bias, Still Refutes the Astrological Hypothesis," in *The Outer Edge: Classic Investigations of the Paranormal,* ed. Barry Karr, Joe Nickell, and Tom Genoni (New York: CSICOP, 1996).

[83] Robert A. Baker, "The Aliens among Us: Hypnotic Regression Revisited," in *The Hundredth Monkey and Other Paradigms of the Paranormal: A Skeptical Inquirer Collection,* ed. Kendrick Frazier (Buffalo, NY: Prometheus Books, 1991).

[84] Carl Sagan, *The Demon-Haunted World: Science as a Candle in the Dark* (New York: Ballantine Books, 1997).

Chapter 3: The Popularity of Conspiracy and Anomalous Beliefs

[1] Betsy Sinclair, Steven S. Smith, and Patrick D. Tucker, "'It's Largely a Rigged System': Voter Confidence and the Winner Effect in 2016," *Political Research Quarterly* 71, no. 4 (2018).

[2] Jack Edelson et al., "The Effect of Conspiratorial Thinking and Motivated Reasoning on Belief in Election Fraud," *Political Research Quarterly* 70, no. 4 (2017).

[3] Katherine Levine Einstein and David M. Glick, "Do I Think BLS Data Are BS? The Consequences of Conspiracy Theories," *Political Behavior* 37, no. 3 (2014).

[4] Katherine Levine Einstein and David M. Glick, "Cynicism, Conspiracies, and Contemporaneous Conditions Moderating Experimental Treatment Effects," unpublished paper (2015).

[5] Eric Oliver and Thomas Wood, "Conspiracy Theories and the Paranoid Style(s) of Mass Opinion," *American Journal of Political Science* 58, no. 4 (2014).

[6] For a more in-depth text on polling and public opinion, I suggest Robert S. Erikson and Kent L. Tedin, *American Public Opinion: Its Origins, Content and Impact* (New York: Pearson, 2014).

[7] Art Swift, "Majority in U.S. Still Believe JFK Killed in a Conspiracy," *Gallup.com,* November 15, 2013.

[8] CBS News, "CBS Poll: JFK Conspiracy Lives," *CBSNews.com,* November 20, 1998.

[9] "8 in 10 French People Believe a Conspiracy Theory: Survey," *France24* (2018).

[10] Swift, "Majority in U.S. Still Believe JFK Killed in a Conspiracy."

[11] Lisa D. Butler, Cheryl Koopman, and Philip G. Zimbardo, "The Psychological Impact of Viewing the Film *JFK*: Emotions, Beliefs, and Political Behavioral Intentions," *Political Psychology* 16, no. 2 (1995).

[12] John W. McHoskey, "Case Closed? On the John F. Kennedy Assassination: Biased Assimilation of Evidence and Attitude Polarization," *Basic and Applied Social Psychology* 17, no. 3 (1995).

[13] Philip J. Klass, *The Real Roswell Crashed-Saucer Coverup* (Buffalo, NY: Prometheus Books, 1997).

[14] Tom Jenson, "Democrats and Republicans Differ on Conspiracy Theory Beliefs," *Public Policy Polling* (2013).

15 Darren Carlson, "Life on Mars? Over a Third of Americans Say They Believe Life in Some Form Exists on the Red Planet," *Gallup.com* (2001).

16 CNN, "Poll: U.S. Hiding Knowledge of Aliens," *CNN.com* (1997), http://articles.cnn.com/1997-06-15/us/9706_15_ufo.poll_1_ufo-aliens-crash-site?_s=PM:US.

17 Linda Lyons, "Paranormal Beliefs Come (Super)Naturally to Some," *news.gallup.com* (2005).

18 Data kindly provided by Conspiracy & Democracy, a Leverhulme-funded project, based at CRASSH, University of Cambridge, from 2013 to 2018. Survey data collected by YouGov. See Hugo Drochon, "Who Believes in Conspiracy Theories in Great Britain and Europe?" in *Conspiracy Theories and the People Who Believe Them*, ed. Joseph E. Uscinski (New York: Oxford University Press, 2018).

19 David Icke, *Children of the Matrix: How an Interdimensional Race Has Controlled the World for Thousands of Years—and Still Does* (Wildwood, MO: Bridge of Love Publications USA, 2001).

20 Jenson, "Democrats and Republicans Differ."

21 John Pollard, "Skinhead Culture: The Ideologies, Mythologies, Religions and Conspiracy Theories of Racist Skinheads," *Patterns of Prejudice* 50, no. 4–5 (2016). Robert Markley, "Alien Assassinations: The X-Files and the Paranoid Structure of History," *Camera Obscura* 14, no. 1–2/40–41 (1997).

22 Sophia Gaston and Joseph E. Uscinski, "Out of the Shadows: Conspiracy Thinking on Immigration," Henry Jackson Society (2018), https://henryjacksonsociety.org/wp-content/uploads/2018/12/Out-of-the-Shadows-Conspiracy-thinking-on-immigration.pdf.

23 "8 in 10 French People Believe a Conspiracy Theory: Survey."

24 Joseph E. Uscinski, Karen Douglas, and Stephan Lewandowsky, "Climate Change Conspiracy Theories," *Oxford Research Encyclopedia of Climate Science* (Oxford: Oxford University Press, 2017), 1–43.

25 Andrew P. Street, "Why Do Australians Believe Silly Things?" ABC News (2017).

26 Marian Tupy, "Europe's Anti-GMO Stance Is Killing Africans," *Reason* (2017).

27 Justus Wesseler et al., "Foregone Benefits of Important Food Crop Improvements in Sub-Saharan Africa," *PLoS ONE* 12, no. 7 (2017).

28 Adrian Dubock, "Golden Rice, Part 3: A Thoroughly Studied GMO Crop Approved by Australia, Canada, New Zealand and the US," *Genetic Literacy Project* (2019); Cameron English, "Quit the Glyphosate Conspiracy Theories," *RealClearScience* (2018).

29 Meron Tesfa Michael, "Africa Bites the Bullet on Genetically Modified Food Aid," *World Press* (2002).

30 Ronald Bailey, "Vermont GMO Labeling Hits Kosher Foods," *Reason* (2016); Ronald Bailey, "New Useless and Costly USDA Bioengineered Food Disclosure Regulations Issued," *Reason* (2018).

31 Eric Oliver and Thomas Wood, "Medical Conspiracy Theories and Health Behaviors in the United States," *JAMA Internal Medicine* 174, no. 5 (2014).

32 Cary Funk, Brian Kennedy, and Meg Hefferon, "Public Perspectives on Food Risks," *Pew Internet* (2018).

33 Jenson, "Democrats and Republicans Differ."

34 "8 in 10 French People Believe a Conspiracy Theory: Survey."

35 Ibid.; Hoang Nguyen, "Most Flat Earthers Consider Themselves Very Religious," *YouGov* (2018).

36 Oliver and Wood, "Medical Conspiracy Theories and Health Behaviors in the United States."

37 Ibid.

38 Jenson, "Democrats and Republicans Differ."

39 Krista Jenkins, "The Best Medicine Is Truth" (2018).

40 David A. Broniatowski, Karen M. Hilyard, and Mark Dredze, "Effective Vaccine Communication during the Disneyland Measles Outbreak," *Vaccine* 34, no. 28 (2016).

41 Ted Goertzel, "The Conspiracy Theory Pyramid Scheme," in *Conspiracy Theories and the People Who Believe Them*, ed. Joseph E. Uscinski (New York: Oxford University Press, 2018).

42 Catrinel Craciun and Adriana Baban, "'Who Will Take the Blame?': Understanding the Reasons Why Romanian Mothers Decline HPV Vaccination for Their Daughters," *Vaccine* 30, no. 48 (2012).

43 Angie Drobnic Holan and Louise Jacobson, "Michele Bachmann Says HPV Vaccine Can Cause Mental Retardation," *Politifact.com* (2011).

44 Mark Dredze, David A. Broniatowski, and Karen M. Hilyard, "Zika Vaccine Misconceptions: A Social Media Analysis," *Vaccine* 34, no. 30 (2016).

45 Hugo Drochon, "Study Shows 60% of Britons Believe in Conspiracy Theories," *The Guardian* (2018).

46 Jenson, "Democrats and Republicans Differ."

47 Lindsay McLaren et al., "Measuring the Short-Term Impact of Fluoridation Cessation on Dental Caries in Grade 2 Children Using Tooth Surface Indices," *Community Dentistry and Oral Epidemiology* 44, no. 3 (2016).

48 Kyle Hill, "Why Portland Is Wrong about Water Fluoridation," *Scientific American*, May 22, 2013.

49 Jenson, "Democrats and Republicans Differ."

50 Jake Blumgart, "What's the Matter with Portland?" *Slate*, May 17, 2013.

51 Marcus Griffin, Darren Shickle, and Nicola Moran, "European Citizens' Opinions on Water Fluoridation," *Community Dentistry and Oral Epidemiology* 36, no. 2 (2008).

52 Oliver and Wood, "Medical Conspiracy Theories and Health Behaviors in the United States."

53 Pride Chigwedere et al., "Estimating the Lost Benefits of Antiretroviral Drug Use in South Africa," *JAIDS Journal of Acquired Immune Deficiency Syndromes* 49, no. 4 (2008).

54 Karen MacGregor, "Conspiracy Theories Fuel Row over AIDS Crisis in South Africa," *Independent.co.uk* (2000).

55 Nicoli Nattrass, "How Bad Ideas Gain Social Traction," *The Lancet* 380, no. 9839 (2012).

56 Drochon, "Who Believes in Conspiracy Theories in Great Britain and Europe?"

57 "8 in 10 French People Believe a Conspiracy Theory: Survey."

58 Laura M. Bogart and Sheryl Thorburn Bird, "Exploring the Relationship of Conspiracy Beliefs about HIV/AIDS to Sexual Behaviors and Attitudes among

African-American Adults," *Journal of the National Medical Association* 95, no. 11 (2003); Laura M. Bogart and Sheryl Thorburn, "Are HIV/AIDS Conspiracy Beliefs a Barrier to HIV Prevention among African Americans?" *JAIDS Journal of Acquired Immune Deficiency Syndromes* 38, no. 2 (2005).

59   David Leiser, Nofar Duani, and Pascal Wagner-Egger, "The Conspiratorial Style in Lay Economic Thinking," *PLoS ONE* 12, no. 3 (2017).

60   Drochon, "Who Believes in Conspiracy Theories in Great Britain and Europe?"

61   Ross Barkan, "'Their Greed Has No End': Bernie Sanders Makes a Surprise Appearance in Manhattan," *Observer* (2015).

62   Drochon, "Who Believes in Conspiracy Theories in Great Britain and Europe?"

63   Steven M. Smallpage, Adam M. Enders, and Joseph E. Uscinski, "The Partisan Contours of Conspiracy Theory Beliefs," *Research & Politics* 4, no. 4 (2017).

64   Drochon, "Who Believes in Conspiracy Theories in Great Britain and Europe?"

65   Ibid.

66   Jenson, "Democrats and Republicans Differ."

67   Ibid.

68   Joseph E. Uscinski and Casey Klofstad, "Commentary: Florida Believes in Conspiracy Theories Too," *Orlando Sentinel* (2018).

69   Oliver and Wood, "Conspiracy Theories and the Paranoid Style(s) of Mass Opinion."

70   Ibid.

71   Will Dahlgren, "British People More Likely to Believe in Ghosts Than a Creator," *YouGov* (2016).

72   Jenson, "Democrats and Republicans Differ"; Public Policy Polling, "Clinton Leads in NC for First Time since March" (2016).

73   Public Policy Polling, "Support for Impeachment at Record High" (2017).

74   "Paranormal America 2017," Chapman University (2017).

75   Ipsos, "Majority of Americans Believe in Ghosts (57%) and UFOs (52%)" (2008).

76   Ibid.; Dahlgren, "British People More Likely to Believe in Ghosts."

77   Ipsos, "Majority of Americans Believe in Ghosts."

78   Dahlgren, "British People More Likely to Believe in Ghosts."

79   YouGov, "Yougov NY Psychics and Mediums," (2017), https://d25d2506sfb94s .cloudfront.net/cumulus_uploads/document/921030f7y9/Copy%20of%20 Results%20for%20YouGov%20NY%20(Psychics%20and%20Mediums)%20227%20 10.30.2017.pdf; Dahlgren, "British People More Likely to Believe in Ghosts."

80   David Moore, "Three in Four Americans Believe in Paranormal," *Gallup.com* (2005).

81   "Paranormal America 2017."

82   Lyons, "Paranormal Beliefs Come (Super)Naturally to Some."

83   YouGov, "Yougov NY Psychics and Mediums."

84   Kathy Frankovic, "Americans Think Ghosts Are More Likely Than Aliens on Earth," *YouGov* (2018).

85   Kendrick Frazier, *Science Confronts the Paranormal* (Buffalo, NY: Prometheus Books, 1986).

86   "Paranormal America 2017."

87   Jenson, "Democrats and Republicans Differ."

88   Joseph E. Uscinski and Casey Klofstad, "New Poll: The QAnon Conspiracy Movement Is Very Unpopular," *Washington Post* (2018); Nguyen, "Most Flat Earthers Consider Themselves Very Religious."

89   "Conspiracy Theories: Separating Fact from Fiction," *Time.com* (2009).

90   Oliver and Wood, "Conspiracy Theories and the Paranoid Style(s) of Mass Opinion."

Chapter 4: The Psychology and Sociology of Conspiracy Theories

1   Amos Tversky and Daniel Kahneman, "Extensional versus Intuitive Reasoning: The Conjunction Fallacy in Probability Judgment," *Psychological Review* 90, no. 4 (1983).

2   Ibid.; Rob Brotherton and Christopher C. French, "Belief in Conspiracy Theories and Susceptibility to the Conjunction Fallacy," *Applied Cognitive Psychology* 28, no. 2 (2014).

3   Paul Rogers, John E. Fisk, and Dawn Wiltshire, "Paranormal Belief and the Conjunction Fallacy: Controlling for Temporal Relatedness and Potential Surprise Differentials in Component Events," *Applied Cognitive Psychology* 25, no. 5 (2011); Brotherton and French, "Belief in Conspiracy Theories."

4   Marta Marchlewska, Aleksandra Cichocka, and Małgorzata Kossowska, "Addicted to Answers: Need for Cognitive Closure and the Endorsement of Conspiracy Beliefs," *European Journal of Social Psychology* 48, no. 2 (2018).

5   Ibid.

6   L. Comsides, "The Logic of Social Exchange: Has Natural Selection Shaped How Humans Reason? Studies with the Wason Selection Task," *Cognition* 31, no. 3 (1989): 187–276.

7   Preston R. Bost and Stephen G. Prunier, "Rationality in Conspiracy Beliefs: The Role of Perceived Motive," *Psychological Reports: Sociocultural Issues in Psychology* 113, no. 1 (2013).

8   Joseph E. Uscinski, "The Psychology behind Why People Believe Conspiracy Theories about Scalia's Death," *Washington Post*, February 19, 2016.

9   Rob Brotherton and Christopher C. French, "Intention Seekers: Conspiracist Ideation and Biased Attributions of Intentionality," *PloS ONE* 10, no. 5 (2015).

10   Cass Sunstein and Adrian Vermeule, "Conspiracy Theories," *SSRN eLibrary* (2008).

11   Ibid.

12   Brendan Nyhan, Jason Reifler, and Peter A. Ubel, "The Hazards of Correcting Myths about Health Care Reform," *Medical Care* 51, no. 2 (2013).

13   Milton Lodge and Charles S. Taber, *The Rationalizing Voter* (New York: Cambridge University Press, 2013).

14   Charles G. Lord, Lee Ross, and Mark R. Lepper, "Biased Assimilation and Attitude Polarization: The Effects of Prior Theories on Subsequently Considered Evidence," *Journal of Personality and Social Psychology* 37, no. 11 (1979).

15 Ryan L. Claassen and Michael J. Ensley, "Motivated Reasoning and Yard-Sign-Stealing Partisans: Mine Is a Likable Rogue, Yours Is a Degenerate Criminal," *Political Behavior* 38, no. 2 (2016).

16 Joanne M. Miller, Kyle L. Saunders, and Christina E. Farhart, "Conspiracy Endorsement as Motivated Reasoning: The Moderating Roles of Political Knowledge and Trust," *American Journal of Political Science* 60, no. 4 (2016). Brendan Nyhan, "9/11 and Birther Misperceptions Compared," *Brendan-nyhan.com/blog* (2009).

17 Tomas Ståhl and Jan-Willem van Prooijen, "Epistemic Rationality: Skepticism toward Unfounded Beliefs Requires Sufficient Cognitive Ability and Motivation to Be Rational," *Personality and Individual Differences* 122 (2018).

18 Jan-Willem van Prooijen, "Why Education Predicts Decreased Belief in Conspiracy Theories," *Applied Cognitive Psychology* 31, no. 1 (2017).

19 Kia Aarnio and Marjaana Lindeman, "Paranormal Beliefs, Education, and Thinking Styles," *Personality and Individual Differences* 39, no. 7 (2005); Kathleen D. Dyer and Raymond E. Hall, "Effect of Critical Thinking Education on Epistemically Unwarranted Beliefs in College Students," *Research in Higher Education* 60, no. 3 (2019).

20 Ricky Green and Karen M. Douglas, "Anxious Attachment and Belief in Conspiracy Theories," *Personality and Individual Differences* 125 (2018); Luigi Leone et al., "Avoidant Attachment Style and Conspiracy Ideation," *Personality and Individual Differences* 134 (2018).

21 Ricky Green and Karen M. Douglas, "Anxious Attachment."

22 Leone et al., "Avoidant Attachment Style."

23 Roland Imhoff and Pia Karoline Lamberty, "Too Special to Be Duped: Need for Uniqueness Motivates Conspiracy Beliefs," *European Journal of Social Psychology* 47, no. 6 (2017).

24 Aleksandra Cichocka, Marta Marchlewska, and Agnieszka Golec de Zavala, "Does Self-Love or Self-Hate Predict Conspiracy Beliefs? Narcissism, Self-Esteem, and the Endorsement of Conspiracy Theories," *Social Psychological and Personality Science* 7, no. 2 (2016).

25 J. Eric Oliver and Thomas John Wood, *Enchanted America: How Intuition and Reason Divide Our Politics* (Chicago: University of Chicago Press, 2018).

26 Neil Dagnall et al., "Conspiracy Theory and Cognitive Style: A Worldview," *Frontiers in Psychology* 6 (2015).

27 Christopher C. French et al., "Psychological Aspects of the Alien Contact Experience," *Cortex* 44, no. 10 (2008).

28 Dagnall et al., "Conspiracy Theory and Cognitive Style"; Hannah Darwin, Nick Neave, and Joni Holmes, "Belief in Conspiracy Theories. The Role of Paranormal Belief, Paranoid Ideation and Schizotypy," *Personality and Individual Differences* 50, no. 8 (2011); Oliver and Wood, *Enchanted America*.

29 Theodor W. Adorno et al., *The Authoritarian Personality* (New York: Harper, 1950).

30 Michael V. Bronstein et al., "Belief in Fake News Is Associated with Delusionality, Dogmatism, Religious Fundamentalism, and Reduced Analytic Thinking," *Journal of Applied Research in Memory and Cognition* (2018); Monika Grzesiak-Feldman

and Monika Irzycka, "Right-Wing Authoritarianism and Conspiracy Thinking in a Polish Sample," *Psychological Reports* 105 (2009); Oliver and Wood, *Enchanted America*.

31. Dagnall et al., "Conspiracy Theory and Cognitive Style"; Ken Drinkwater, Neil Dagnall, and Andrew Parker, "Reality Testing, Conspiracy Theories, and Paranormal Beliefs," *Journal of Parapsychology* 76, no. 1 (2012).

32. Daniel Freeman and Richard P. Bentall, "The Concomitants of Conspiracy Concerns," *Social Psychiatry and Psychiatric Epidemiology* 52, no. 5 (2017); Rob Brotherton and Silan Eser, "Bored to Fears: Boredom Proneness, Paranoia, and Conspiracy Theories," *Personality and Individual Differences* 80 (2015).

33. Darwin, Neave, and Holmes, "Belief in Conspiracy Theories."

34. Roland Imhoff and Pia Lamberty, "How Paranoid Are Conspiracy Believers? Toward a More Fine-Grained Understanding of the Connect and Disconnect between Paranoia and Belief in Conspiracy Theories," *European Journal of Social Psychology* 48, no. 7 (2017).

35. K. M. Douglas et al., "Understanding Conspiracy Theories," *Advances in Political Psychology* 6 (2019).

36. Eric Oliver and Thomas Wood, "Conspiracy Theories and the Paranoid Style(s) of Mass Opinion," *American Journal of Political Science* 58, no. 4 (2014).

37. Sean Richey, "A Birther and a Truther: The Influence of the Authoritarian Personality on Conspiracy Beliefs," *Politics & Policy* 45, no. 3 (2017).

38. Joseph E. Uscinski and Joseph M. Parent, *American Conspiracy Theories* (New York: Oxford University Press, 2014).

39. S. B. Thomas and S. C. Quinn, "The Tuskegee Syphilis Study, 1932 to 1972: Implications for HIV Education and AIDS Risk Education Programs in the Black Community," *American Journal of Public Health* 81, no. 11 (1991).

40. Spike Lee, "Spike Lee on Real Time with Bill Maher" (HBO, 2007).

41. Wiktor Soral et al., "The Collective Conspiracy Mentality in Poland," in *Conspiracy Theories and the People Who Believe Them*, ed. Joseph E. Uscinski (New York: Oxford University Press, 2018); Claassen and Ensley, "Motivated Reasoning and Yard-Sign-Stealing Partisans."

42. Emily Gaudette, "Starbucks Continues So-Called 'War on Christmas' with Lesbian Positive Ad," *Newsweek* (2017).

43. Michal Bilewicz and Ireneusz Krzeminski, "Anti-Semitism in Poland and Ukraine: The Belief in Jewish Control as a Mechanism of Scapegoating," *International Journal of Conflict and Violence* 4, no. 2 (2010).

44. Anna-Kaisa Newheiser, Miguel Farias, and Nicole Tausch, "The Functional Nature of Conspiracy Beliefs: Examining the Underpinnings of Belief in the *Da Vinci Code* Conspiracy," *Personality and Individual Differences* 51, no. 8 (2011).

45. Steven M. Smallpage, Adam M. Enders, and Joseph E. Uscinski, "The Partisan Contours of Conspiracy Theory Beliefs," *Research & Politics* 4, no. 4 (2017).

46. David Brion Davis, *The Slave Power Conspiracy and the Paranoid Style* (Baton Rouge: Louisiana State University Press, 1969).

47. Daniel Jolley, Rose Meleady, and Karen Douglas, "Exposure to Intergroup Conspiracy Theories Promotes Prejudice Which Spreads across Groups," *British Journal of Psychology* (2019).

Chapter 5: The Politics of Conspiracy Theories

1   Niccolo Machiavelli, *Discourses on Livy*, trans. Harvey Mansfield and Nathan Tarcov (Chicago: University of Chicago Press, 1996).

2   Alexa Liataud, "White House Acknowledges the U.S. Is at War in Seven Countries," *Vice News* (2018).

3   Medea Benjamin, "America Dropped 26,171 Bombs in 2016. What a Bloody End to Obama's Reign," *The Guardian* (2017).

4   S. B. Thomas and S. C. Quinn, "The Tuskegee Syphilis Study, 1932 to 1972: Implications for HIV Education and AIDS Risk Education Programs in the Black Community," *American Journal of Public Health* 81, no. 11 (1991).

5   Joel Rosenblatt, "Champagne Remark May Cost Lawyer $289 Million Bayer Award," *Bloomberg* (2018).

6   Jan-Willem van Prooijen and Mark van Vugt, "Conspiracy Theories: Evolved Functions and Psychological Mechanisms," *Perspectives on Psychological Science* 13, no. 6 (2018).

7   Cory Clark et al., "Tribalism Is Human Nature," *Current Directions in Psychological Science* (2019).

8   Brian Dunning, *Conspiracies Declassified: The Skeptoid Guide to the Truth Behind the Theories* (Avon, MA: Adams Media, 2018).

9   Paul Karp, "Conspiracy Theorist David Icke Hits Back after Australia Revokes Visa," *The Guardian* (2019), https://www.theguardian.com/news/2019/feb/20/conspiracy-theorist-david-icke-hits-back-after-australia-revokes-visa.

10 David Icke, *Human Race Get Off Your Knees: The Lion Sleeps No More* (Isle of Wight: David Icke Books, 2010), 142–43.

11 Ibid., 194–95.

12 http://content.time.com/time/specials/packages/completelist/0,29569,1860871,00.html.

13 Jim Marrs, *Population Control: How Corporate Owners Are Killing Us* (New York: William Morrow, 2015), 2.

14 http://archive.larouchepac.com/node/22617.

15 https://larouchepac.com/20160421/it-was-your-bloody-hand-unleashed-911-queen-elizabeth.

16 Dina Shapiro, "The Risk of Disease Stigma: Threat and Support for Coercive Public Heath Policy," APSA Pre-Conference on Political Communication of Risk (Seattle, WA, 2011).

17 Jim Fetzer and Mike Palecek, eds., *Nobody Died at Sandy Hook* (US: Moon Rock Books, 2015).

18 "8 in 10 French People Believe a Conspiracy Theory: Survey," *France24* (2018).

19 Brenton Tarrant, "The Great Replacement," unpublished manifesto (2019).

20 Jennifer Williams et al., "Christchurch Mosque Shooting: What We Know So Far," *Vox.com* (2019).

21 Jan-Werner Müller, *What Is Populism?* (London: Penguin UK, 2017).

22 Marrs, *Population Control*, 21.

23 Joseph Gershtenson, Jeffrey Ladewig, and Dennis L. Plane, "Parties, Institutional Control, and Trust in Government," *Social Science Quarterly* 87, no. 4 (2006).

24 Justin McCarthy, "Highest GOP Satisfaction with U.S. Direction since 2007," *Gallup.com* (2018).

25 Lydia Saad, "Americans Say Economy Is 'Most Important Thing Going Well,'" *Gallup.com* (2018).

26 Joseph E. Uscinski and Joseph M. Parent, *American Conspiracy Theories* (New York: Oxford University Press, 2014).

27 Steven M. Smallpage, Adam M. Enders, and Joseph E. Uscinski, "The Partisan Contours of Conspiracy Theory Beliefs," *Research & Politics* 4, no. 4 (2017).

28 Paul Lazarsfeld, Bernard Berelson, and Hazel Gaudet, *The People's Choice* (New York: Columbia University Press, 1944).

29 Bernard Berelson, Paul Lazarsfeld, and William McPhee, *Voting: A Study of Opinion Formation in a Presidential Campaign* (Chicago: University of Chicago Press, 1954); E. Katz and Paul Lazarsfeld, *Personal Influence, the Part Played by People in the Flow of Mass Communications* (New York: The Free Press, 1955); Lazarsfeld, Berelson, and Gaudet, *The People's Choice.*

30 Jeffery L. Bineham, "A Historical Account of the Hypodermic Model in Mass Communication," *Communication Monographs* 55, no. 3 (1988).

31 Angus Campbell et al., *The American Voter*, unabridged edition (Chicago: The University of Chicago Press, 1960).

32 Donald P. Green, Bradley Palmquist, and Eric Schickler, *Partisan Hearts and Minds: Political Parties and the Social Identities of Voters* (New Haven, CT: Yale University Press, 2002).

33 Steven E. Finkel, "Reexamining the 'Minimal Effects' Model in Recent Presidential Campaigns," *Journal of Politics* 55, no. 1 (1993).

34 Charles G. Lord, Lee Ross, and Mark R. Lepper, "Biased Assimilation and Attitude Polarization: The Effects of Prior Theories on Subsequently Considered Evidence," *Journal of Personality and Social Psychology* 37, no. 11 (1979).

35 Ibid.

36 John W. McHoskey, "Case Closed? On the John F. Kennedy Assassination: Biased Assimilation of Evidence and Attitude Polarization," *Basic and Applied Social Psychology* 17, no. 3 (1995).

37 Matthew A. Baum, "Partisan Media and Attitude Polarization," in *Regulatory Breakdown: The Crisis of Confidence in U.S. Regulation*, ed. Cary Coglianese (Philadelphia: University of Pennsylvania Press, 2012).

38 Alessandro Bessi et al., "Science vs. Conspiracy: Collective Narratives in the Age of Misinformation," *PLoS ONE* 10, no. 2 (2015).

39 Maxwell E. McCombs and Donald L. Shaw, "The Agenda-Setting Function of Mass Media," *Public Opinion Quarterly* 36, no. 2 (1972).

40 Dietram A. Scheufele and David Tewksbury, "Framing, Agenda Setting, and Priming: The Evolution of Three Media Effects Models," *Journal of Communication* 57, no. 1 (2007).

41 Amy E. Jasperson et al., "Framing and the Public Agenda: Media Effects on the Importance of the Federal Budget Deficit," *Political Communication* 15, no. 2 (1998).

42 Kevin Arceneaux, Martin Johnson, and Chad Murphy, "Polarized Political Communication, Oppositional Media Hostility, and Selective Exposure," *Journal of Politics* 74, no. 1 (2012).

43 Joseph E. Uscinski, *The People's News: Media, Politics, and the Demands of Capitalism* (New York: New York University Press, 2014).

44 John Zaller, *The Nature and Origins of Mass Opinion* (Cambridge: Cambridge University Press, 1992).

45 David E. Broockman and Daniel M. Butler, "The Causal Effects of Elite Position-Taking on Voter Attitudes: Field Experiments with Elite Communication," *American Journal of Political Science* 61, no. 1 (2017).

46 Ibid.

47 Michael Tesler, "How Democrats Derailed Marijuana Legalization in California," *Washington Post—The Monkey Cage* (2014).

48 Ted Marzilli, "Cain's Candidacy Splits Pizza Scores," *YouGov: BrandIndex* (2011).

49 Andrew Gelman and Gary King, "Why Are American Presidential Election Polls So Variable When Votes Are So Predictable?" *British Journal of Political Science* 23, no. 4 (1993).

50 Campbell et al., *The American Voter.*

51 Smallpage, Enders, and Uscinski, "The Partisan Contours of Conspiracy Theory Beliefs."

52 Herbert McClosky and Dennis Chong, "Similarities and Differences between Left-Wing and Right-Wing Radicals," *British Journal of Political Science* 15, no. 3 (1985).

53 Eric Oliver and Thomas Wood, "Conspiracy Theories and the Paranoid Style(s) of Mass Opinion," *American Journal of Political Science* 58, no. 4 (2014).

54 Smallpage, Enders, and Uscinski, "The Partisan Contours of Conspiracy Theory Beliefs."

55 P. R. Bost, "The Truth Is around Here Somewhere: Integrating the Research on Conspiracy Beliefs," in *Conspiracy Theories and the People Who Believe Them*, ed. Joseph E. Uscinski (New York: Oxford University Press, 2018).

56 Uscinski and Parent, *American Conspiracy Theories.*

57 James Pickard, "Corbyn Lashes Out at Financial Sector 'Speculators and Gamblers,'" *Financial Times* (2017).

58 Paula Dwyer, "Everything Is 'Rigged,'" *Chicago Tribune* (2016); Ross Barkan, "'Their Greed Has No End': Bernie Sanders Makes a Surprise Appearance in Manhattan," *Observer* (2015).

59 Rich Lowry, "Bernie's Conspiracy Theory," *National Review* (2015).

60 David Leiser, Nofar Duani, and Pascal Wagner-Egger, "The Conspiratorial Style in Lay Economic Thinking," *PLoS ONE* 12, no. 3 (2017).

61 Robert A. Dahl, "A Critique of the Ruling Elite Model," *American Political Science Review* 52, no. 2 (1958).

62 Ibid.

63 Ibid.

64 Martin Gilens and Benjamin I. Page, "Testing Theories of American Politics: Elites, Interest Groups, and Average Citizens," *Perspectives on Politics* 12, no. 3 (2014).

65 Peter K. Enns, "Relative Policy Support and Coincidental Representation," *Perspectives on Politics* 13, no. 4 (2015).

66 Daniel Kurt, "Are You in the Top One Percent of the World?" *Investopedia* (2019).

67 Lowry, "Bernie's Conspiracy Theory"; Bernie Sanders, "Gambling on Wall Street," *Politico.com* (2009).

68 Sarah Ann Gordon, *Hitler, Germans, and the "Jewish Question"* (Princeton, NJ: Princeton University Press, 1984).

69 Michael Wood, Karen Douglas, and Robbie Sutton, "Dead and Alive: Beliefs in Contradictory Conspiracy Theories," *Social Psychological and Personality Science* 3, no. 6 (2012).

70 Christina Prignano, "Here's How People Are Reacting to Elizabeth Warren's 'Wealth Tax' Proposal," *Boston Globe* (2019).

71 Christopher Daly, "For Vermont's Sanders, Victory Followed Long Path," *Washington Post* (1990).

72 Jim Tankersley, "Sorry, Bernie Sanders. Deodorant Isn't Starving America's Children," *Washington Post* (2015); Sam Frizell, "Bernie Sanders' Long History with Alternative Medicine," *Time.com* (2016).

73 Oliver and Wood, "Conspiracy Theories."

74 Paul Rosenberg, "QAnon, Tampa and Donald Trump: Not All Conspiracy Theories Are the Same," *Salon.com* (2018); Paul Krugman, "Attack of the Crazy Centrists," *Washington Post* (2014).

75 Smallpage, Enders, and Uscinski, "The Partisan Contours of Conspiracy Theory Beliefs"; Casey Klofstad et al., "What Drives People to Believe in Zika Conspiracy Theories?" *Palgrave Communications* 5, no. 36 (2019).

76 Joseph E. Uscinski and Casey Klofstad, "New Poll: The QAnon Conspiracy Movement Is Very Unpopular," *Washington Post* (2018).

77 Rob Brotherton, Christopher C. French, and Alan D. Pickering, "Measuring Belief in Conspiracy Theories: The Generic Conspiracist Beliefs Scale," *Frontiers in Psychology* 4, Article 279 (2013).

78 Michael J. Wood, "Some Dare Call It Conspiracy: Labeling Something a Conspiracy Theory Does Not Reduce Belief in It," *Political Psychology* 37, no. 5 (2016).

79 Joseph E. Uscinski, Casey Klofstad, and Matthew Atkinson, "Why Do People Believe in Conspiracy Theories? The Role of Informational Cues and Predispositions," *Political Research Quarterly* 69, no. 1 (2016).

80 Ibid.

81 Uscinski and Parent, *American Conspiracy Theories.*

82 Brendan Nyhan, "9/11 and Birther Misperceptions Compared," *Brendan-nyhan .com/blog* (2009).

83 David Weigel, "Trump's Foes Say He's a 9/11 Truther. Truthers Would Disagree" (2016).

84 Tom Jenson, "Democrats and Republicans Differ on Conspiracy Theory Beliefs," *Public Policy Polling* (2013).

85 Art Swift, "Majority in U.S. Still Believe JFK Killed in a Conspiracy," *Gallup.com*, November 15, 2013.

86 Larry J. Sabato, *The Kennedy Half-Century: The Presidency, Assassination, and Lasting Legacy of John F. Kennedy* (New York: Bloomsbury Publishing USA, 2013).

87 Uscinski and Parent, *American Conspiracy Theories.*

88 Ibid.

89 Jack Edelson et al., "The Effect of Conspiratorial Thinking and Motivated Reasoning on Belief in Election Fraud," *Political Research Quarterly* 70, no. 4 (2017).

90 Uscinski and Parent, *American Conspiracy Theories*.

91 Ibid.

92 Ibid.

93 Paul Krugman, "Who's Crazy Now?" *New York Times* (2006).

94 Paul Krugman, "Attack of the Crazy Centrists," *Washington Post* (2014).

95 Bob Bryan, "Krugman: It's Looking More and More Like the Election Was Swung by the FBI in Virtual 'Alliance with Putin'" (2016).

Chapter 6: President Trump, the Internet, Conspiracy, and Conspiracy Theory

1 J. Eric Oliver and Wendy M. Rahn, "Rise of the Trumpenvolk: Populism in the 2016 Election," *ANNALS of the American Academy of Political and Social Science* 667, no. 1 (2016).

2 Alan W. Bock, "Ambush at Ruby Ridge," *Reason* (1993).

3 Ibid.

4 Ibid.

5 Richard Lei and George Lardner Jr., "Seige Guided by Hastily Revised Rules of Engagement," *Washington Post* (1995).

6 Bock, "Ambush at Ruby Ridge."

7 Jesse Walker, "Ruby Ridge Is History, but the Mindset That Led to Ruby Ridge Is Thriving," *Reason* (2012).

8 Bock, "Ambush at Ruby Ridge."

9 Walker, "Ruby Ridge Is History."

10 Bock, "Ambush at Ruby Ridge."

11 Arthur M. Simon and Joseph E. Uscinski, "Prior Experience Predicts Presidential Performance," *Presidential Studies Quarterly* 42, no. 3 (2012).

12 Jose A. DelReal, "Here Are 10 More Conspiracy Theories Embraced by Donald Trump," *Washington Post* (2016).

13 Maxwell Tani, "The Conspiracy Candidate? 13 Outlandish Theories Donald Trump Has Floated on the Campaign Trail," *Business Insider* (2016).

14 Callum Borchers, "How on Earth Is the Media Supposed to Cover Trump's Wacky JFK-Cruz Conspiracy Theory?" *Washington Post* (2016).

15 Joseph E. Uscinski, "Lots of Americans Agree with Donald Trump about 'Rigged Elections,'" *Washington Post* (2016).

16 Mallory Shelbourne, "Trump Claims Voter Fraud without Evidence, Says 'I Won the Popular Vote,'" *The Hill* (2016).

17 Nancy L. Rosenblum and Russell Muirhead, *A Lot of People Are Saying: The New Conspiracism and the Assault on Democracy* (Princeton, NJ: Princeton University Press, 2019).

18 Matthew D. Atkinson and Darin DeWitt, "The Politics of Disruption: Social Choice Theory and Conspiracy Theory Politics," in *Conspiracy Theories and the People Who Believe Them*, ed. Joseph E. Uscinski (New York: Oxford University Press, 2018).

19 Matthew D. Atkinson, Darin DeWitt, and Joseph E. Uscinski, "How Conspiracy Theories Helped Power Trump's Disruptive Politics," *Vox.com*, May 2, 2017.

20 Dan Cassino, "Fairleigh Dickinson University's Publicmind Poll Finds Trump Supporters More Conspiracy-Minded Than Other Republicans," news release, May 4, 2016.

21 Naomi Oreskes, "The Scientific Consensus on Climate Change," *Science* 306, no. 5702 (2004).

22 Joseph E. Uscinski, Karen Douglas, and Stephan Lewandowsky, "Climate Change Conspiracy Theories," *Oxford Research Encyclopedia of Climate Science* (2017).

23 Stephan Lewandowsky et al., "Recurrent Fury: Conspiratorial Discourse in the Blogosphere Triggered by Research on the Role of Conspiracist Ideation in Climate Denial," *Journal of Social and Political Psychology* 3, no. 1 (2015).

24 Stephan Lewandowsky et al., "Seepage: Climate Change Denial and Its Effect on the Scientific Community," *Global Environmental Change* 33 (2015).

25 Gene Maddus, "Harvey Weinstein Hired Investigators to Spy on Accusers, *New Yorker* Reports," *Variety* (2017); Matt Wilstein, "Bill O'Reilly Lashes Out at Critics in Conspiracy-Laden Glenn Beck Interview," *The Daily Beast* (2017); Jennifer Bendery, "Roy Moore Is Fueling a Crazy Conspiracy Theory about George Soros," *Huffington Post* (2017).

26 Paula Dwyer, "Everything Is 'Rigged,'" *Chicago Tribune* (2016); Ari Berman, "The Democratic Primary Wasn't Rigged," *The Nation* (2016).

27 From analysis of data collected by: Hugo Drochon, "Study Shows 60% of Britons Believe in Conspiracy Theories," *The Guardian* (2018).

28 Max Ehrenfreund, "What Is Hillary Clinton Trying to Say with This Ad about Donald Trump and Putin?" *Washington Post* (2016).

29 Ben Mathis-Lilley, "Watch Hillary Shred Trump on Releasing His Taxes," *Slate* (2016), http://www.slate.com/blogs/the_slatest/2016/09/26/hillary_clinton_s_effective_shot_at_trump_over_tax_releases.html.

30 Joseph E. Uscinski and Joseph M. Parent, *American Conspiracy Theories* (New York: Oxford University Press, 2014).

31 Nicholas Fandos and Adam Goldman, "Barr Asserts Intelligence Agencies Spied on the Trump Campaign," *New York Times* (2019).

32 Matt Taibbi, "Taibbi: On Russiagate and Our Refusal to Face Why Trump Won," *Rolling Stone* (2019).

33 McKay Coppins, "How the Left Lost Its Mind," *The Atlantic* (2017).

34 Glenn Greenwald, "Beyond Buzzfeed: The 10 Worst, Most Embarrassing U.S. Media Failures on the Trump-Russia Story," *The Intercept* (2019).

35 Ibid.

36 Glenn Greenwald, "Robert Mueller Did Not Merely Reject the Trump-Russia Conspiracy Theories. He Obliterated Them," *The Intercept* (2019).

37 Ross Barkan, "Will Rachel Maddow Face a Reckoning over Her Trump-Russia Coverage?" *The Guardian* (2019).

38 Jonathan Chait, "Will Trump Be Meeting with His Counterpart—or His Handler?" (2018).

39 Ibid.

40 Jonathan Chait, "I Wrote an Article Suggesting Trump Was Compromised by Russia. I Was Right." *New York Magazine* (2019).

[41] Joseph E. Uscinski, "Down the Rabbit Hole We Go!" in *Conspiracy Theories and the People Who Believe Them*, ed. Joseph E. Uscinski (New York: Oxford University Press, 2018).

[42] Charles Stewart III, "Donald Trump's 'Rigged Election' Talk Is Changing Minds. Democrats' Minds, That Is." *Washington Post* (2016).

[43] David Drucker, "Romney Was Right about Russia," *CNN.com* (2017).

[44] Joseph E. Uscinski, "If Trump's Rhetoric around Conspiracy Theories Follows Him to the White House, It Could Lead to the Violation of Rights on a Massive Scale," *Impact of American Politics & Policy Blog* (2016); Atkinson, DeWitt, and Uscinski, "How Conspiracy Theories Helped."

[45] Alfred Moore, "On the Democratic Problem of Conspiracy Theory Politics," in *Conspiracy Theories and the People Who Believe Them*, ed. Joseph E. Uscinski (New York: Oxford University Press, 2018).

[46] Scott Shackford, "Backpage Founder's 93 Charges Lack Actual Sex-Trafficking Claims," (2018); Nick Gillespie, "Are Google and YouTube Evil? No, but Don't Let That Get in the Way of Your Feelings," *Reason* (2019).

[47] Ezra Klein, "Facebook Is a Capitalism Problem, Not a Mark Zuckerberg Problem," *Vox.com* (2019).

[48] Brendan Nyhan, "Fake News and Bots May Be Worrisome, but Their Political Power Is Overblown," *New York Times* (2018).

[49] Nick Gillespie, "Are Google and YouTube Evil? No, but Don't Let That Get in the Way of Your Feelings." *Reason Magazine*, June 11, 2019. https://reason.com/2019/06/10/are-google-and-youtube-evil-no-but-dont-let-that-get-in-the-way-of-your-feelings/.

[50] As of May 12, 2019.

[51] Adrienne LaFrance, "Going Online in the Age of Conspiracy Theories: A Video Claiming *Back to the Future* Predicted 9/11 Is the Latest in a Long and Often Bizarre Tradition of Questioning Key Moments in History." *The Atlantic*, October 21, 2015.

[52] Jared Keller, "'The Internet Made Me Do It': Stop Blaming Social Media for Our Behavioral Problems," *Pacific Standard* (2017).

[53] According to data obtained from Alexa.com on May 12, 2019.

[54] Uscinski and Parent, *American Conspiracy*.

[55] Alessandro Bessi et al., "Science vs. Conspiracy: Collective Narratives in the Age of Misinformation," *PLoS ONE* 10, no. 2 (2015).

[56] Uscinski and Parent, *American Conspiracy*.

[57] Steve Clarke, "Conspiracy Theories and the Internet: Controlled Demolition and Arrested Development," *Episteme* 4, no. 2 (2007).

[58] Cass R. Sunstein, *Conspiracy Theories and Other Dangerous Ideas* (New York: Simon & Schuster, 2014).

[59] Carl Sagan, *The Demon-Haunted World: Science as a Candle in the Dark* (New York: Ballantine Books, 1997), 5.

Index